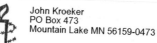

The ABUSE of POWER

The ABUSE of POWER

A Theological Problem

JAMES NEWTON POLING

ABINGDON PRESS
Nashville

THE ABUSE OF POWER: A THEOLOGICAL PROBLEM

This book is printed on recycled acid-free paper.

Library of Congress Cataloging-in-Publication Data

Poling, James N. (James Newton), 1942–
The abuse of power : a theological problem / James Newton Poling.
p. cm.
Includes bibliographical references and index.
ISBN 0-687-00684-8 (pbk. : alk. paper)
1. Sex crimes—United States. 2. Adult child sexual abuse victims—United States. 3. Power (Christian theology) 4. Self. 5. Community. 6. God. 7. Theology, Practical. I. Title.
HQ72.U53P65 1991
261.8'33153—dc20 91-18019
CIP

93 94 95 96 97 98 99 00 01 02—10 9 8 7 6 5 4

MANUFACTURED IN THE UNITED STATES OF AMERICA

To

LAUREE HERSCH MEYER

who challenged me
to shed my patriarchal ways
and become a full human being

ACKNOWLEDGMENTS

I wish to acknowledge my indebtedness during the research and writing that led to this book:

To co-author, Karen, and all survivors of sexual violence who have trusted me with their stories.

To family, who have taught me so much about life, love, and power: Nancy Werking Poling, Christina Poling, Nathan Poling.

To students and clients, who have taught me about theology and experience.

To colleagues who have made important contributions to my research by reading and critiquing my manuscript: Lauree Hersch Meyer, Melanie May, Toinette Eugene, Thomas Troeger, Marie Fortune, Riet Bons-Storm, Ellen Wondra.

To colleagues who encouraged me and gave me crucial support and ideas: Han van den Blink, Jay Gibble, Rob van Kessel, Gilbert Bond, and those in the Society for Pastoral Theology.

To mentors: Bernard Loomer, John Cobb, Marjorie Soule.

To teachers and supervisors: Wesley Brun, Tom Ryan, Kit Miles.

My thanks to the following for sabbatical study leaves: Bethany Theological Seminary, 1985–86; Colgate Rochester Divinity School, 1990.

To readers and editors: Ulrike Guthrie, Rex Matthews, Thomas Troeger, Nancy Poling.

CONTENTS

CHAPTER ONE

HEARING THE SILENCED VOICES

A twelve-year-old girl tells the pastor that her father, a Sunday school teacher, has been sexually molesting her since she was four years old.

The brother of a deacon is arrested for raping his five-year-old son.

The pastor in a nearby church has to leave his parish because he engaged in sexual relations with three female parishioners.

Several prominent religious figures are "caught" in exploitative sexual relationships with women and fall from power.

The local and national news is filled with the stories of the sexual abuse of women and children.

Pastors and theologians, as moral and religious leaders, are the recipients of questions:

—Why are we suddenly hearing so much about sexual exploitation of children and women? Is there an increase in this problem?
—Is sexual violence unusual or is it typical of human morality?
—If sexual violence is a serious problem why have the church and society been silent?

We are hearing a lot about sexual violence because many women are beginning to break the silence and tell about their experiences. The taboos about speaking the truth are being set aside, and shocking stories are being heard. Experts estimate that 20 to 40 percent of all children experience some form of sexual violence before age eighteen, and that more than half of all women have experienced a rape or attempted rape in their lifetime.[1] Even more disturbing is that most sexual violence is perpetrated within families and by persons who are trusted leaders in communities. Sexual violence is a far-reaching problem with very destructive consequences for many people.

There may have been an increase in sexual violence in recent years, though more research needs to be done. Studies show that younger women have experienced more sexual abuse than their mothers and grandmothers.[2] Changes in society such as the breakdown of cohesive local communities, the increasing isolation of many individuals and families, the sexualization of culture, and the greater tolerance for violent behavior may all have contributed to this increase.[3] However, research also shows that sexual violence has been a problem in previous centuries.[4] So we are facing a serious problem that has existed for many years, and one that is increasing. Sexual violence raises serious questions about the morality of human beings. Some scholars have suggested that violence against women and children is a highly symbolic and significant aspect of Western culture. Through sexual violence, sanctioned forms of social control of women and other marginal groups are being expressed.[5] Sexual violence has been a taboo subject for a long time. The terrible suffering of victims has been silenced by public attitudes and policies; some victims maintain their silence for decades and many never tell. Recently, adult survivors have discovered new power to speak about their suffering and their hope. In small support groups, women, especially, have begun to ask why they are such frequent victims of sexual violence.[6] As they speak, the tangled web of taboos is coming unraveled. Silence does not protect the victims; it perpetuates victimization. Without the protection of silence and taboos, sexual violence is unmasked for what it really is—the evil of abuse of power.

Power is a complex term with personal, social, and religious connotations. At a personal level, all persons have some power by virtue of being alive, along with an inner drive to use this power to become all they can be. Some are denied the chance to exercise their power because of oppression. Others use their power for destructive ends. Society dictates how power is distributed. Institutions and ideologies determine who has privilege to be dominant and who must defer. Some persons are given great power to make choices for themselves and other people and are protected from the consequences of their choices. But many are denied the power to control even their own bodies and minds, and their choices are circumscribed by others. These inequities create the occasions for abusive behaviors and unjust power arrangements. Religion serves to define the nature of power and its legitimate uses.

Religious leaders must choose whether to collude with the dominant culture as sanctioning agents of abusive power or to be prophetic critics of the way power is distributed and defined. Sexual violence can serve as a test for understanding the nature of power and its destructive and creative potential in an unjust society. Chapter 2 discusses the nature of power more fully. This study is committed to understanding the suffering and hope of survivors with a goal of radically transforming the structures of power in society.

Chapters 3 and 4 of this book explore stories of persons for whom sexual violence has been a central reality. Many courageous survivors have found words to express their suffering and hope in new ways. They have overcome the victimization of the past and have found new power to live, through connections with other survivors. Survivors are opening the eyes of those who are willing to see the abuse of power that has destroyed so many persons and families in our communities.

Recovering perpetrators is a term used in this study for the few men who have confessed their crimes of abuse and violence, have begun to face the consequences of their destructive behaviors, and have committed themselves to an indefinite period of restitution and change through psychotherapy and education. I focus on male perpetrators because statistically they are in the majority (80 to 95 percent of sexual violence is committed by men), and because of my own experience working with men.[7] Though only a very small percentage of all male abusers are trying to change their destructive behaviors, it is important to study this group to understand the dynamics of all abusers.

The later chapters engage in theological reflection on issues of sexual violence against women and children in our society. Certain theological questions have become apparent through my research that need further exploration.

First, the prevalence of sexual violence raises questions about human nature. Most sexual violence occurs in the family and in other human relationships based on trust and intimacy. If a father can rape his daughter, if a husband can rape his wife, if a pastor can rape a parishioner, is there any limit to violence? We must try to understand the human self and spirit in relation to experiences of such betrayal and destructiveness so that we can protect ourselves and our communities against evil. Equally important is the resilient hope that springs up in survivors of such extreme abuse.[8] We need to understand those persons who are terrorized with sexual violence but keep up their struggle for integrity and wholeness. The theological question here is the capacity for good and evil in the human personality. Chapter 6 will explore the nature of the human self in the midst of suffering and hope.

Second, the silence of church and society on sexual violence raises questions about the nature of community. Sexual violence against women and children has been a widespread phenomenon for centuries, and it seems to be getting worse in modern times. Even though both church and society claim to be concerned about human suffering and injustice, society is ineffective in facing and dealing with this problem, and the church has kept a deadly silence in spite of its ethic of concern for all persons. New communities of support for survivors of sexual violence are being organized outside traditional institutions, showing that the human search for community persists in spite of the failure of community. The theological question is the nature of human community itself. Where is the community in which all persons can grow into their own integrity and be affirmed for the strength of the gifts they bring to the body, recognizing that all members of the community are both strong and weak? Chapter 7 explores the nature of community with its potential for good and evil.

Third, the structure of oppression in sexual violence raises questions about God. The voices of those suffering from sexual violence have been ignored in most theological discussions about the relationship of God and humans, sometimes giving the impression that God is uncaring. Many survivors of sexual violence have great difficulty with traditional images of a male God who requires obedience to dominant powers even in situations of great injustice. New definitions of the relation of love and power are coming from counter-communities of resistance to evil. The search for a God of love and justice is strong in some survivors of sexual violence, and they are leading a discussion about reformulated understandings of God. Chapter 8 will explore the nature of God in relation to the creative and violent potential of creation itself.

HEARING SURVIVORS OF SEXUAL VIOLENCE

This study attends to two groups silenced by present patriarchal structures of society: children and women.[9] A hermeneutical principle in this research is that those with the least power can reveal the most about the nature of the good and unmask the abuse of power. Those who are in positions of power need to hear the voices of those who suffer from abuse or deprivation just as surely as those who suffer cry out to be heard. Only through this kind of conversation can humanity be restored to both oppressed and oppressor.[10]

How my eyes were opened. The decision to focus my research on survivors of sexual violence evolved from personal experience in my life and ministry. I first encountered the reality of sexual violence as a pastor. A young woman told me that she had been sexually molested over many years by both her father and her grandfather. I had never been confronted by an evil like this. In my shock I was no help to her.

Later, a fifteen-year-old girl, a member of the youth group, told me that her father, a Sunday school teacher, was touching her breasts and saying he wanted to have sex with her. This time I got professional consultation and confronted the father. The girl received counseling until she was able to leave home and protect herself. But because of my naivete about the seriousness of these cases, I did not report the father and he faced no consequences for his abuse.

Part of my struggle in these two events was the extent to which I personally identified with the men in these families. Like me, they were respected leaders in church and community. The privilege they assumed in relation to their children had an uncomfortable resemblance to my own attitudes about power in my family and community. This was one of my first clues that issues of gender and power were interrelated in my own personality and in the community.

As a beginning seminary professor in 1979, I began to hear frequent stories from Master of Divinity students about their own experiences of sexual and physical violence at the hands of church-going, respected parents, mostly fathers. I also heard stories from students who were sexually approached by pastors and counselors in the church. Many students came to seminary to find healing for sexual abuse, which was ignored and trivialized in their families and congregations. Christians are universally opposed to coercive sex, but there is little ethical discussion about the effects of sexual violence on victims. The fact that these students could find no one to address their psychic pain indicates a strong taboo against open discussion of such suffering. Even as I listened, I realized that I was one of the silent leaders who kept such abuse a secret. It was many years before I gained the courage to begin speaking about the evil I saw.

For four years I taught a seminary course called "Evil and Aggression," which focused on sexual violence along with racism and the holocaust of World War II as examples of destructive behavior. The students in these courses began to teach me about the interrelationship of personal and family violence with race and culture. Several students were very articulate about how the isolation and hatred expressed within their families were reflecting class and racial hatred in society. Black and Hispanic students disclosed their own struggles with violence and showed me how social institutions and ideologies had concrete consequences in their own childhood experiences. The courage of these students persuaded me to sharpen my social analysis of sexual and family violence. I became convinced that the injustices perpetrated against women, persons of color, and underprivileged classes were crucial to understanding the roots of sexual violence.

Finally, I discovered that one of my mentors in the ministry had a history of sexually abusive behaviors toward seminary students and women in the church. I was shocked by this discovery because I had trusted this man as much as anyone. Many persons, including me, had ignored the signals that something was wrong in his understanding of the ethical use of power. His victims were betrayed by his destructive behaviors and by the conspiracy of silence that protected his abuse of power. This disclosure increased my sensitivity to the sexual abuse of power by professionals, to whom many women trust their vulnerabilities and spiritual growth.[11] The voices of survivors of sexual violence were compelling to me because of the courage and hope they expressed in seeking healing. It was only with deep grief and sadness that they shared the stories of abuse within their families and churches. These witnesses showed great courage in talking to someone about their pain and grief, and their stories revealed a tremendous resilience of hope in the midst of obstacles to their healing.

I was horrified at my own complicity and the complicity of the church in the silence about such an obvious evil. None of the students had ever heard any public discussion of the evils of sexual and physical abuse. They had not been encouraged to disclose their stories even when they had the courage to speak. Yet they continued to look to the church as a center of hope in the midst of evil. I began to focus on this ambiguity in my own life and to critically examine the church and the larger society that created the conditions giving rise to this problem.

As these voices of the survivors of sexual violence gained power in my own spirit, I realized my inadequacy to understand and to provide the expertise they needed for their healing. I decided to seek further therapy for myself and additional training in work with the survivors of sexual violence. During my training I had my first encounter with molesters, men who had been convicted of criminal sexual abuse of children. I was shocked to see such evil organized into individual personalities. Most of these men were so narcissistic that they were unable to understand that the needs of children were different from their own needs. Many of them actually thought that children enjoyed the sexual contact. They knew their behavior was "wrong" because of the social taboo, but they often felt they had done no harm. I was beginning to see the depth of violence in these men. Part of the horror included the unmasking of my own violent potential. I discovered similar attitudes of dominance and entitlement in myself and my clients. How could men be so blind to the destructiveness of our abuse of power?

I was also shocked to hear about the childhood suffering of these molesters. Every man I interviewed had lived a life of terror himself. Most were victims of sexual violence, physical violence, or severe deprivation. Each one had his own tale of suffering to tell. They were silenced as children so that they could not speak of the terror they knew. I became aware of how little ability I had to speak of my own childhood pain. I had silenced my own inner child to avoid facing the suffering in my own life. The violence of these molesters against others was a continuation of what they had learned about relationships in the past. Society was reaping the harvest of its abuse and neglect of children of previous generations. Some research indicates that my experience may not be typical. David Finkelhor has summarized research that shows a significant number of perpetrators were not sexually abused as children. There are multiple reasons why men become sexually violent, including social expectations for the behavior of men. These factors will be examined to supplement the limitations of my experience.[12]

Through sharing with survivors and clinical work with recovering perpetrators, I became convinced of the need to investigate the issue of sexual violence to its social and religious roots.

I am impelled to understand the extreme suffering of women and children subjected to sexual violence. As a minister I am disturbed that the moral witness of the church on the issue of sexual violence is almost completely missing.

I am impelled to explore the resilience of hope in the human spirit. Women survivors are finding courage to speak about their suffering in the midst of secrecy and silence. A few recovering perpetrators are beginning to find the strength to seek healing. New communities of survivors, counselors, and support groups have recently sprung up in response to the evil of sexual violence.

The stories of the survivors of sexual violence are being heard in new ways in this generation. My research depends on these voices. I hope that because of increased knowledge about sexual violence church and society will become more engaged with the courage of survivors and more committed to justice.

THE QUESTION OF MY ACCOUNTABILITY

I grew up as a white, heterosexual male in the fifties in Southern United States culture with its embedded sexism, racism, and classism. Both my parents are college educated, and all my siblings are well educated. I am an ordained Protestant minister and a professor in a seminary. I have been married for twenty-seven years to a woman who is white and educated. We have reared two children, who are both college graduates. On every index of social privilege, I am at or near the top. This means that in understanding the structures of power from the underside, I am vastly handicapped. I have little or no knowledge of what it is to be marginal, excluded from the centers of power on a systematic basis.

Through the sensitivities I have gained from my work with survivors of sexual violence, I have learned something about the limits of my social location. I have usually identified with the dominant culture and assumed that I understood things better than most other people. But I have slowly come to see that others have insights that are crucial to my own life and well-being. In writing this book, I have been in dialogue with those who can correct my distortions and help me say what needs to be said. One of these persons is Karen, a survivor of sexual violence. This project has been for her a way to give voice to her suffering and hope. I have changed many of my perceptions herein because of her responses.

I have maintained accountability for my work on this project in specific and disciplined ways. During my training and research in sexual violence, my therapist and supervisors were women who are well aware of the sexism of our culture and its history. They frequently confronted me with my distorted ideas of women and children. Issues of class were predominant in my clinical and personal work. I also submitted one draft to six women, who are credited in the acknowledgments. All of these women have the expertise and authority to challenge distortions, such as those they found in my work. As a group they represent diversities of race and culture that have sharpened the social analysis. Significant portions were altered in order to respond to their criticism. Finally, my editor is a woman with European roots who has guided me through blind spots at several crucial junctures.

My work with issues of sexual violence has resulted in my own experiences of transformation. I have been teaching and counseling survivors and perpetrators of sexual violence for five years. My perspective on myself and the world has been completely changed by this experience. In the interests of truth, I have learned to look at church and society imaginatively through the eyes of survivors. I am horrified by what I have seen, and these perceptions have transformed my own spiritual journey. Without the courage and trust of many survivors I would have been unable to write this book.

In spite of my attempts to be accountable, I am aware that my privileged position in society prevents my experiencing the full impact of sexual violence as experienced by women. Finally, I am accountable to you, the readers, as you challenge any distortions that warp the truth.

METHODOLOGY

This study follows the methods of practical theology, an emerging discipline of theology that involves theological reflection on the relation of God and humankind as it arises out of the ministry practice of the church. After initial definitions of key terms, like power and abuse as these relate to its personal, social, and religious levels, the study focuses on in-depth case histories that are based on the testimony of survivors themselves. These stories are then analyzed with critical theories that identify systematic distortions and the search for resilient truth in the midst of extreme suffering. From this analysis come theological affirmations, which are used to transform the ministry practice of the church in the future. This rhythm of practice and reflection is central to practical theology. I have identified some of the reasons why the testimony of survivors and recovering perpetrators became compelling in my research. In a similar way, certain critical theories have become central to my analysis, namely, process theology, psychoanalytic theory, and feminist and African-American sociology and theology. These theories have been chosen partly because they offer significant insights into the understanding of sexual violence, and partly because they have become central to my own understanding of human reality. A more detailed discussion of methodology can be found in chapter 9.[13]

A central theologian in this study is Bernard Loomer, who died in 1985 after teaching many years at the University of Chicago and with whom I studied in 1978 at Claremont, California. Professor Loomer referred to his own theology as Process/relational, and identified himself as a part of the empirical wing of process thought. He was primarily interested in concrete, historical actuality as opposed to abstract, theoretical study, and identified God closely with the actual world. His basic concepts were process and relationality, and he believed that the interaction of these two primordial forces would lead to a revolution over Enlightenment thought. The structure of his theology will become more clear during this study.[14]

SUMMARY OF CHAPTERS

This book is about power and the abuse of power as it is manifested in sexual violence toward women and children. This study will focus on the structures of domination in the personal, social, and religious areas of human life that produce suffering. We will also learn about the resilience of hope in survivors and the new communities of healing that are being created.

Chapter 2 discusses power and abuse of power. The study of sexual violence as a form of abuse gives us clues about the nature of power, and how abuse of power leads to human suffering and evil.

Karen is a survivor of sexual violence both in childhood and as an adult. She has struggled to understand her story in the midst of painful healing. She corresponded with me over a year to put her story into a theological context and chapter 3 relays her testimony.

The story of Sam in chapter 4 is a portrait made out of stories I have heard about recovering perpetrators. Sam's is the fictional story of a victim who became a molester and attempted to recover from his sexually violent behaviors and attitudes. He represents the very small group of men who have broken the taboos by speaking about what it is like to be a man who has sexually abused others. Sam is not a typical molester, because he confessed his crimes and sought healing, a most unusual phenomenon among perpetrators. It is hoped this story will help us begin to make sense of this evil.

Chapter 5 discusses Freud's classic case of Judge Schreber. In 1903 Schreber wrote his *Memoirs,* which tell the story of his adult mental illness and his attempts to find healing. The debate about this case has become an important discussion about the long-term personal and social consequences of child abuse.

The later chapters of the book turn to an analysis of the personal, social, and religious issues of the abuse of power. Chapter 6 explores how abuse of power becomes organized as an evil force in individual and family life, and how the self deals with the long-term consequences of abuse. Chapter 7 is about the search for community among survivors. Abuse of power is one result of the breakdown of community life. Instead of providing resources and hope, community becomes the source of oppression through its institutions and ideologies. Finding a community of justice and love is a goal of survivors.

Chapter 8 stretches our minds the farthest by asking about abuse of power as a theological problem. For many survivors, religion is a mixed blessing. In their struggle for wholeness, victims see that the church and society, reluctant to hear the suffering of children, have supported their parents. As children, they were introduced to a God who expected them to be good and to honor their parents. More deeply, some survivors see that the patriarchal images of God sanction the structures of the privileged even when they abuse their power. Yet in the healing process, survivors search for a God of love and power. This chapter explores the images of God's power and love that hinder healing and suggests revised images of God that can emerge in the process of healing.

Chapter 9 examines the implications for ministry and practical theology. The evil of sexual violence in our day has not been fully faced by church or society. This chapter will discuss some principles for changing ministry practice and briefly discuss the theological method underlying this study.

CHAPTER TWO

POWER AND ABUSE OF POWER

Those who have experienced sexual violence are the victims of abuse of power. Children are vulnerable to adult abuse of power because they lack understanding and resources for self-protection. Some children are physically overpowered and raped by men who have no concern for their well-being. Some are sexually exploited and then intimidated into silence by being made to fear for their safety or the safety of their family. Some children are manipulated over long periods of time into gratifying the sexual needs of a molester, usually a trusted family member. The use of threats and rewards to exploit a child's vulnerability is abuse of power. All sexual contacts between adults and children are destructive because of the power inequities between them.[1]

Women are vulnerable to assault and manipulation because of the power of men. Some women are raped because they lack the physical strength and other resources to protect themselves on the streets, on dates, in marriage, or in other relationships. Rape is coercive sexual contact without consent.[2] Some women are manipulated into sexual relationships because of great power inequalities. In certain professional relationships such as employer-employee, counselor-client, doctor-patient, and pastor-parishioner, men have resources they can use abusively to exploit the vulnerabilities of women in a patriarchal society.[3] When the oppressions of race and class are added, the possibility of abuse of power is increased. Persons with power disadvantages are vulnerable to exploitation.[4]

In order to understand the various forms of abuse of power through sexual violence, we must understand the nature of power itself. This section explores normative definitions of power that will inform later analysis.

POWER IN ITS IDEAL FORM

Within a process-relational view of reality, power in its ideal form is virtually synonymous with life itself. To live is to desire power to relate to others.

> If power is roughly defined as the ability to make or establish a claim on life, then . . . power is co-extensive with life itself. To be alive, in any sense, is to make some claim, large or small. To be alive is to exercise power in some degree.[5]

When we feel powerful, we know that we take up physical and social space and that our being is effective in some sphere. We can move objects and influence people according to our goals. A baby knows beginning power when it gains the ability to move its arms at will and gets a positive response from an adult. As adults we feel a sense of power when we engage in successful cooperative activity with others to pursue a goal. In this perspective, power is the ability to act in effective ways with the objects and people that make up our perceived world. To the extent that people or institutions deprive a person of the power to live, that person is rendered powerless and her life is limited.

Power is often misunderstood as a one-way effect on others. But power is actually organized by the relational webs of which we are a part. Our ability to act in effective ways depends on our connections with other persons, and with the institutions and ideas that form the basis of our experience. Power is gauged by the complexity of the relationships that can be contained in an interaction. "Power is relational, i.e., the relative amount of power we have is determined in relation to other persons."[6]

The web of relationships determines the nature of power. Two basic principles of life are interrelated. There is the creative energy that is the basis of everything that is, what Meland calls "the Creative Passage."[7] There is the web of relationships into which this energy is structured, what Loomer calls "the relational web."[8] When these two aspects are seen together, we get an image of the "power of existence-as-a-relational-process."[9]

> Relational power . . . is the ability both to produce and to undergo an effect . . . the capacity to sustain a relationship . . . the capacity to sustain complex and mutually internal relationships that encompass . . . the concrete lives of individuals and groups.[10]

When power is seen as the energy of the relational web itself, then power can be understood as the ability to sustain internal relationships and increase the power of the relational web as a whole.

In the relational web of the family, the good-enough parent is one who can accept the many spontaneous moods of the infant without undue censorship. Whether the child is happy or sad or angry, the parent can accommodate the mood, seeing it as appropriate within certain limits. The inadequate parent is one who is comfortable with only a small range of feeling and is intolerant of variation. Some parents are threatened by infantile rage and become abusive in order to eliminate these unwanted feelings.

The power of the individual is enhanced when the web of relationships is benevolent and encourages the most creativity. This gives the person the potential ability to participate fully in the relational web, to allow one's being to absorb as much experience as possible, and to have such an effect on self and others that the whole relational aspect of life is enhanced and enlarged. Healthy internal relationships are mutual relationships in which self and other are continually transformed. As each participates in the interior experience of the other, the relationship is enlarged and the subjective reality of each individual is enriched. Rita Brock uses the term "erotic power" to refer to this creative energy of relationships.

> Erotic power is the power of our primal interrelatedness. Erotic power, as it creates and connects hearts, involves the whole person in relationships of self-awareness, vulnerability, openness, and caring. . . . Erotic power involves inner and outer worlds in a knowing that is multilayered and a causality that is multilateral and intertwined. . . . Erotic power is the energy that produces creative synthesis, and is enhanced by the relationships that emerge from creative synthesis.[11]

In its ideal form, power as the ability to engage in internal relationships is virtually synonymous with life itself. In this sense, power is potentially nearly identical with sexual energy. Erotic power, or sexual power, is the holistic expression of communion and freedom between persons in ways that are appropriate to their relationships. Sexual violence is both a violation of the telos of sexuality and an abuse of power.

For the individual, the ability to embrace the contradictions and tensions that are a part of life requires great strength. There is inequality in the parent-child relationship. A child, unable to determine its world apart from the parent, depends on benevolent relationships. In spite of the inequity, parent and child can increase mutual intimacy and freedom. The parent-child relationship has the potential to be one of the most intimate experiences in a person's life. The interior of one's subjective life is interrelated and intertwined with another. The relationship is internal for both persons. The child attaches to the parent and allows herself to be molded to the inner life of that adult. The parent attaches himself to the child and allows the child to remake his inner experience. From such an experience, both parent and child have a sense of periodic communion, and such an intense relationship opens up new options for both in the future through personal growth. The child has the chance to become a full person with the ability to relate to many other people through language and other symbols. The adult has the chance to rework subjective experiences and regain the forgotten knowledge of a child's world.

Relational power for the individual person as just described depends on a just and creative social environment. Society is organized into institutions and ideologies, which control the resources humans need for a good life. Walter Wink distinguishes the outer forms of social power, namely institutions, from the inner forms of social power, namely ideologies and shared assumptions:

> The New Testament's "principalities and powers" is a generic category referring to the determining forces of physical, psychic, and social existence. These powers usually consist of an outer manifestation and an inner spirituality or interiority. Power must become incarnate, institutionalized, or systemic in order to be effective. It has a dual aspect, possessing both an outer visible form (constitutions, judges, police, leaders, office complexes), and an inner, invisible spirit that provides it legitimacy, compliance, credibility, and clout.[12]

Power as defined in this study has both a personal and a social dimension. At the personal level, there is a drive for power to actualize the self through the relational web. This power can be denied by the person's set of circumstances or it can become distorted toward evil. But choices for the individual derive from social institutions and ideologies as these are sanctioned by religious assumptions and world views. We will see how power is organized as we further explore the self and social and religious circumstances later.

The ideal direction of power in human life that is undistorted by sin and evil is toward communion and enlarged freedom; in the relational process, human bonding grows stronger and individuals and groups increase their freedom. "Loving power undistorted by evil in human experience is interaction characterized by sensitivity which moves toward communion with self, others, and God, and by creativity which moves toward enlarged freedom for self, others, and God."[13]

ABUSE OF POWER AS EVIL

One of our questions is why society has organized power so that inequity becomes the occasion for injustice and why some individuals abuse their power in destructive behaviors such as sexual abuse. Daniel Day Williams suggests that the temptation to abuse power arises from human fear and arrogance.

> We are created for communion with God and our neighbour in a life which offers communion on terms which require courage and trust in a future we cannot see, which postpones fulfilment and does not allow every kind of immediate gratification. When we discover the risks involved in being human in the great community we are anxious, and when we do not find the hope of communion we are desperate. We willingly deny the fullness of our humanity in order to gratify some part of it. . . . It is not a long step in the logic of emotion to will to destroy the sensitivity of life itself, to turn against ourselves and everything which symbolizes full humanity. We kill what we love because we refuse to love on the terms which life gives.[14]

Abuse of power for the individual is motivated by fear and by the resulting desire to control the power of life. This fear and arrogance are then used to create societies in which structures of domination create special possibilities for the privileged at the expense of shared power for all persons. The power that is intended by God for everyone who lives is used to destroy relationships in exchange for control. Rather than live in insecurity, some persons choose to create structures that dominate and control others for personal gratification and false security.

This describes the dilemma of the abusive parent within the social circumstances of parental privilege. Most parents have expectations of a bright future in their children. Yet the challenge of parenting a fragile being through all the developmental crises to fulfillment of these dreams requires "courage and trust in a future we cannot see, which postpones fulfillment and does not allow every kind of immediate gratification."[15] Parents must discipline their own impulses in favor of long-term goals that can only be imagined. All parents become frustrated with the complexity of this task and occasionally fail to adhere to their goals. Many parents try to mold their children in certain, narrow directions to meet their own needs. Some parents turn against their children in a systematic way and try to break their spirits and destroy their claim on life. All parents abuse their power at times in relation to the children they care for. They lack the strength and discipline to engage creatively the complex processes of development. Some parents abuse their power in extreme ways that lead to psychic or physical death. They would rather destroy their children than face their own failure and disappointment in life. "We kill what we love because we refuse to love on the terms which life gives."[16] A society that creates the conditions for such parental abuse of children is unjust.

Loomer refers to such abuse of power with the term "unilateral power," that is, the presumed ability to produce an effect on another with only minimal impact on the self:

> As long as one's size and sense of worth are measured by the strength of one's capacity to influence others, as long as power is associated with the sense of initiative and aggressiveness, and passivity is indicative of weakness or a corresponding lack of power, then the natural and inevitable inequalities among individuals and groups become the means whereby the estrangements in life become wider and deeper. . . . We tend to trample on or remain indifferent to those people whom we feel we can safely ignore.[17]

The evil of unilateral power can be seen in abusive parent-child relationships. In our society, where the isolated nuclear family is considered more important than the rights of children, parents have almost god-like power over the development of their children. Yet, in the long run, the exercise of unilateral power by a parent over a child destroys the parent's future as well as the child's. Parent and child form a relational web in which both can increase or decrease the quality of their lives in concert with each other. Because of the power inequities the parent can determine the future for the child. Any interaction that decreases the possibilities for the child also decreases the possibilities for the parent. For example, if, to stifle the child's increasing power, a parent refuses to educate a child, the future possibilities for both are limited. The child loses the chance for an expansive world. The parent loses the opportunity to be in relationship with someone who can bring new ideas and creativity. In a less extreme case, if parent and child cannot communicate because the parent is threatened by new ideas, then the experience of education will not become internal to their relationship. Both parent and child are diminished by this restriction on their relationship.

Social power inequalities become occasions for the abuse of power. Those who are powerful can organize societies in such a way that those who are vulnerable are denied the full resources that life has to offer. Abuse of power relies on institutions and ideologies.

The family is an ideological construct and institution in society that structures domination in certain ways. In the relationships between parents and children in Western societies, parents are given almost omnipotent control over their children as long as they don't attract the attention of outside authorities. A father can sexually abuse his daughter for many years without interference if he can prevent outsiders from finding out. Even symptoms in the child will often be ignored if the family is respectable and well-socialized. The overwhelming power of parents is socially defined and protected. Suffering children who act out or who complain are often not believed because the family is perceived as a sacred institution which cannot easily be challenged unless the family is poor or marginal. The ideology of family is one of the structures of domination and control that create the conditions for abuse of power.[18]

Patriarchy, the unjust power relationships of men and women perpetuated by ideologies and institutions, is another structure of domination that creates the conditions for abuse of power. Rita Brock describes how patriarchy is exemplified in the interpersonal relationships of men and women:

> Women in patriarchy find themselves on the downside of power hierarchies. . . . The masculine and feminine views of power remain split into two sides of a dualism as polarized opposites. The two views of power depend on each other in a gender-stratified system of dominance and submission. Exploiter male and exploited female go hand in hand, just as powerful, controlling parent and abused child fit a system of hierarchical power. . . . Both dominance and compliance confuse personal power with

> positional power. Positional power has to do with our status in social relationships and the extent to which our interpersonal world has emphasized control.[19]

What appears to some to be an equal struggle between men and women is actually a structure of domination in which women have fewer resources and choices to protect themselves from abuse. Within the ideology and institutionalized power of patriarchy, women are denied fundamental resources needed for equality, survival, and well-being. For example, a woman who is faced with a physically abusive husband has to deal not only with his physical strength, but also with her need for protection and resources for herself and her children. Before seeking legal action, she must face the likelihood that she will not receive justice from the police and courts if she seeks help. If she finds herself alone as a single parent, she may lack the resources for self-support. These overlapping inequalities make her vulnerable to physical attack without resources to protect and fend for herself. This is a situation of abuse of power because inequalities become the occasion for her life to be circumscribed and damaged by a man whose abuse is protected by social attitudes and institutions.

Racism is another structure of domination that creates the conditions for abuse of power. Racism means that a particular group of persons are denied resources needed for life because of race or color.

> Racism is understood as a system of attitudes, behaviors, and assumptions that objectifies human persons on the basis of color, and that has the power to deny autonomy, access to resources, and self-determination to those persons, while maintaining the values of the dominant society as the norm by which all else will be measured.[20]

Communities that are victims of systemic racism are denied economic, educational, and other resources. In order to justify such inequalities, persons of color are often blamed for their own suffering. Chapter 7 discusses how sexual violence against women of color has been used as a terror tactic in a racist society, and how false rape charges against men of color have justified lynching, capital punishment, and extended imprisonment for many. Individual abuse of power because of race actually depends on the social organization of power that protects those with privilege and endangers those who are made marginal by the dominant culture.

There are other structures of domination and control—institutionalized abuse of power—that are minor themes in this study, namely, classism (the oppression of the poor and working classes), heterosexism (the oppression of gays and lesbians), and imperialism (the oppression of poor nations by the overwhelming economic and military power of the richer nations). Structures of domination mean that the power of creation is not being used to enhance communion and enlarged freedom for all persons. The many "-isms" must be analyzed and criticized for their distortion of the use of power. Combining gender, racial, and class analysis will sharpen our perception of the way abuse of power is organized and maintained.

Social injustice is a major source of human suffering. All persons are dependent on the social organization of resources such as food, housing, education, medical care, safety, and other things that make human life possible and beautiful. When the organization of families and societies deprives persons of the resources they need, the result is hunger, medical crisis, violence, and exposure. Owing to their poverty and class, women and children most often suffer the systemic abuse of power. In addition, women who are abused are often isolated even further by trauma and denied access to the resources they need for survival and well-being.

Another type of suffering occurs when the ideologies and institutions of society create "blind zones," in which interpersonal violence is tacitly permitted and is not redressed. Certain relationship systems are regarded as normative and therefore are not open to scrutiny. This protection, or social approval, does not, however, protect victims, only perpetrators. There are common rationalizations for such violence: "Parents must hit their children in order to teach them to be good citizens." "Men hit women in order to show them who is boss." Certain professions, such as the ministry and medicine, often function as havens to protect perpetrators at the expense of victims. The extent and consequences of such abuse are denied and treated as interpersonal difficulties rather than as the abuse of power.

Social injustice and individual abuse of power are evil. They harm the power of life itself within the relational web. Power so used stifles the possibility of mutuality and interdependence. Abuse of power not only destroys individuals, it also destroys the web of relationships on which all life depends. "Abuse of power is denial of communion and denial of freedom for self, others, and God."[21]

THE REDEMPTION OF POWER

When one begins to see the extent of the organized abuse of power in families and societies, one can despair about the future. Individuals have a perverse capacity for misusing the power of life against others and organizing society in unjust ways. Much power for life is organized into institutions and ideologies that encourage destructive activity. Is there any remedy for this tragic state of affairs?

> [Humans are] created for communion but [they lose] it and [they lose] the power to recover it. If we believe that in spite of [human] failure love can be recovered we have the triple theme of the Christian Gospel. [Humans bear] the image of God who is love. [Human] love falls into disorder; but there is a work of God which restores [human] integrity and . . . power to enter into communion. Every Christian theology is an elaboration of this theme.[22]

In a world where evil as abuse of power is so dominant, how can at least some power be redeemed to serve its original purposes? If evil cannot be eliminated, then perhaps there is a power of redemption that can resist the total abuse of power.

In my work with some survivors, I have been impressed by the resilience of their hope. In the midst of the worst terror and destruction, the spirits of some do not completely lose courage. There are many others whose spirits and resistance are broken and their lives shattered; for these there may be no redemption unless society is entirely transformed. Those with resilient spirits can teach us about both the evil of abusive power and the source of hope in an unjust world. The resistance of individuals and groups thus becomes a source of hope for all humanity.

> The term *resistance* . . . thematize[s] the particular form of authentic human existence which emerges from reflection on the historical and religious experience of victims of historical domination. Resistance is to be understood as the maintenance by the victims of any shred of humanity in situations of massive and systematic dehumanization.[23]

When victims of sexual abuse defend their inner psyche against abuse through whatever symptoms they need, they are resisting dehumanization. When survivors reject society's ignorance and seek healing, they are resisting the abuse of power that is intended to destroy them. Victims and survivors of sexual violence struggle to maintain their humanity "in situations of massive and systematic dehumanization." This resistance is based on the primal hope of everyone in the relational web for communion and freedom, even in the midst of evil and injustice. We can choose to live in solidarity with survivors of sexual violence for clues about resistance to power abuse, which can provide a basis for faith in a God of love and power.

In human resistance to the abuse of power, we see analogies to Jesus' resistance to the power and principalities of his time. For many resilient spirits through the ages, Jesus has been an inspiring figure of hope in the midst of evil. Jesus has also been appropriated through the centuries to support the powers of evil and violence. Discovering the Jesus who can reveal God's power and love and clearing away the distortions that would make Jesus into one who sanctions abuse of power is one of the challenges of modern theology. In this way abuse of power is a theological problem.

I have seen the redemption of God's power in the stories and courageous actions of survivors of sexual violence. Their stories have inspired me. Their voices are testimony to the resilient God who has been revealed in Jesus Christ.

Power in its ideal form is the energy of life itself as it is organized into the relational web that includes us all. This primal relational power is distorted through human sin by individuals and societies into abuse of power and is the cause of much human suffering. Through resistance to the abuse of power and the work of God's love in Jesus Christ, the human spirit is made resilient. We search for the resilient hope of the human spirit, which can resist abuse and create new communities for the restoration of communion and freedom of self, others, and God.

CHAPTER THREE

KAREN: SURVIVOR OF SEXUAL VIOLENCE

In several years of teaching and pastoral counseling, I have been engaged in conversation with survivors of child sexual abuse. I first heard Karen's story in a workshop on child abuse where she told of her childhood and adult experiences of sexual violence. Writing and speaking have become a part of her healing, and she identifies many of the important issues for those she addresses. By way of letters and phone calls, we began a conversation that lasted eighteen months. What follows first is her speech to a national group in the church. The second part of the chapter includes excerpts from her letters to me, which give more detail about some of the events covered in the speech. Even though there is some repetition of material, the changed context gives useful insight into her healing experiences. Karen gives an interior picture of the suffering that comes from abuse of power and the resilient hope in the human heart.

KAREN'S SPEECH

When I was four years old I was sexually molested by someone I knew and had learned to trust. That someone was my father. When one is so young it is easy to believe what adults say and do to you is right, even if it is wrong. It is easy to get caught up in promises and special secrets. It is easy to become a victim, again and again.

In the morning of my life, my right to a happy, carefree childhood was stolen. Instead of the spontaneous play of childhood, I became quiet, never cried, and was the "good one." Inside I knew pain and humiliation, fear and distrust. My childhood years were offset by repeated physical and emotional violations of my body. To cope, I buried the experiences beyond the level of consciousness. My mind helped me survive by forgetting. As I passed through my teenage and young adult years, I was ravaged by fears of men, depression, and a deep sense that something was not right. I was aware of something "missing" but could never identify the "it" or the cause of "it." I felt I was being followed by a heavy, mysterious shadow.

When I was thirty-five I was raped by an acquaintance—someone I knew and trusted. He was a nationally recognized minister who was well known and respected by the ecumenical church. The experience left me psychologically anesthetized. I was unable to comprehend this devastating, humiliating experience. He threatened me and told me to keep silence. I did, for six years. Yet, my body and mind adopted their own ways to cope with the trauma. To manage the high anxiety, sleepless nights, nightmares, and fear, I invested myself in a doctoral study program. Unconsciously I drove myself to busyness. As long as I remained busy, no one would suspect the fear and torment that inhabited the deep crevices of my body.

Upon completion of my doctoral studies, I was not swift enough to leap into as equally demanding a project. Before I knew it, my body began to tell the story. I became desperately ill and was hospitalized. The accumulated trauma of incest and rape numbed my ability to feel. I was ill and in pain, yet I could not recognize or feel it.

Later, a sermon on anger prompted me to seek counseling from my pastor. He wisely referred me to a special therapist. Somehow in all the pain, I chose to search for wholeness. With the compulsion of a detective solving a masked hold-up, I was driven to find that which invaded my life and stole my childhood, my womanhood, and myself. I was insistent from the beginning that my therapy be holistic. I worked with my therapist, physician, and pastor. I sincerely believed that all parts of me worked together, and the damage I had sustained affected all parts of myself. One part must work with the other in order to heal effectively.

I must admit I didn't know what I was getting into. If I had known that healing would hurt so much, I would likely have chosen not to heal. My therapy was anything but traditional. One of the first things I was asked to do was to journal and draw and paint. "I'm not an artist," I complained, but I began to write profusely and, surprisingly, I began to draw. When I couldn't find the words to write, I drew. Drawings emerged from dreams and from budding memories. I drew my pain. And I wrote. I wrote my dreams, my thoughts, and the memories that surfaced. I wrote poetry and psalms. I wish to share my first psalm, written early in my painful journey:

My God, my God
Why have you forsaken me?
My body cries out.
My hands are in knots
My neck is pained with tension
My chest is tight, breathing is labored
My stomach grows with unrest
My mouth is dry
My eyes will not close with sleep
My ears ring
My mind is pregnant with unrest
My legs are curled, the muscles crying with tightness
My heart beats on while pain abounds
Oh God, my God
Where are you now?

My spirit longs for thee
for the peace that comes with rest
for the peace that arrives on the footsteps of truth
for the peace that comes with the healing of brokenness
for the peace that comes with the release of the pained soul from bondage
for the peace that creeps in when I can share the depths of my pain with trusted ones.

Oh God, my God
release the wells of my eyes
break down the remaining walls of my defense
destroy the fear that enfolds my being
awaken the courage to continue to reach out, to unfold

Grant me patience, Lord, to endure
—the time required for healing
—the pain of the width and depth of my emotion
—the pain of aloneness
—the search for truth and understanding
—the search for meaning

> O God. I feel like the abandoned child, hardening myself to survive because I feel so alone. I cry out again—please enfold me in your arms and wrap me with care. Melt my defenses. Help me to surrender to complete trust in significant others so my story can be told and I can find the things that make for peace. I pray that through this death I may find life.

I also began to write letters to my pain, to various parts of my body, to my anger—all those parts of me I had ignored. In my writing I began to invite anger, pain, and memories into my conscious life so that I could meet them and learn from them. I wanted them to speak to me. I began to ask many questions of them, and in time, received many answers. In reality, those parts of me asked questions and provided answers that I didn't want to hear. But they were necessary to my healing. The journal became a vital part of me. I could write and draw experiences I couldn't speak. Filled with pages of words and pictures, it became the synthesis of my story.

My therapist also encouraged me to express my anger. This was *new* for me for I had learned early as a child *not* to express feelings, particularly anger. I was asked to make a stuffed animal and I did—in the image of a male—complete with all vital body parts. Then I was instructed to beat it—and I did. Now on my third tennis racket, the animal is nearly mutilated. I also began to play racquetball once or twice weekly. I had an excellent partner, one who coached me to swear, to name the men, and to slam the ball against the wall with all the intensity of the reservoir of my anger. A game of racquetball is one of the most therapeutic uses of one hour for me.

When I refused medication to bring on the needed sleep, my physician wrote a prescription for a running program for me. It was most effective. Within two weeks I began to sleep.

Though angry and bitter, I also had within me the small child who was never comforted and held as a child, particularly in times of distress. My therapist recommended "holding therapy." Sometimes it was my husband. But most other times I engaged the compassionate services of a female friend, who held me, sang to me, or played soothing music while she wrapped me in a blanket and rocked me in her lap. My husband bought me a teddy bear, my first, for my forty-fourth birthday. I slept with it for many nights and still take it with me when I sleep in unfamiliar places. My husband also bought me a kitten. This cat intuitively knows she is a comforter for me.

Also in therapy I learned to meditate, to go deep within to the core, to listen to the small quiet voice within. I learned to trust the wisdom of my body, to follow its direction. I learned to recognize that my body was telling me how to heal. With meditation, I also learned to visualize and I employed the techniques learned from Carl and Stephanie Simonton, Bernie Siegel, and my therapist to heal parts of my broken body.

Like most sexual abuse survivors, I really began to heal when I began to remember. I remembered the rapes (there was more than one by the same man) of six years earlier and later remembered the childhood incest of forty years earlier.

Early in the healing process I learned that most perpetrators deny their wrong. Eight months into therapy I confronted my rapist. He denied everything. Later I went to my parents to share the story of the rapes and the childhood molestations. I asked them for support during my struggle to heal. Instead, I received denial of the sexual abuse and no support for healing. In fact, my father's advice was "If we forget about this, it will go away." The denials ripped to shreds the beliefs I had about family and friends. It hurt deeply to hear denials from people who were supposed to love me and care about me. I felt abandoned and betrayed, again. I identified with the psalmist who made references to being in the pit, overcome with a sense of powerlessness. I remembered Joseph, also in the pit, crushed by the betrayal of those he once trusted. I was in a state of inertia. Henri Nouwen calls us the "walking wounded." Even though I chose to be in counseling, most movements and changes were feared and experienced as painful and more disruptive to my life. Time seemed like an eternity in which I existed. My body was gorged with pain—at times nearly unable to move. Frequently I felt my only choice was to die.

At the advice of my therapist, I turned to the church for help. With the assistance of my pastor, I chose five persons to be my support group. Care was given to choose people who could provide confidentiality, compassion, and encouragement to endure the arduous journey ahead of me. This group became my safety net. When we were together, I knew I was in a safe place to be me, to tell and re-tell my story, to be heard and believed. I looked forward to our meetings every two weeks. The time spent together gave me the encouragement and hope I needed to run the race. In between meetings, members of the group would call or stop by to see me. We cried together, prayed together, and celebrated victories and growth. This group was and still is my "church." We continue to meet on a regular basis; however, the support has widened to include us all. For clergy or members of the helping professions, I recommend this type of group. Rape and incest are afflictions that are difficult for us to share in church, at work, or in the marketplace. Victims need to be nurtured more openly, as they are when there is divorce, death, or illness. Yet, care must be exercised as to how they receive care and where it is safe to share grief.

While the small support group served my needs to be nurtured and cared for, the larger church became the target for much of my anger and bitterness. As I began the process of remembering, I had memories of learning the Bible verse "Honor thy Father and Mother"—of placing a sticker on a chart to reward my memorization of this verse. I remember my Sunday school teacher telling us that parents love you and protect you and know what is right for you. She also told us that parents would "be there" for you. We could go to them and they would listen and respond to us. Additionally, she told us that God is like a loving parent and will always protect us from harm. It was in the church that I learned not to question the behavior of adults. It was this very teaching that laid the groundwork for the accumulated layers of guilt and shame. That teaching coupled with the threat "you would never tell" sealed a story so deep inside that parts of it still have yet to emerge after four-and-a-half years of therapy.

Angry as I was, I continued to attend church and participate in a variety of roles. Yet I was aware of a growing sense of uncomfortableness. I was attending the same church the perpetrator of my childhood abuse was attending. In addition, a former pastor who had displayed inappropriate sexual behavior toward me when I earlier asked for help also attended the same church. And finally, the man who raped me was called into service by the larger church and cited for his contributions to the church. Sunday after Sunday, I would watch or hear these men called out and lifted up by the church. My body ached with the inconsistency of behavior in their lives. I soon recognized I was being victimized by the church again. After three years of internal struggle I slowly withdrew from the church. It was just this past spring that I finally left.

It was difficult to decide to leave a church after forty-six years, but I was finally able to do it without guilt and fear. It was the right decision for me and one supported by my pastors. I have high regard for pastors who can be sensitive to and supportive of the needs of a member. As I have widened my circle of contact with other sexual abuse victims and survivors I have learned from many of them that their pastor did not believe their story and essentially prevented any healing from occurring within the church. We need to enable pastors to hear the story of sexual abuse and respond with compassion and understanding. In addition, we must face the truth that abuse occurs within the church and among members of the church. We must not toss aside or ignore this devastating event that occurs in the lives of many young children and adults.

Healing is painfully slow and difficult. Both therapists I have worked with have suggested a seven-to-ten-year recovery process. I have struggled to overcome guilt and shame, finally being able to admit I did not invite the experiences of childhood abuse or rape. I am still working on remembering parts of my story. I continue to express anger and rage, which are essential to my healing. I have learned to trust some people. And I still grieve for the losses, not only for me but for the rest of my family as I have struggled with healing. I can now cry in a limited fashion, and my self-confidence and self-esteem are fairly restored.

Incest and rape are not about sex. They are about power and control. It's about big people over little people, superior over subordinate. To heal requires that I gain a sense of control in my life. I've gained enough control to make the transition from victim to survivor. The healing process is long but I've surrendered to the fact that being in the process of healing is a respectable and legitimate place to be. I deserve to heal. My greatest victory has been to break the promise and tell my story. I have been able to use the power of writing and speech to transform, to change anger, fear, shame, and guilt into useful tools for cutting away lies and deception.

The more I hear and read my own story, the more the truth of it all becomes a part of me. Thank you for letting me hear it one more time.

EXCERPTS FROM KAREN'S LETTERS

What is abuse of power and how does it get organized in the family? First, there was the threat from my father not to tell anyone. This threat was indirectly given in statements such as, "You would not tell your mother. This could hurt her." What child wants to intentionally hurt her mother? So, the secret was kept. Sheer size of a father can quiet any child. A child can never win, sizewise, when conflict occurs. Since my father committed the molestation during the night, in the dark, many times nothing was said—I did not know who he was. He appeared as a monster. No one paid attention to my comments about a monster in my bedroom. Of course, such things do not exist!

Second, I do not know to this day whether my mother ever knew the abuse was occurring. Her comments lead me to believe she did not know. If she did know, she pretended not to know. My father represents a well-known family—a family of seven children, all raised by their mother after the father died when my father (the oldest) was a teenager. There is so much respect for this family, for their strength in adverse times and for their survival. People see my father as a decent, respectable man. Such a man, in my mother's eyes, would never think of committing such an act as sexual abuse. My mother is quiet and passive, and does not speak up for herself or her rights. Nor does she question my father; he is always right. My mother cannot allow herself to entertain any other possible qualities of my father. In many respects, mother held power over me because "your dad knows best."

Third, I needed the love of my parents and I desperately wanted to please them. I was reminded to be good, to do good and never cause "trouble" for adults. Ironically, it was all right for adults to cause trouble for children! I was a pleasing child as well as extremely guilt-laden. I always sensed and carried a tremendous burden of guilt when I caused the least inconvenience for someone. While in college, my roommate shouted at me one time, "Why do you always say I'm sorry! I cannot stand the frequency with which you say that." The sense of guilt followed long overdue into my adult life. For years I felt responsible for every little thing that went wrong.

My overwhelming dependence on my parents stemmed from the fear I had of this unknown monster in my bedroom. Even though they provided no support for their scared child, I still looked to them for protection. Still unaware the abuser was my father, it seemed safe to assume protection from him and my mother. The strange thing was, even though I depended on them for protection, I did not get it. This compounded my fear, yet I felt less worthy of asking for protection. *No one* put me to bed—I went up the stairs by myself to the lonely bedroom in a dark, old farmhouse. Essentially, no one was there for me as a child. There was no one to verbalize my fears to, no one to cuddle me and soothe me, *no one, no one, no one.* After a few attempts to ask for support, I was told to be a big girl and go to bed. I did not want (or could not want) them to know I was not big, so I walked off into the scary night by myself. I recall being so afraid of the dark night, thunderstorms and loud noises, but I never asked anyone for support. I was afraid, but more afraid to risk asking for support only to be rejected again. In my mind I clearly was not worth their effort to support me. My coping strategy was to numb myself and turn all feelings inward. In short, the abuse that was happening to me in the night had to be my fault. My parents did not see or hear my fright so I must be causing it. My father frequently referred to other people in such ways as, "He's crazy, What a dumb guy," etc. All these kinds of comments. By doing so in front of me, I rapidly learned that my dad was the good guy, the smart guy. Little did I understand that his putdowns were a cover for himself. Again, such statements caused me to uphold my dad rather than question him.

In a recent state of deep relaxation and trance, I found myself in the room where I attended Sunday school as a four- or five-year-old child. I stood in front of a poster on the wall, which had all the names of my classmates listed. Beside our names were stickers, placed in a row after we had memorized certain Bible verses. I heard myself repeating "Honor thy Father and Mother." While I sat on the floor with my classmates, our teacher told us about the goodness of parents; they love us, feed, clothe, and protect us from *all* harm. I learned early, while being abused, that my parents kept me from harm. The church taught me to be grateful to parents and to trust they would always protect me. Again, when I was five, my young mind would not let me think that my father could be anything but good.

My reaction to this remembering has been anger. In recent weeks it has been nearly impossible to attend church. I recognize my anger at church leaders who taught me to believe that whatever my parents did was right and good for me. What child can question the church? God, like parents, loves us and protects us from harm. The message was clear. The church, then, as now, must accept responsibility for silencing those subject to abuse.

During fourth grade (the abuse was in its sixth year), I began to complain of headaches every day. After several weeks of the same complaint, my teacher evidently contacted my mother who in turn took me to an eye doctor. He asked me all kinds of questions about seeing near and far, performed a typical exam, and then pronounced nothing was wrong with my vision. Again, *no one* ever questioned me any more about the headaches. I was returned to school with the report of fine vision. The headaches continued; however, I ceased to complain, choosing instead to repress the pain. Eventually the headaches were no longer known to me. When teachers, parents, and the church did nothing to hear my cry, I concluded I certainly was not worth voicing the cry. My mother did not like complainers. My body accumulated more and more layers of hardness so that the feelings could not be felt. Of course, I ceased to hurt anymore and therefore, did not bother anyone. I wanted to be good and liked, not troublesome.

I think my silencing was largely a part of society's belief that young children are of little value. What they say is unimportant, certainly not of reason, logic, or truth. In some respects, I feel the same because of my gender. Women tend not to be respected as ones who can be rational, logical, or truthful. When nursery school teachers are acquitted and jurists say they just did not believe the stories children told, it appears that children are not yet believed to say much of value.

I developed a "false self" in order to survive. By early adolescence, the real me remained unknown to my conscious mind. There was a fascination on my part to set out on a journey to discover my "true self." I began to read the works of several persons who seemed to be respected as those who knew how to discover oneself. I bought books, read, underlined, and journaled. These people offered hope and wisdom to me, such an infant on my journey. I hung on to their words and applied them to my own struggle. My therapist continued to recommend readings to me. Through my reading I connected with others who had struggled and survived, but most important of all, I sensed no regrets on the part of authors regarding their circumstances. They took the events of their lives and created meaning. I sensed their satisfaction in plodding, taking small steps, and later, being able to reflect and evaluate the distance traveled. Obviously, the satisfaction came *after* much of the plodding and traveling!

Survivors did not place limits on what they did to try to survive. I ceased saying "I cannot" and began to test my limits. My limits appear to have no end; when I get within reach, new limits beckon. I am fascinated with where I am being led. Clearly, I am "in motion." Why not? What compels me? An inner sense, a drive, that all my struggle is for a purpose yet to be defined. It's the fascination of the unknown that compels me to continue.

My moment of transformation was like the story in Genesis. Creation occurred following the time of nothingness. Out of chaos came the new, the fresh. I also had my "genesis moment," a time of being in the dark surrounded by chaos. It was at that point that death looked inviting. Pain was too great. My therapist challenged my thinking by suggesting that the most creative moments often follow times of despair, of dark. I was fascinated with the imagery. I keenly felt the chaos, the despair, the pain that accompanies birth. I was intrigued by the idea of creating meaning out of chaos. Literally, my mind became full of images of creation—turbulence, wind, dashing seas, lightning, and crashing thunder. I asked for direction. The pain advanced, I groaned and the birth was in process. It was a long labor! Incidentally, this all happened once I surrendered to my illness.

Once I stopped fighting the story, I was caught up in it, content to trust the forces. I surrendered my need to control my creation and liberation, and allowed myself to follow. This was not an easy transformation to make, since abuse victims feel they have had no control. Therefore, it was important to keep control. It was a member of my support group who finally convinced me I could survive *if* I gave up the need to control my journey. She encouraged me to trust the process, another difficult thing to do since I had learned never to trust anyone.

After so many years of avoiding the pain, I was convinced by my therapist to acknowledge pain, to sense it, listen to it, and draw my story from it. I allowed myself to move from numbness into pain, and I remained with the pain a long time. It was a vital part of me I had not met. I wrote to the pain, drew pictures of it, talked with it, even scooped it up and held it in my hands at times, stroking and nurturing it. The pain was me and it helped me discover more of me. Throughout all this time, my therapist would never allow me to medicate the pain.

My physician and my pastor were the first to know the truth of my life. First I trusted my physician. Soon after, my pastor preached a sermon on anger, and I was eventually able to tell him. Both observed that I was visibly quite ill and rapidly getting worse. The difference was they asked questions beyond the routine questions. They did not reject me. When I stumbled with an answer or could not find the words to answer, they read my body language. They both were extremely sensitive men. Their training had taught them to listen to the words *and* the body. By this time my body was so ill they knew there was meaning beneath the surface. Interestingly enough, for all my hurt by men, I was able to respond to these two men at the outset. Part of the reason they gained my fractured trust early was that both of them, in different settings, clearly articulated they would not touch me or hurt me in any way. They respected me as a woman who had been devastated by men. They knew their boundaries. I was weak and sick; yet I was able to respond to their caring because I sensed they would *not* hurt me. They believed me, listened to me, and I, being so hungry for *someone* to hear me, began to believe they had my best interests at heart. Also, I was clearly *dying*. When someone cared enough to attend to me, I risked reaching out.

In my search for community, it was important to find the right people to be in my support group; people who, above all, respected confidentiality. I found people who could listen, share, and confront when I needed to be confronted. Most likely, their unconditional love drew me inside their circle and kept me there. I had learned only conditional love as a child. To be loved unconditionally was new. The group provided safety for me, again something contradictory to my upbringing. Parents are supposed to protect children from harm. In my case, the direct harm was done by my father. I had no sense of protection or safety. It took a long period of time to gain a sense of safety within my group. As I write this, I realize there are some parts of my story that I have not yet shared with this group. In fact, some parts have never been shared with anyone, not even my therapist. I have yet to find the courage to write or tell the whole story. That's part of the conflict between the two selves—one self is bravely on a journey while the other self is still afraid to move forward, to trust. I keenly sense that conflict and think that is the source of much of my personal unrest yet today. One limit I still retain is the fear of telling the rest of the story. Trust is an issue. Fear is an issue. I have not gained the strength to let all the terror be known. Perhaps I am not ready to be consciously aware of all the terror. I guess this is part of the journey—knowing there is likely a detour ahead, where I will have to shift routes and deal with the story yet to be known. When that time comes, my group will be there for me.

I have grown angrier at the church and the ideals it perpetuates because of two incidents that happened recently. These show you how difficult it is for me to see the church as a place of community. In fact, because of these two incidents, I lack any feeling of safety in the church.

Several weeks ago, we had communion during the worship service. A group of people from one church school class had been invited to serve communion. To my horror, one of the communion servers was our former pastor, the one who made sexual advances toward me when I first decided I needed counseling. (After his overpowering advances, I did not seek help for another three years.) I could not bear to see him "chosen" for this act in the worship. In the same worship service, my pastor made reference to the "poignant story of one woman's story of abuse" during his sermon. He was referring to my article in a recent church publication. I froze. Here, in one sense I was lifted up, and yet I had to sit through church and be served communion by one of the three men who had sexually devastated my life. I felt the contradictions. I was angry. How does a church continue to love both of us—the abuser and the victim? I found a member of my group after church and we went to a quiet place where I sobbed and sobbed.

Two weeks later, a similar incident occurred in which a well-meaning gentleman shared an issue raised in our church magazine in which the hunger in a third world nation was the feature story. He named the missionaries to whom "we need to send money to support their good work." Well, the missionary named was the man who raped me, the one who held me hostage and raped me more than once, only to turn me loose and say, "Do not tell anyone."

This church was not a place for me. I could not feel safety or find peace in a place where the innocent cry inwardly with despair and the perpetrator is uplifted. I was convinced I could never feel safe within the walls of this church. I appreciate my current pastor, for he has been one of the gentle souls who has guided me in the past four years. In both of the above cases, he was unaware that the two events were going to occur. He felt my pain and understood my need to leave. Am I angry at God, or the people who make up the church? My feelings toward God are numb. I confess I fear God. I feel very much alone and wonder whether there is a loving God out there for me.

Two weeks ago, I made the decision to leave our church. Presently, I do not attend any church, preferring instead to spend Sunday mornings alone in my own private meditation at home. It seems to be the right decision for now, and I could finally reach it without guilt and fear. It took me a long time, but I was finally able to "know and feel" the rightness about the decision. . . .

Recently, after telling my story to a national church group, a woman in the audience raised a question regarding my spiritual life. She said, "You seem so spiritual a person. Who, or what, is your image for spiritual contact?" First I appreciated being referred to as spiritual, especially because I have left the church. That confirms my belief that one's spiritual development is not confined ever to a building or place or set of rituals or a group of people. I responded with some of my most recent thinking in this area. My image is that of a being, neither male nor female. The being is faceless. It has wide spreading arms, draped with a filmy robe that opens up and out to me. I refer to it as the Great Healing

Spirit. I like it. When I close my eyes in need to contact a spiritual being, this is what I image. It serves me very well at this point.

It is with hope that I choose to walk into the future. In a recent dream I found myself selecting new trees to be planted in the yard of my childhood home. I was adamant about choosing trees that would flower and bloom. Perhaps this was a foretelling of the time to plant anew upon the graveyards of the past. Trees are symbolic of growth and strength. With time, they sink their roots deep, enabling them to weather many storms. Trees are also symbolic of death and life; it is only through the cycle of dying that they emerge anew. I ponder the meaning of this dream, caught up in the image of newness at the scene of a long ago tragedy. Therein lies hope. Out of profound darkness comes light, and inherent in it all is meaning.

CONCLUDING COMMENT

In order to make sense of sexual violence, the voices of victims and survivors must be given priority. It is they who endure abuse and violence while society keeps silence. The truth can only be known when their voices are clearly heard. Their strength is needed for the whole community. Karen has spoken as one survivor. She adds her voice to the thousands of women who are beginning to speak about the terror of their lives and their agonizing recovery in a society that continues to deny the reality of sexual violence.

It is difficult to hear the voices of survivors like Karen. In order to hear her story we have to imagine ourselves as small and helpless in a destructive situation with no understanding or support. Such feelings of helplessness are frightening for us. They remind us how dependent we are on the benevolent attitudes and behaviors of others. Our feelings of being competent and in control are fragile. Listening to survivors puts us in touch with the fear of our vulnerability in a dangerous world.

Listening to Karen is inspiring because of her resilient hope in the midst of evil and death. If hope is possible in her life of terror, then it is possible for others who seek new life.

CHAPTER FOUR

STORIES OF RECOVERING PERPETRATORS

In order to understand how abuse of power is organized, we need to hear the voices and testimonies of those who know sexual violence first-hand. We have listened to a survivor who had the courage to speak about her suffering in the midst of society's denial and taboos.

We also need to hear the truth about sexual violence from those few men who are trying to recover from their addiction to power and are willing to be vulnerable with their inner psychic processes. This testimony is difficult to obtain because so few men have the courage to share their stories. In this chapter we try to hear from perpetrators. In the midst of their distorted cries for help are clues to the need all men have to change their basic perceptions about power. By listening for the truth in the midst of evil, perhaps we can begin to see certain beliefs held in common by all men that sometimes lead to abuse and which require radical transformation.

MY PERSONAL STORY

Several years ago I began working as a psychotherapist with incestuous families.[1] In the agency where I practiced I was one of only three men in a staff of fifteen. I was assigned to a perpetrators' group and worked with child molesters in individual and group psychotherapy. When I moved to a new city, I continued the same kind of work.[2]

It was a shock to hear the stories of molesters and to be in the presence of such disturbed and dangerous men. As a therapist I had to be clear about limits both inside and outside therapy. The ethical responsibility of the therapist is high and remains a constant issue. A therapist must work in partnership with other professionals in social work and law to provide for the safety of women and children. It is difficult to set up adequate accountability for perpetrators of sexual violence so that the abuse does not continue during treatment. Professionals who work with this population need to be alert to the extreme danger; there must be legal consequences for violations based on information from other family members. Denial and rationalization are defenses commonly offered by perpetrators that make the truth nearly impossible to discern. All perpetrators lie to avoid the consequences of their crimes. Male therapists need to understand that they are not adequately sensitive to abuse by men and therefore need feedback from and accountability to female therapists.

When legal and therapeutic limits are put in place to discourage further abuse, and when instructional efforts are organized to challenge the cognitive distortions, therapy then includes listening to and interpreting the pain of these men. They are out of touch with the emptiness and isolation of their own lives, and they externalize their problems by blaming others. They feel entitled to emotional control of the women and children in their families and resent any interference from child protective agencies, courts, and therapists. In order to work with this population, one must be firm about the consequences of violating limits and patiently wait for the fragile growth of trust in the midst of manipulation and rationalizations. These factors make clinical work with perpetrators difficult and challenging.

I have never been able to give a good answer for why I work with child molesters. I wonder if it is not because I grew up in a traditional middle-class culture in the United States in which emotional pain was denied. My parents had survived sad childhoods of their own and they were determined to make things better for their children. The culture of the fifties encouraged conformity and offered prosperity for those who were the most socialized. I was the oldest child and most anxious to please. So I grew up as an achiever with many strong feelings that had to be repressed. I have struggled in my own psychotherapy to mend my childhood wounds.

There is something about working with molesters that keeps me in touch with my own primitive feelings. Molesters put me in touch with impulses that have been repressed, with my own unconscious violence that controls so much of what I feel and do. My own growth and understanding from this work have been important.

Another motive for my work with molesters is critique of culture. The culture of the fifties was controlling and numbing. Individuals were taught to sacrifice their own impulses in exchange for social respectability and success. The cost for individuals was not only the loss of feeling and integrity, but also a blindness to social injustice. American culture depends on the uncritical cooperation of its people. Working with child molesters breaks through my anesthesia toward the injustice of culture.

A child molester is a frightening example of how society fails to hold men accountable for their abuses. Research shows that "the combined conviction rate for . . . child sexual abuse is 1 percent."[3] When estimates of unreported cases are added, the accountability of men for their crimes of sexual violence is abysmally small. To the extent that men are protected from the consequences of their crimes against those who are vulnerable, the culture bears responsibility for the violations of women and children. Many molesters are confused by the consequences that follow arrest and conviction because they were but exercising the privileges men are expected to have in the family. Through my work in this area, I have been able to uncover some of the lies that protect the powerful at the expense of the vulnerable. My gain is an awareness of society's wrongs that breaks through my own numbness toward social evil.

Working with molesters has also challenged and transformed my theology. As a follower of process theology, I have a radical empirical view of the relation of God and the world. I believe that God is present in every moment of experience, working to increase intensity and harmony. Perhaps I accepted this view of reality because of my own feeling of distance from God. I want to believe that God is present in a personal way even though often I cannot feel it.

In working with child molesters, however, the problem of evil cannot be ignored. In the presence of such human destructiveness, it is impossible to retain a naive doctrine of the goodness of God. Individual and social evil is so apparent in child sexual abuse that it challenges any easy conception that God's grace is available to all. Where is God's justice and love in the life of a man who has raped a child? Within child molesters, within their families, and within a society that ignores the extent of child abuse, evil is organized and powerful. Other examples of extreme evil such as the holocaust and American slavery may reveal patterns similar to those of sexual violence. There seems to be no limit to evil when the structures of domination rule the world. The tragedy of human suffering when evil is in control is enormous. The relation of evil and goodness in God is a puzzle that is not easily solved when we face the full implications of sexual violence.

Where is the hope in a God of love and power when one has perpetrated evil? Here recovering perpetrators have been my teachers. In some men who choose the arduous road to healing and want to make a radical change in their lives, I have seen a resilient hope that has not completely died. This courage of the human spirit in the face of the internal power of evil is remarkable. If hope is still present in some of these men, then perhaps hope is still possible in a society that invented slavery and nuclear weapons. One recovering perpetrator suffered severe sexual abuse as a teenager and was arrested just as he was making the transition to abusing others. One of his counselors told him that he had one chance in a thousand to recover. He said, "I do not plan to be a statistic." The resiliency of his spirit cannot be explained by any theory. A few molesters have a determination to face the evil in their own lives and have not given up hope for themselves. This may be validation of faith in a God who is resilient in the presence of evil.

FINDING THE STORIES OF PERPETRATORS

I have been unable to co-author a chapter with a perpetrator because I have found none with the courage to speak the truth about his life in public. Therefore I have made a second choice—to report my own perceptions about perpetrators. In addition to my clinical work with molesters, I have been immersed in reading and have discussed the dynamics of incestuous families with other therapists in workshops and conferences. I have heard hundreds of stories about the various issues that arise out of this population. From my experience as a whole, I have created stories and fictitious characters that describe some of the pain and rage I have witnessed. I have tried to discern general patterns, and I have filled them with fictitious content. In this way I have been true to my oath of confidentiality, yet I am able to share some of my general perceptions. Nothing I say is the story of any single person who has shared with me.

One additional caution about the following stories. I have been working as a psychotherapist with individuals and families for seventeen years, including training in several intensive programs.[4] I continue to work under supervision after five years' experience with perpetrators of sexual abuse. It is important that pastors and other untrained counselors not underestimate the difficult clinical issues of this population. This story is meant to serve as instructive material, not as a guide for clinicians.

THERE IS NO TYPICAL STORY

The fictional story of Sam which follows represents one of the more optimistic case studies and shows that the issues are difficult to face and resolve even under optimal conditions. There are several ways in which this composite case presentation does not give an accurate picture:

First, Sam's story gives a distorted view because most molesters do not acknowledge what they have done, and most never seek or take the opportunity of therapy. Most who do begin therapy do not respond positively to treatment. Even after years of therapy, most molesters still maintain some denial about the significance of their behaviors. Denial is the typical defense against accountability for sexual violence and is the most serious problem blocking molesters from the treatment they need. Sam is unusual because he gradually began to face the truth about his life and stayed in treatment over a long period of time in spite of his pain and depression.

Second, Sam's story gives a distorted picture because it seems to imply that "abuse victims become abuse perpetrators."[5] Most molesters I have known have been abused or deprived as children, and their sexual violence as adults seems to be a repetition of their own trauma. Evidently there is an important relationship between trauma in childhood and becoming abusive as an adult.[6] However, research has shown that "most children who are molested do not go on to become molesters themselves. This is particularly true among women, who whether victimized or not rarely become offenders."[7] It is also true that many men who have been victims of child sexual abuse do not become molesters. Clearly, sexual violence results from multiple causes in need of more complete study, including social factors and male socialization, which will be examined more closely later. My own experience, as reported here, indicates a high prevalence of sexual and other trauma during the childhood of molesters, but this conclusion may be premature.

Third, this story does not explore adequately the question of why child sexual abuse is primarily perpetrated by men rather than women.

There are clear differences in the way men and women are socialized as children and in the expectations for male and female behavior in the adult culture. Women are often victimized as children, and have to cope with their subordinate positions in the adult world. Their behaviors are circumscribed by the limitations of patriarchy and inequality. Men are socialized to be dominant in interpersonal relationships, and they are excused for their abusive behaviors. Men abuse children because they are not held accountable for their actions, and because they choose to inflict suffering on others. The differences between men and women is a leading research issue for this study.

Fourth, Sam represents only one of many types of molesters. There have been several attempts to categorize the types of molesters.[8] If one thinks of molesters as a group along a continuum, at one end are those men like Sam who molest infrequently, usually under stress, and for whom the prognosis is only fair even under optimal treatment conditions. Some in this group receive help because of psychic pain under other diagnoses such as alcoholism, depression, or suicidal ideation, without ever revealing their history of sexual violence. At the other end of the continuum are those violent molesters, for whom there is no known treatment, who rape or kill children they do not know.

In between these extremes there are molesters with every diagnosis and many different patterns. There is no correlation between the symptom of child sexual abuse and any particular psychological pathology, or between child sexual abuse and social class. The population of child molesters is much larger and more complex than the public realizes. In order to understand why child sexual abuse is so widespread, we must listen to the testimonies of survivors as they describe the consequences of growing up in such terror. Hearing the voices of survivors will give us clues to the phenomenon we are trying to understand and treat. In addition we must hear the destructive images and inner pain of the molesters themselves. Until we can begin to identify the individual and social causes of sexual violence, we will not be able to prevent the widespread prevalence of this evil.

SAM: A RECOVERING PERPETRATOR

Sam grew up pretty much on his own with few attachments that he could count on. His father left home before he started to school and he does not remember any positive contact with him. As an adult he learned that his father had died in his early fifties of alcoholism. Because Sam's mother could not manage the four children after the departure of Sam's father, Sam and his siblings spent several years in foster care. It was here that he first remembers being mistreated. He was beaten for minor offenses, and has a vague recollection of being molested by the older children in the family, but he is not sure. Sam's early life was characterized by family instability and unreliable adult relationships.

Sam was greatly relieved when his mother remarried and collected the children. Things were better for a short time—at least there was greater financial stability. When Sam was nine, his step-father promised him what seemed a significant sum of money if he would "give him a blow-job." He felt forced by the situation to comply since he did not know how to protect himself. This incident was repeated several times before his step-father stopped. Extreme distance characterized their relationship after that. Later he was also molested by his mother's brother, who forced Sam to masturbate him to orgasm. Sam was terrified by these experiences and unable to talk to his mother because his relationship with her was difficult and she always sided with adults against him.[9]

These incidents of sexual abuse led to increasing depression and isolation from peers and adults. He had difficulty concentrating on his school work and was frequently in trouble with teachers at school. He made one friend in fifth grade, but this friend moved away at Christmas and Sam never saw him again. When he was fifteen Sam began abusing alcohol as a form of relief from the daily pain and loneliness. When he used alcohol he became enraged and got into fights, which occasionally got him into trouble with the police. He spent several nights in jail, and spent several months in the local detention center for boys. At age seventeen he had his first sexual encounter with a girl in an abandoned car at the back of her father's lot, an experience that had very little meaning for him.

After high school Sam worked in a factory on the assembly line, where he met Peggy, an equally immature woman his own age. They started dating and decided to get married when she became pregnant. Their second child, a girl, died of a heart defect when she was one year old. Sam was devastated because he identified so strongly with this frail child, who reminded him of his own lost self. Soon after her death, Sam lost his job, and the family lived on unemployment for a year.

When he could not find work, and Peggy went to work as a waitress,

Sam was alone with his five-year-old son, Johnny. Sam had no understanding of the deep crisis he was in. This was the year he first touched his son sexually. At first it was rough play and tickling, but later Sam was touching Johnny's genitals and masturbating in front of him. In Sam's mind, his son seemed to enjoy the attention and did not mind the touching. The sense of power and excitement for Sam was intoxicating. Here seemed to be the admiration and physical contact that he had always longed for, but had never experienced. One day while they were playing, he forced his penis into his son's mouth. It seemed good for a moment, but then Sam remembered with horror his own experience with his step-father. He stopped, cried, and promised his son that he would never do anything like this again. In his preoccupation with his own shame, he did not notice the devastating effect of this event on his son, who began to have nightmares, physical symptoms, and phobias at school and home.

The next week while he was playing with Johnny, Sam abused his son again. This time he was frightened that he would get into trouble. He cried and forced his son to promise that he would never tell anyone what had happened. His son was terrified and promised he would never tell.

It was several months before Sam played with his son again. But when he thought the danger was over, he began touching his son again. Once the pattern started, Sam did not stop. He began abusing his son on a weekly basis. Sam started drinking again to try to deal with his pain and escape the horror his life was becoming.

One day when he was at the tavern, two policemen arrested him and took him to the station. They said there had been a report from the nursery school teacher that he was molesting his son. At first Sam denied everything and blamed his son for being a liar, but later that night he confessed.

He was arrested and kept in jail for several days while child protective services worked out an arrangement for the family. They decided that Sam could be released on the condition that he have no contact with his son, that he find his own apartment, and that he participate regularly in the program of a sexual abuse treatment agency.

The next day Sam was interviewed at the agency, placed in an orientation group with Peggy and other couples from incestuous families, and assigned to me, his therapist. I saw him about three weeks later. He was very cooperative in the first session, relieved to be out of jail, to have a chance to keep his family together, and relieved to no longer be molesting his son. He felt mistreated by the police, the courts, and the guards at the jail. He was angry, scared, and willing to do anything our agency wanted him to do. He told a lot about his life, including detailed descriptions of molesting his son, as well as detailed stories about his own sad childhood. At one level he wanted help. He was desperate and hoped that our agency would be able to fix his life. There was an initial family session in which Sam apologized to his son and to Peggy and took responsibility for his misconduct. This was a first, tentative step to help his son avoid self-blame, which would require much follow-up later. Peggy was devastated that the man she loved had become so destructive. She was given support, her own therapist, and other resources to help her cope with this crisis in her life.

After a few weeks, Sam was impatient. He heard from other men in the therapy group that the separation from the family often lasted twelve to eighteen months, and that not infrequently there was a divorce. When he shared his perception that his son enjoyed the touching and playing, the counselors confronted him with his rationalization and confusion about his son's real needs. Peggy vacillated in her feelings for him. One day she never wanted to see him again; the next day she helplessly called him and pleaded with him to visit even though it would violate the court order. He did not know whether he wanted to stay married to her or not. He did miss his son terribly and could not understand why his counselors said it was best not to see him for now.

The limitations set by the courts, the county child protection agency, and the treatment center rules infuriated him. He felt he was being treated like a child rather than an adult. His feelings of helplessness often turned to rage, though he was careful not to let his counselors see him angry. The "system" had disrupted his position of dominance and taken away "his" family, which he had abused to compensate for the deficiencies of his empty self. This phase of resistance and avoidance of responsibility lasted many months. He made few comments in therapy group, and talked, in individual therapy, about how lonely he was without his family. His possessive feelings toward his family were a part of the pattern that provided the rationale for abuse. He also talked about being unemployed, about his concern over finances, about his in-laws. In fact, he discussed many things except the sexual abuse of his son and his other abusive patterns. The initial euphoria about the opportunity to get well gave way to depression.

One day he came to the therapy group after he had been drinking. The counselors took him aside and said that if he came to therapy group again after drinking, he would not be able to continue. He would have to make up his mind whether he wanted to be in the program.

In individual counseling, Sam complained about how the therapy group counselors were unfair, how they did not really care about him, and how they did not understand how hard it was for him. I listened and asked him to tell me how bad he really felt. He broke down and cried in a different way from how he had cried before. This time he seemed to be crying not only out of fear and desperation, but also out of a deeper sense of despair about his whole life. Four months into treatment he was finally beginning to feel something and find a few words to express himself. He became more active in the therapy group and asked for time to discuss his situation.

In the meantime, Sam had found a job as a carpenter's assistant with a contractor who built porches and remodeled rooms. At the end of two months' work, Sam had not yet been paid. His boss owed him two thousand dollars and was not sure when he could pay up. Sam came to a session one night and told me he was planning to assault his boss because he believed he would never be paid. He was enraged that someone would do this to him. What he did not see was his own inability to make sound judgments for himself. He could not see that he should have quit after two weeks when it became apparent that he was not going to be paid on time, or that he should have seen the signs of mismanagement much sooner. He also did not see that controlling his impulses was one of his therapeutic issues and losing control could not be blamed on external circumstances. Being in a situation where he felt humiliated and abused was too close to his own inner pathology, and he responded with fantasies of violence.

Explanations did not help. He seemed a potential danger to his boss. After thinking about this situation and talking it over with my supervisor, I decided to tell Sam that I needed to call his boss to tell him about the potential danger. I explained that this would serve two purposes: It might protect his boss from physical harm, and it might help Sam to contain his rage in this situation. An assault charge would jeopardize his probation, his marriage, and his treatment. I said I was willing to provide support as he tried to work out this conflict, but that I needed to take action to protect others and to help him in a situation fraught with danger. It is crucial for therapists to know the limits of confidentiality, especially when the health and safety of others is at risk.

I called his boss to warn him that Sam was telling me he was in danger of becoming violent. The next day, Sam confronted his boss with his feelings of being mistreated. They worked out a compromise that involved getting paid part of the money right away and the rest a week later. When Sam came to the next session, he was feeling much better about himself. A situation that would have led to the kind of fighting he indulged in as a teenager had been averted. Sam was beginning to learn new ways of behaving. He started taking more assertive action in the therapy group around a number of topics.

After about a year of treatment without serious incidents, Sam began to get restless about living alone in an apartment. He felt that he had cooperated with treatment, had not violated his court orders, and yet was not moving toward being reunited with his family. There had been occasional family sessions, and he was engaging in weekly supervised visits with his son. Sam's assertiveness toward the counselors and courts was different from the complaining of many months earlier. This time he was asking for help, and he was willing to compromise. It was the policy of our agency that recommendations to the court about reuniting incestuous families be made by the staff in consultation with all counselors, social workers, and probation officers.

Of first priority was the victim and his counselor. Johnny was now six years old and attending first grade. His ability to play during therapy had gradually improved, and he had made the transition to school without serious incident. But he remained a fragile, easily discouraged, and depressed little boy. The sexual abuse had severely interrupted his development, and he was greatly deficient in impulse control, peer skills, and ability to concentrate on goals. He was afraid of adults and had a negative view of himself and the world around him. The counselor thought that the father-son relationship might still be salvaged, but was skeptical about reuniting the family. Much more work needed to be done in family therapy before Johnny could tolerate his father's presence on a full-time basis.

Peggy's counselor was also skeptical. She had seen small progress in this inadequate and fragile woman, who often fell into helplessness in a crisis. Peggy had also grown up in a dysfunctional family where she was alternately neglected and abused, and she was depressed about the death of her daughter and the terror of discovering that her husband had sexually abused their son. She did not yet have the strength to oppose her husband directly. In the few family sessions, the counselors could see that Sam remained dominant in the family, and he was still unable to see his wife and son as separate people with needs different from his. However, all the counselors agreed that some interpersonal work could be added to individual and group therapy. Regular marital and family sessions were added.

The increased emotional load was difficult for Sam and Peggy. Sam could tolerate very little confrontation about his abusive behaviors. Peggy was still terrified and felt unsafe with him. They had few skills for expressing their feelings to each other and for resolving conflicts between them. The gains they had made in talking with their counselors did not easily translate into effective marital communication. One week Sam missed all his therapy sessions with no explanation. Peggy had not heard from him, and he had not called his counselors. Two weeks passed before Sam showed up at his counseling session, red-eyed, unshaven. He had driven fifty miles to a nearby town, had slept several nights in his car, then stayed with a friend from work. He said he was "thinking"—about whether he wanted to be married to Peggy, and whether he could live with himself as a father who had molested his son. He had not been able to answer either question, but he realized that he really had nothing else to do. Running away was appealing, but it did not solve anything. He missed seeing his counselors and visiting his son. His attachments helped him through a most difficult time.

Peggy was enraged by Sam's absence. Just as she was beginning to trust him a little and to make a few demands, he let her down. Now he was the helpless one who could not stand any confrontation. This crisis began to shift some of the power dynamics of their relationship. Peggy began to see that she was stronger than she had thought, and that Sam had his weaknesses. These insights contributed to their marital therapy.

A crucial issue in the treatment of an incestuous family is whether the non-abusing parent is strong enough to protect the children. Child molesters cannot be fully trusted to put the child's interest ahead of their own, even after years of treatment. This makes the role of the mother critically important. This image of family life is very far from that of a healthy functioning family unit where the adults are partners in the nurture of their children. Until now, it appeared that Peggy was unable to oppose Sam in any important conflict. But Peggy's counselors helped her to see that she had survived as a single parent for more than a year now, and that she had enforced limits on Sam's behavior. Now she had survived his absence and kept functioning. This provided a basis for strengthening her role in the family in the future.

After six more months of therapy, the counselors at last decided there was enough change to warrant the risk of reuniting the family. Certain rules had to be negotiated first, including the rule that Sam would not be alone with his son until unsupervised visits were approved by the counselors. This meant that Johnny had to stay with his grandmother whenever Peggy was at work. Regular progress was made over the next two years up to the end of court probation. After probation, Sam and Peggy decided to remain in therapy on a somewhat reduced schedule. They faced many difficult problems hidden from them during the first eighteen months of crisis. Now they had to face the problems of every family—developing patience for one another in the midst of the stress of modern life, making adjustments for the changing developmental needs of their child, negotiating satisfactory times of intimacy and enjoyable activities, resolving conflicts of values and priorities. They discovered that life was more difficult and more interesting than they had earlier thought. As far as I know, there was no repetition of Sam's molesting behavior during the three years of treatment. No one knows the long-term prognosis of child molesters.

THE ORGANIZATION OF ABUSE OF POWER IN PERPETRATORS

Sam's story gives only a bare outline of his life, and it does not explain the process by which he became a perpetrator of sexual violence against his son. In this chapter we begin a preliminary analysis of themes in the lives of men who have sexually abused women and children. These themes will be expanded and elaborated in later chapters on the self, community, and religion.

For men there is no clear correlation between childhood experiences of abuse and becoming an adult perpetrator. Some men who have been victims of sexual violence do not become perpetrators. They become survivors with personal pain. They may have self-destructive symptoms that continue the effects of the abusive patterns of their childhood trauma, such as substance abuse, but they do not engage in the extreme abuse of power that we know as child sexual abuse. As sexual violence is identified as a problem that can be treated, more men who have been victims will identify themselves and seek help. This will provide research for understanding how men overcome victimization without becoming abusers.[10]

Some men who have not been victims of sexual violence become perpetrators of sexual violence on others. This means that there are motives at work in sexually violent behaviors that cannot be attributed only to individual pathology. Some of the implications of sexual violence and gender will be explored in later chapters.[11]

Some men like Sam who have been victims of sexual violence develop into abusers who act out their trauma on those who cannot protect themselves. One of the questions of our research is why some victims become perpetrators.

More men than women become perpetrators. Some estimates are that 80 to 95 percent of sexual violence is perpetrated by men.[12] Whenever we uncover a gender difference this extreme, we must try to account for the difference. We need to ask why men are more likely to become perpetrators of sexual violence than women.

These questions cannot be fully answered here. There are many theories about why some men become perpetrators, and why more men than women are sexually violent. David Finkelhor has devised a four-factor analysis that will inform our discussion later. He suggests that there are "four preconditions that needed to be met before sexual abuse could occur":

1. A potential offender needed to have some motivation to abuse a child sexually.
2. The potential offender had to overcome internal inhibitions against acting on that motivation.
3. The potential offender had to overcome external impediments to committing sexual abuse.
4. The potential offender or some other factor had to undermine or overcome a child's possible resistance to the sexual abuse.[13]

The importance of Finkelhor's theory is that, where there is inadequate accountability, there is the potential for sexual violence in any man, regardless of individual history or previous abuse. A conviction stemming from this study is that the analysis of causes for sexual violence by men must be made in three areas: individual and intrapsychic, social institutions and ideologies, and religion. The last part of this section is organized around four intrapsychic themes that seem to be present to some extent in the population of men who become perpetrators of sexual violence: sexualized dependency, destructive aggression, the grandiose self, and inability to respect limits.

These themes will be explored in later chapters with the help of critical theories from psychoanalysis, feminism, and liberation theologies. They begin to help us understand the process by which some men become perpetrators of sexual violence and the connection of this process with the stereotypes of what it means to be male and female in United States culture.

We also need to know if there is any hope that the abuse of power in sexual violence can be understood and justice can be found for the thousands of victims. We need to know if there is any hope of transformation for men for whom abuse of power through sexual violence has become a way of living.

Sexualized Dependency

One way to understand a man who has molested children is that he has a dependency disorder.[14] Something is wrong internally with his ability to meet his needs for love and nurture with other adults. He sexualizes his emotional needs and projects them onto children. He feels that he is justified in meeting these needs by abusing persons who are vulnerable, and he is confident that he will not be held accountable for his crimes.

There are several reasons why children may be likely targets of such projections. First, children are vulnerable unless protected by adults. Many children are unprotected and thus are defenseless against adults who want to use them for inappropriate needs. Second, because of their youth and innocence children seem, for some men, symbolically closer to the source of life. To an adult whose inner life is empty, the spontaneity and energy of children can mistakenly seem to be the fullness of life.[15]

In terms of childhood history, many molesters grow up in situations where basic dependency needs are unmet. Robert grew up in a home where his parents and grandparents were active alcoholics. One of his earliest memories was trying to separate his mother and grandmother from physical fights. The men in the family were usually gone, and he felt responsible for trying to keep the two women from killing each other.

When he was eight or nine, his uncle would take him fishing and camping in the mountains. He loved his uncle because he felt included in the male subculture. Unfortunately, his uncle also molested him, leading to a lifetime of confusion about intimacy and sexuality. Sexual abuse became something that he had to tolerate in order to be accepted by men.

When he was ten, Robert was sent to a foster home along with his younger brother. In this home, Robert became enthralled with his foster father and his foster brothers. They treated him like a little man, included him in their activities, and gave him a sense of positive worth. Unfortunately, his foster mother would give the two boys long baths in which she would spend many minutes painfully cleaning their genital areas. Robert hated these baths and the confusion and pain he experienced. In his child's mind, he thought that sexual abuse was something that went along with normal family life.

Robert's story illustrates a phenomenon that occurs in the childhood of some child molesters. The most important relationships in his life included sexual abuse. He internalized sexual abuse as a part of nurturing and acceptance.[16] In his mind, sexual abuse became identified with love. This led to confusion in his psychic life between love, sexuality, and abuse.

As an adult, he was seriously injured in an industrial accident and spent eighteen months in recovery, without his usual preoccupation with work to distract him from his inner pain. He lacked the inner strength to cope with his crisis and turned to the form of nurture he knew as a child himself—molesting. He raped his eleven-year-old step-daughter. In his distorted mind, sexual contact with a child met his need for someone who was completely accepting and non-threatening. It seemed like the love he had known as a child.

Although he felt some fear after each incident of abuse, his need for closeness with someone was so distorted, and his inability to connect with other adults was so severely limited, that it seemed to him the only way he could survive. Through threats and secrecy, he was able to continue the abuse for three years until his wife found out and confronted him.

Although there is nothing in this story that explains why Robert molested a child, there are certain themes that can be identified as contributing factors. For Robert, becoming a perpetrator became a "repetition compulsion"[17] for meeting dependency needs that had become sexualized in his own childhood. Because important attachment figures in his childhood molested him, Robert internalized abuse as a distorted form of interpersonal closeness. He molested a girl because she was defenseless against his power in a society that ignores child abuse, and because he could rationalize that it did not harm her.

One reason men are more likely than women to become child molesters is that sexualized dependency is more consonant with predominating images of what it means to be male. Some scholars have suggested that growing up in a patriarchal society means that men and women learn very different ways of expressing dependency needs and sexuality.[18] It is much more acceptable for a woman to be vulnerable, to allow herself to be taken care of by another person. Women are encouraged to share feelings and touch with others without fear of loss of identity.

Being loved like a child often feels contradictory for men, who think they are supposed to be strong and autonomous. Denial of dependency needs in some men takes an aggressive sexual direction. The paradigm of rape in which the man is in complete control of the other is a more comfortable way of being physically close for someone who is incapable of intimacy.[19] The need for touch is met without the terrifying possibility of vulnerability to another. A "real man" must be dominant in every relationship.

In Robert's story, we can see this confusion. As a child, he became attached to a man who expressed his affection through sexual abuse, and Robert needed this affection so much that, in his young mind, affection and sexual touching became synonymous, and all the more easily in a society that confuses intimacy and sexuality. When he was an adult in crisis and depression, he sought intimacy with a child who was defenseless against his initiative. He felt as though he could talk and be himself with this eleven-year-old girl in a more complete way than with any adult he knew. Raping a child as a way of expressing intimacy is a caricature of what it means to be male in United States' society.

Destructive Aggression

Another way to understand the child molester is to recognize that he has an aggressive disorder.[20] Something is wrong in his ability to protect the self or pursue a goal without hurting another person. He has difficulty understanding that he is acting in destructive ways toward others and does not understand the consequences of his aggression on others, especially in a society where there is so little accountability for such crimes.

John was sexually abused by a neighbor. Through severe threats and bribes of money, alcohol, and drugs, this man was able to keep John entrapped for many years. The relationship with the molester became the center of John's life. It is a clear case of "identification with the aggressor."[21] Because of his own impoverished relationships and his psychic immaturity, John was helpless to get out of this destructive relationship. He survived by internalizing the abuse at the core of his personality.[22]

One of the principal characteristics of his abuse was the constant threat of violence and death. The molester was sadistic in his treatment and verbally explicit in his threats. He backed up his threats by keeping loaded guns around the house.

As an adult, John adopted the same personal style. He molested a child while under the power of his molester, and was a danger to children in general because of his history of sexual abuse and drug addiction. Whenever John was frightened or unbalanced for any reason, he became threatening toward others. His inappropriate aggression was a sign that he was losing his internal balance. He became enraged and nearly out of control whenever he was afraid. Because of his fragile state, every situation was fraught with great danger. Because his rage was his best defense, he lashed out at authority whenever he felt threatened.

Destructive aggression is especially dangerous when molesters are with children. Some perpetrators are sadistic when they are with someone they judge less powerful.

The sexual abuse of a child is always a violent act. In order to sexually abuse a child, the adult has to override all the signals from the child that this behavior does not correspond to the child's needs. No matter how damaged a child is, or how starved she or he is for adult affection and acceptance, any truly sensitive adult can see that the child needs something besides sexual contact.[23]

> Sexual violence is, first and foremost, an act of violence, hatred, and aggression. Whether it is viewed clinically or legally, objectively or subjectively, violence is the common denominator. Like other acts of violence (assault and battery, murder, nuclear war), there is a violation and injury to victims. The injuries may be psychological or physical. In acts of sexual violence, usually the injuries are both.[24]

The child molester has a problem because he cannot see the child as separate from himself. He lacks empathy. If he wants something, he distorts his perception until he thinks it is something the child wants also. His aggression is unneutralized and he treats the child as an extension of his needs.[25] If he wants something, he feels he should have it, especially if the other is unprotected and can put up no effective defense.

Since destructive aggression is more consonant with the dominant images of what it means to be male in United States culture, this may help us understand why more men than women engage in sexual violence. The image of a man who gets what he wants without regard for the other is a stereotype of male competence. The "real man" is one who does not tolerate resistance to meeting his needs. If he meets resistance, he turns to threats and violence. Any resistance is perceived as an attack on his masculinity and must be destroyed.

Some child molesters imitate this supermacho image in their social behavior. They boast of their power and their lack of tolerance for any opposition. Their macho demeanor is actually in direct contrast to their symptoms of abusing children. They deliberately choose the most helpless, defenseless persons in society on which to dump their rage. They are far from being men who are not afraid of anything. Their disordered aggression is hidden and secret, but they are macho only around children.

Other molesters are not supermacho in their presentation of self; some, in fact, are very deferential. But such good behavior is not to be trusted. They are frightened of anyone with authority and may act respectfully. But outside the eyes of authority, and in the presence of someone who is vulnerable, they become tyrannical and controlling, expressing the deep rage that they carry hidden all the time.

The Grandiose Self

Another way to understand child molesters is that they have a narcissistic disorder.[26] Something is wrong in their ability to accurately evaluate self and other. According to Kohut, one of the biggest challenges facing any person is maintaining narcissistic equilibrium or balance between self and other. Any imbalance tends to lead to devaluation of either self or other and an inability to foster an accurate perception of both self and other and their interrelationship.

When an abused person experiences narcissistic imbalance, there is a regression to infantile images of the grandiose self and the omnipotent object. The grandiose self is the self who is never wrong and is entitled to whatever privilege and pleasure is available in an interaction. The omnipotent object is the demanding, all-powerful other against whom there is no defense. In the state of imbalance, there is a life-and-death battle between self and other. The grandiose self who is not satisfied can become enraged and destroy the other. The omnipotent object who is not obeyed can annihilate the self.

Bob's life was organized around fear of the omnipotent object. He was extremely deferential in therapy, with his counselors, and with his bosses at work. He tended to present himself as worthless. In his childhood, he was treated in a mean and cruel way. He has memories of playing beside the railroad track right up to the last minute before curfew. Then he would try to sneak up to his room without attracting his father's attention. Frequently his father heard him come in and would call him into the living room for extended sessions of humiliation and abuse. His father would tear him down in every conceivable way.

Afterward Bob would go to his room alone and fantasize about being on the train whose whistle he could hear in the background. As an adult he became a train buff because these fantasies were his solace in childhood. His childhood life can be understood by the categories of the omnipotent object and the worthless self.

Bob married a woman who was abusive like his father. She would frequently humiliate Bob, but she eventually tired of him and divorced him. It was during weekend visits with his nine-year-old son that Bob repeated his own childhood trauma. Even though he had not been molested himself, on several camping trips he raped his son during the night. It was his attempt to turn the tables and humiliate someone else the same way he had been humiliated. It is often puzzling that a person who has suffered the humiliation and injury of abuse would perpetuate the same experience on another victim. Many women and men take care never to abuse anyone because they remember the pain of their own experience. But many men pass their trauma on to others in a cycle of violence that seems unending.

Other molesters have had similar experiences of childhood humiliation. They defended against abusive situations by identifying with the grandiose self. They felt that their family was wrong to mistreat them, and they felt justified in hating them and their arrogance. In a sense they identified with the grandiosity of their abusers and incorporated extreme narcissism into their self-presentation. In their adult life, some molesters give the impression of complete fearlessness about the consequences of their actions. They are ready and willing to abuse anyone who stands between them and the goals they set. They despise the devalued object from the perspective of his grandiose self.

This tendency to see life as a competitive life-and-death battle between self and other is a stereotypically male way of organizing the world. In this perceptual world, whenever two persons are interacting, one must be dominant and the other subordinate. If they find themselves in the subordinate position, they must be deferential to avoid harm or challenge very carefully. If they are in the dominant position, they feel they can do whatever they want against the other without consequences. The possibility that persons could work together in a cooperative way without one or the other being destroyed seems impossible. Violence becomes a way of enforcing their power. Either they become the victim of abuse of power, or they victimize others. There is no other alternative.

Inability to Respect Limits

One of the most troublesome areas in working with molesters is setting limits and establishing appropriate boundaries.[27] It is obvious that a man who molests a child does not know how to set limits on his own destructive behaviors, and does not respect the boundaries that other persons need in order to survive. Therapy with molesters is often a tug of war over who is responsible for what. The molester will blame the therapist for cooperating with authorities and creating more damage than the molestation did in the first place. Keeping limits and boundaries confused is one of the skills of molesters.

After many months of therapy, Paul said to his wife, "Cindy was running around with only a towel on, giving me the eye, you know the way she does. I'm not the only one to blame for what happened." His wife responded: "But Cindy was only seven years old!"

After many months of therapy, Paul still felt that he was not responsible for molesting his step-daughter. His ability to set limits on his own behaviors and respect the boundaries of others was still defective. His perspective was informed by five years of involvement, from age ten to fifteen, in sibling incest with an older brother and a younger sister. The values of his home life in terms of sexual attitudes and behaviors and exposure to pornography were so distorted that he was unable to understand the full extent of his guilt for what he had done.

Establishing realistic objectives for one's life is also difficult for molesters. In ten years Paul had worked at any one job no longer than six months. He was unable to set and accomplish realistic and fulfilling goals. Part of the motive for molesting his step-daughter was to compensate for the feeling of failure in the rest of his life.

Male abuse of power in our culture means that many men have trouble setting appropriate limits when they are in a dominant position. Hierarchically organized business and education means that the power at each level is checked by accountability to the power at the next higher level. But within the limits of the job, each power level is able to do what it needs to do to get the job done. This means that whenever there is a power differential, there is danger that someone will be controlled or damaged as long as it does not threaten the assigned task.

Women complain of serious sexual harassment in the workplace. Because such abuse is misunderstood as the sexual play between men and women rather than intimidation, harassment is often not considered a serious problem. Paul did not consider his sexual abuse of Cindy to be a serious problem because, in his mind, she wanted it as much as he did and because it did not interfere with anything else in the family. He was enraged that outside authorities would interfere in his life and limit his access to Cindy. The male sense of entitlement to abuse of power, especially in relation to women and children, is a widespread social problem.

WHERE IS THE HOPE?

Given the above description of individual and social pathology of sexual violence directed against children, is there any hope that sexual violence can be stopped and that perpetrators can be held accountable for their crimes? So far our society has not shown the kind of determination required to understand and respond adequately to this problem.

The courage of survivors who are breaking the silence and speaking about their suffering and healing gives hope. They are already changing the assumptions against which we all understand this problem. Stories of survivors need to be told in many settings until the public begins to understand the scope and tragedy of sexual violence.

The community of therapists and health care workers who are willing to work with victims and perpetrators in order to find answers gives hope. This book is only one of many that have been written in the last ten years to try to respond to issues of sexual violence. Many persons are dedicated to changing our society concerning the issue of sexual violence.

Some recovering perpetrators who show unusual courage in facing their own pathology give hope. We continue our search for hope by hearing stories that represent some hope within the group of molesters themselves.

One group for whom there seems to be hope is adolescent molesters.[28] Young men aged 12 to 21 who are just beginning to make the transition to perpetrators may be amenable to treatment before their abusive patterns become deeply entrenched. Most adolescent molesters have been victims of sexual violence who didn't get help when they most needed it, that is, when they were first molested as children. Someone should have provided treatment at that time so that the confusion could be sorted out and they could discover that adults could really care about their pain and would protect them, not abuse them. But perhaps they can get help before they have firmly established a pattern of hurting others through sexual violence. Often they are anxious to talk with someone about what has happened to them, and try to sort out identity questions.

One of the most difficult clinical issues with this group is autonomy, which is a very distorted issue during the time one is trying to become a man in American society. Young men of this age are very protective of their autonomy, and their right to make their own decisions has to be encouraged in therapy or therapy will fail. This can be hard because some of their ideas about the meaning of autonomy are immature and underdeveloped. In spite of its difficulty, there is a possibility that, with proper help, these young men can temper their abusive behaviors in the future.

There is some basis for hope in molesters who are forced into treatment by the threat of prison. Often they express a desire to become whole when counselors are available within a controlled environment. Once structures that prevent further abuse are in place, some are relieved to be able to talk about their lifelong agony and their fears of hurting children in the future. We need further research about the combination of safeguards and therapy that will work with this group.

ISSUES FOR COUNSELORS

For me, working with child molesters creates more intense countertransference than any work I have ever done.[29] This is caused especially by my unresolved perplexities around sexuality and aggression. In order to engage in therapy with anyone, it is necessary to imaginatively enter their world and understand the way it is organized. With molesters this means trying to understand the wish to sexually exploit others and the desire to be violent. One of the most troubling discoveries I made was that I sometimes envied my clients because they indulged these wishes.

For molesters, there is an absence of healthy sexuality, which includes consent, caring, and mutuality. Child molesters are so incapable of nurturing satisfying interpersonal attachments that they can molest someone they love without understanding the destructive consequences. But their symptoms do not satisfy the human hunger for affirmation and connection. Working with child molesters has forced me to see how I am often inept at nurturing satisfying interpersonal attachments and how my sexualized fantasies are a substitute for connection with real people. Such exploitative sexual fantasies indicate how entrenched male dominance is in our culture. It has been frightening to recognize my own pathology around issues of sexuality, and this knowledge has forced me to sharpen my ethical sensibilities in my own relationships.

In molesters rage and destructive aggression are often defenses against the deep hurt caused by childhood abuse and the continuing inability to differentiate self and nonself in relationships. Being in the presence of unneutralized aggression and rage has been a terrifying experience for me because it threatens to demolish my fragile defenses against my own rage and the hurt it protects. With these clients, it is difficult to listen to the stories about what they did to children partly because they trigger fears of my own aggressive impulses. I have had dreams about molesting children. Occasionally I have experienced the full force of client rage in a session. These experiences have created terror and then anger as a second reaction. I have had fantasies of being hurt by clients and of hurting them. For many men, violent fantasies are not unusual and they indicate that the need to control is written on the male psyche. In a sense molesters present themselves as targets for a justifiable rage. But for these clients, rage is not an indulgence in the same way it would be for me. They have never experienced caring limits, but instead have experienced destructive intrusiveness interspersed with severe deprivation. Beneath their rage is a desperate wish to be bonded to someone who does not fragment in the same way they do and thus is strong enough to be both firm and caring in the presence of their rage.

One reason I am so uncomfortable with molesters is that I fear the fragmentation they exhibit and I wish to reject them as if they were the cause of my fragmentation. This is related to my real struggle to face my own fragility. Rejecting them is easier than admitting to myself that I am unintegrated and that my psychic self is only minimally held together by an intellectualized ego and a rigid superego. How much do I really know about my own symbiotic dependency and destructive aggression? I have found out that my professional identity often serves a defensive function in keeping my ugly parts hidden and sustaining the myth that I am a caring, humble person and interested only in helping those less fortunate. I am grateful that my work with child molesters has provided a mirror that enables me to be more honest with myself than I was capable of being before.

Where is the hope? On the surface, hope is not apparent. Thousands of persons live in hell every day because they are victims of sexual violence. We live in a society that is only beginning to examine this horror and its prevalence. The church has been silent about this evil and has much work to do before it will begin to comprehend its severity. Beneath the surface, however, there are glimmers of hope that are inspiring. A growing community of survivors and their counselors are understanding more and more about the causes and consequences of sexual violence. A small group of recovering perpetrators and their counselors are exploring a frontier that could change the face of modern society. In the following chapters we will continue to try to understand the issues of sexual violence and what the Christian gospel can say to this area of human suffering and hope.

CHAPTER FIVE

THE SCHREBER CASE: METHODS OF ANALYSIS

THE SCHREBER CASE

In 1903 Daniel Paul Schreber published his *Memoirs of My Nervous Illness,*[1] in which he reported on the history of his mental illness over twelve years of his adult life. He was a successful and apparently healthy individual until age forty-two when he suffered an illness that required psychiatric hospitalization. Part of the historical interest of the case is that Judge Schreber was a member of the first generation to be treated by the new science of psychiatry in a modern hospital.

His case was made famous when Sigmund Freud published a commentary on Schreber in 1911. For the psychiatric community, the case became a classic study of the etiology and structure of paranoia, a most difficult illness to diagnose and treat. Although we must read Freud critically because of his legacy of negative theories about women, homosexuals, and others, he was a genius at listening to the suffering of individuals and finding universal meaning in their stories. He introduced revolutionary ideas about what suffering means for persons and for society. Freud helps us understand that listening to individual suffering can be a subversive act because it means listening for the pain that is taboo in a particular community. Part of the strength of his studies is that he took the time to understand the testimony of persons labeled crazy, and in doing so he started a debate about the nature of suffering and hope in an oppressive society.[2]

In 1951 William Niederland published his discovery that Daniel Paul Schreber, a judge, had a famous father, Daniel Gottlieb Moritz Schreber, a physician.[3] Dr. Schreber was an important author in the field of health and child-rearing. This provided the opportunity for a unique historical comparison of a parent's theory of childrearing and an autobiographical report of the adult child's psychotic experience. Both the father and the son wrote books. More recent commentaries have explored the social and religious issues of this case.[4]

The importance of this case for our purposes is that it gives an analysis of abuse that informs our case studies. Review of this discussion will help us begin to understand the long-term consequences of abuse of power and the social and religious climate that fosters violence against women and children. It will also help us to see how society misunderstands and misinterprets the suffering of victims who have been silenced.

The Memoirs of Daniel Paul Schreber

Judge Schreber describes the onset of his illness:

> I have twice had a nervous illness, each time in consequence of mental overstrain; the first (while Chairman of the County Court of Chemnitz) was occasioned by my candidature for parliament, the second by the extraordinary burden of work on taking up office as President of the Senate of a Court of Appeal in Dresden, to which I had been newly appointed.
>
> The first of the two illnesses commenced in the autumn of 1884 and was finally cured at the end of 1885, so that I was able to resume work as Chairman of the County Court at Leipzig. . . . The second nervous illness began in October 1893 and still continues [published in 1903].[5]

Both hospitalizations occurred during times of great stress in his life, the first after losing an election for Parliament, the second soon after appointment to a position with much increased responsibility. His illness was a severe one, generally understood today as paranoid schizophrenia. He was suicidal, he couldn't sleep, he was catatonic (locked in a rigid body position) for days at a time, and he suffered disturbing hallucinations. He had to be restrained often and spent many days in a padded cell so that he could not hurt himself or others. During his involuntary hospitalization his treatment consisted of rest, drug therapy, and conversation with his physician, Dr. Flechsig.

In his *Memoirs* Judge Schreber gives an account of his subjective experiences during the illness. He says that he managed to survive by constructing an elaborate religious delusion that explained his sufferings and gave him a sense of hope in his life.

Schreber believed that his suffering was caused by persecution from God. In his delusion, "The human soul is contained in the nerves of the body. . . . God to start with is only nerve, not body, and akin therefore to the human soul."[6] Normally there is little contact between God and humans because of the danger that God could get stuck in the human nervous system. Therefore, communication between God and humans normally occurs during dreams, occasional miracles, and after death, when human nerves enrich the soul of God.

But something went wrong in Schreber's case. God became attracted to Schreber's nerves and became stuck there in violation of the "Order of the World," that is, in violation of God's usually fair way of relating to humans. The result was incredible physical and emotional suffering for Schreber, which he called "soul-murder." God also was in jeopardy because God had compromised God's responsibility for order and justice. The only solution to this cosmic dilemma was that Schreber's body be transformed into the body of a woman for the redemption of the world. This change would allow the union of God and Schreber to create a new race of humans and better harmony between God and the world.

> The scales of victory are coming down on my side more and more, the struggle against me continues to lose its previous hostile character, the growing soul-voluptuousness makes my physical condition and my other outward circumstances more bearable. And so I believe I am not mistaken in expecting that a very special palm of victory will eventually be mine. I cannot say with any certainty what form it will take. As possibilities I would mention that my unmanning will be accomplished with the result that by divine fertilization offspring will issue from my lap, or alternatively that great fame will be attached to my name.[7]

Schreber's delusion explained his many years of enormous suffering as persecution from God. He found a solution to his pain: transformation into a woman whose suffering would issue in salvation for the world. Schreber's suffering was justified as a sacrifice for all humanity, an expectation of coming fulfillment. Apparently the delusion and his writing enabled him to survive as well as he did, even though he was never considered cured or normal in his lifetime. The *Memoirs* are Schreber's account of his suffering and his hope.

Freud's Commentary

From this summary, many would agree with the psychiatric diagnosis of paranoid schizophrenia, which indeed was supported by every medical person who knew Mr. Schreber. Sigmund Freud's 1911 commentary on the *Memoir* turned Dr. Schreber from an ordinary mental patient into a famous case.[8] The question of how an apparently healthy, functioning adult could become so ill was one of the puzzles that preoccupied Freud's research. In addition, Freud had a special interest in paranoia, an especially difficult mental illness to understand and treat.

Freud himself never met Dr. Schreber, but he argued that since paranoid patients often do not tell about their subjective experience in therapy, a published testimony is even better and may give insight into the internal structure of this illness.

> Thus Freud for the first time made the content of mental symptoms understandable. . . . Only since Freud replaced philosophical and psychological speculation by providing a new technique for investigating the unconscious mind, has it been possible to speak of a pathology of the mind.[9]

In brief, Freud's interpretation can be summarized as follows. Freud identified what, to him, seemed the most important aspects of Schreber's illness: the feelings of being persecuted, and his religious delusion, "his belief that he has a mission to redeem the world, and to restore [human]kind to their lost state of bliss."[10] Freud identified two parts of the delusion as being most important, "the patient's assumption of the role of Redeemer, and his transformation into a woman."[11] As one might expect, Freud decided that the sexual imagery was the more basic.

> For we learn that the idea of being transformed into a woman (that is, of being emasculated) was the primary delusion, that he began by regarding that act as a piece of persecution and a serious injury, and that it only became related to his playing the part of Redeemer in a secondary way.[12]

In the crisis of mid-life, Judge Schreber felt intense longing for his father, who had recently died. These eroticized images frightened him because he feared he was a homosexual. He experienced sleeplessness, suicidal impulses, and inner panic, which led to his hospitalization. He recovered from the first episode and returned to normal life. But nine years later his feelings erupted again and his condition deteriorated much more rapidly. This time he defended himself against his fear of homosexuality by devising delusions of being persecuted by his physician. He projected his fears about homosexuality into fantasies of being sexually assaulted by Dr. Flechsig. This was the worst part of his illness.

Gradually this delusion was replaced with a more grandiose fantasy about persecution by God. If God was persecuting him, perhaps there was some purpose in his suffering. In the end, Judge Schreber believed that he was called to be the redeemer of the world and that sexual pleasure would be a part of his role. As Freud summarizes:

> It was impossible for Schreber to become reconciled to playing the part of a female prostitute towards his physician; but the task of providing God himself with the voluptuous sensations that he required called up no such resistance on the part of his ego. Emasculation was now no longer a disgrace; it became "consonant with the order of things," it took its place in a great cosmic chain of events, and was instrumental in the re-creation of humanity after its extinction.[13]

From this case Freud devised his theory that homosexual fears were the basis of the paranoid disorders. Because this view is still influential in psychiatry today, there is danger in Freud's idea that homosexuality is a cause of mental illness. This prejudice has led to much fear of sexual feelings and fantasies and has contributed to the oppression of gays and lesbians in our time. Whenever we work with Freud we must separate the genius of his methods from his prejudices, which have damaged our culture.

Freud had a genius for unraveling many threads of thought and feeling in the life of an individual. Freud believed that persons experiencing great suffering could be understood and treated. He has given us methods and theories for listening to persons who are usually abandoned and marginal, namely, the mentally ill. Freud did not shrink from the suffering he uncovered in the individual, but pressed on to find theories that would adequately explain such evil. He believed a will to live lay hidden behind psychiatric symptoms, a will that, no matter how distorted, if understood and interpreted, could restore hope in the individual. We will return to this perspective in chapter 6.

The Psychotic Son and the Abusive Father

In 1951, another aspect of the Schreber case opened up and initiated a dramatic debate about the consequences of child abuse. William

Niederland discovered that Judge Schreber was the victim of child abuse, and that this data had not been taken into account by Freud or in other commentaries on this case. Schreber's father was a famous physician whose writing influenced a whole generation of parents in the nineteenth century concerning their attitudes toward children, and discovery of this material reorganized the analysis of this case study.

> The main body of Dr. Schreber's educational system is condensed in his oft-repeated advice to parents and educators that they use a maximum of pressure and coercion during the earliest years of the child's life. He emphasizes that this will prevent much trouble in later years. At the same time, by subjecting the child to a rigid system of vigorous physical training and by combining methodical muscular exercises with measures aimed at physical and emotional restraint, both bodily and mental health will be promoted.[14]

The data Niederland uncovered was used by Morton Schatzman in a similar interpretation.[15] Schatzman based his interpretation on the one-to-one correlation between the sadistic treatment by the father and the psychosis of the child. He suggests that many of the delusions of persecution in Schreber's *Memoirs* are actually memory-traces of abuse during childhood. Although Schreber had mental amnesia about his early childhood experiences, his body still held the physical and emotional wounds.

As if it were not enough to believe that all independent will of the child must be ruthlessly crushed, the most sadistic techniques of the father were wire and strap contraptions to coerce perfect posture and rigid positions while eating, studying, and even sleeping. Both Niederland and Schatzman reproduce diagrams from Dr. Schreber's books that document severe physical and emotional abuse. One leather harness was wrapped around the arms and across the chest to prevent the child from turning over while sleeping at night. Dr. Schreber believed that rigid, balanced posture was essential for health. He also designed a metal pole and head belt to hold the child's head perfectly still and straight while reading and studying.[16]

Using information that was not available to Freud about Schreber's probable childhood torture, Niederland and Schatzman identify Judge Schreber as the victim of severe child abuse. Niederland tries to remain true to Freud's interest in the process of internalization, which focuses on the subjective meaning of events for the individual. Schatzman is less reluctant to blame the father for his son's mental illness and to see the delusions of the *Memoirs* as a protest against his mistreatment. Both Niederland and Schatzman go on to link such sadistic treatment with German philosophies that contributed to the Nazi holocaust.

The importance of Niederland and Schatzman for our purposes is their exploration of how abuse is organized in the family and how hope for justice does not die in the interior life of abused children, even after many decades of suffering. Judge Schreber sought relief from his trauma and risked being diagnosed as mentally ill in order to recover his health. He was never able to fully resolve the internal conflict between the rage at his suffering and his hope for healing, even though he had delusions of some pleasure late in life.

Feminist Commentaries

There have been other protests against Freud's interpretation. What about the images of men and women? Freud interprets Schreber's psychosis as a fear of being emasculated and turned into a woman. Several researchers have reread the original *Memoirs* and discovered positive images of what it means to be female.[17] They argue that though Schreber does fantasize being turned into a woman and being sexually abused, this does not immediately translate into fear of castration or emasculation. In fact, being transformed into a woman leads to pleasure and potential productivity. For Freud, as for patriarchy, femininity does equal emasculation. But for Schreber, at least in his so-called psychotic state, "To be a woman means in fact nothing less than to be a human being."[18] "The basic fear is that he will be turned into a woman within the exploitative structures of this world, turned over to others for sexual abuse."[19]

In brief, the feminist case is that Schreber's resistance and protest is not only against his father's abuse, but also against the ideology of patriarchy, which implicitly sanctions such abuse through its devaluation of women and the human character traits they represent.

> What was threatening to Schreber was not his "latent homosexual impulses," but the realization—in body and mind—that his soul had been murdered, that his will and spirit had been broken and torture inflicted on his body. He comes to the realization—in a symbolic way to be sure—that his father, believing in the evilness of human nature, softness, comfort, pleasure and maternal love, had systematically attempted to destroy these aspects of his soul. . . . In a sense he suffers from his culture's distorted

> view of human nature as this view was transmitted to him through his father's beliefs and methods. What "breaks through" when Schreber becomes psychotic is, thus, the denied and repressed side of his humanity—femininity, softness, the desire to feel some comfort and pleasure in his body, and his long repressed willfulness or autonomy.[20]

Schreber's father had tried to destroy all that was human in this child and had performed a kind of psychic surgery. The feminist argument is that whenever a social ideology identifies a group as less than fully human, whether children, women, racial minorities, religious groups, or others, it is committing soul-murder against the spirit of its people. There is a tendency to overlook the consequences of family and sexual violence for individuals and for society. But when we listen to the testimonies of victims such as Judge Schreber and the child and adult victims of today, we learn that personal violence can damage and even kill the soul. The tendency to divide people into good and evil groups creates structures of oppression, which are destructive of the souls of all persons.

Judge Schreber is trying to overcome the distorted sexual images of his culture.

> The condition of voluptuousness he seeks is neither male nor female, but rather a state of BLESSEDNESS, an Order of the World in which "all legitimate interests are in harmony." With that sentence Schreber deserves a place among the great mystics and the great utopian socialist philosophers. His psychological idiosyncracies remain interesting, but . . . they are in essence irrelevant to the articulation of his philosophical discourse.[21]

In this case we can see how the stereotypical attitudes of male and female distorted Judge Schreber's choices. He tried hard all his life to live up to the rigid role expectations of male achievement and control. But at mid-life he was overcome with deep needs to express his rage, his fears, and his sexuality in more holistic ways. We need to attend to how gender roles restrict the creative development of full human potential, and how our unconscious expectations create oppressive structures that lead to poverty and abuse for women and children. Schreber's protest against the price of oppression for men was a form of resistance to patriarchy.

The importance of the feminist commentary in this study is that it elaborates on how suffering becomes organized as a result of social ideology and describes how resistance and hope are expressed in the symptoms people use to seek wholeness.

Religious Commentaries

Lucy Bregman suggests that while the above interpretations are interesting, they all ignore Schreber's own testimony, that he claimed to have discovered a new revelation about the nature of God. In Schreber's delusion, God is a problem. Usually God can only deal with people after they are dead, and God uses the energy from dead souls to create pleasure. But God has made the mistake of becoming attracted to the nerves of Schreber and has become stuck there. The connection between God and Schreber is pleasurable for God but torture for Schreber, and the future of the world is in danger unless this symbiosis can be resolved. Thus the responsibility for helping God and saving the world depends on Schreber, who must allow his body to be transformed into the body of a woman.

> Through the "cultivation of voluptuousness" Schreber hoped to restore those nerves of God that became attracted to his body to their lost state of Blessedness ("soul-voluptuousness"). God Himself will exist once again in harmony with his creation.[22]

In this religious vision, Bregman suggests that Schreber has identified a basic problem in Western theology.

> This eschatological, erotic vision uses strange and idiosyncratic language. But the message may be less strange to us: a God deeply implicated in oppression and exploitation, is doomed. Such a God is culpable, for in siding with power and dominion, He has lost all claim on our loyalties. Yet instead of angry protest against the God-of-authority, Schreber insists that God cannot betray His own creation, for "the Order of the world carries its own remedies for healing the wounds inflicted upon it."[23]

The God Schreber knew through the tyranny and torture of his father's abuse and later through the religious sanction of the culture in which he was a successful judge was a God who could not be tolerated. For small children such as Schreber and Karen, the parent is a god whose power cannot be challenged because of the child's overwhelming dependency. If the parent is abusive, then the power discrepancy results in soul-murder, especially if there are no nurturing figures to counteract the violence.

For Judge Schreber, father was omnipotent and unreachable, much like the God of the church. When Schreber became a successful adult, a judge, in his culture he learned that his father's behavior was sanctioned by that culture through the authority of the Father-God. But unconsciously, the child cannot tolerate an abusive Father whose authority is unquestioned. In one part of the soul, resistance to such destructive authority builds. For Judge Schreber, there was a connection between his childhood abuse and the tyrannical God worshiped by his culture, a God who was not accountable for any of his words or deeds. The God of theology felt the same temptation to be a petty tyrant that the omnipotent father in an incestuous family feels. The abusive father can be abusive because there is no corrective or limit to his authority.

In some ways, the abusive family reflects a theology in which God's power is distorted and uncorrected by love and relationship to the creation. Bregman asks, "But what of the sins committed by the Father against His children?"[24] Schreber is reaching for a doctrine of God in which the children have a right to question God's authority. His vision does include a constructive alternative.

> Schreber defines "the Order of the World" not as an impersonal entity "higher than God," but as "the lawful relation which, resting on God's nature and attributes, exists between God and the creation called to life by Him." In other words, this relationship binds God Himself to act on behalf of the created order or to suffer the consequences of arbitrariness and discord. We today might refer to this as an "ecological" theology, in sharp contrast to the traditional stress on God's transcendence and dominance over the world. . . . He was trying to speak of a transcendent Eros that includes all creation, but the God-language he knew was the language of paternal authority, just as the only language of "woman" he knew was of sensuality and exploitation. Few of Schreber's contemporaries were aware of the moral threat of such language, its religious and psychological consequences.[25]

For our purposes, Bregman has supplied a link between this case and religion. Through her analysis, we begin to see connections between the depth of individual pain and suffering and the religious hope that will not die. One of the tasks of religion and theology is to form and transform culture. The secret suffering denied voice by a society is a critical commentary on a society's religion. Judge Schreber could not acknowledge his questions about God's authority in a society that would not acknowledge the suffering of his childhood. He heard the sanction of his father's abuse as sanction of God's omnipotence. He could vent his psychic pain, his protest against patriarchy, and his resistance to a patriarchal God only through his psychosis. Since there was no public forum for his questions about God, he created a private delusion that acknowledged his persecution by his father, by his physician, by his distorted patriarchal image of being male, and by an uncaring God. And in his psychotic delusion he came closer to a theology of hope that acknowledged and integrated his suffering and his full humanity than any theology he had encountered through church or culture.

It would not be an exaggeration to say that the prevailing image of God in the family and culture of Schreber contributed to the evil and suffering of Judge Schreber during his lifetime and especially during eighteen years of psychosis. The heart of Bregman's argument is that the current debate about the relational, ambiguous God is prefigured in the delusions of Schreber. He had no language for his religious intuitions and so deviated from the acceptable norms of the culture in order to put his troubled soul back together. In his idiosyncratic theology he discovered a new relation between God and humans that was characterized by pleasure and voluptuousness.

HOW IS POWER ORGANIZED IN HUMAN EXPERIENCE?

Judge Schreber was an abused child whose full symptoms of suffering were not expressed until many decades later. The seventy-five-year development of this case study provides clues to the structures of dominance and the depth of human suffering that result from the abuse of power. Five types of analysis are involved in understanding power and abuse of power. Exploring these types will help us understand today's cases of sexual violence against women and children.

Organization of Power in Individuals

Freud has discovered something about how power is organized in individual personality. He is sometimes criticized because he was so focused on intrapsychic issues that he missed the social realities around him. But he did courageously open up the subjective experience of the individual for understanding.

Freud could not divorce his mind from the possibility of a death instinct in the greatest depths of personality because of the amount of destructiveness he saw there. But in spite of such a dreadful possibility he assumed that even the death instinct had a logic that could be followed and eventually understood. He concluded that love and hate are so completely intertwined in the human heart that they can never be successfully separated, but that the effort to sort them out and neutralize the destructive possibilities can never be given up. So he tried not to shrink back no matter how awful the suffering he saw.[26]

One of the issues of our research is to discover the relationship between good and evil in the individual spirit. In individuals who have perpetrated sexual violence, we seem to see persons in whom evil is systematically organized. We have to face the possibility that sometimes evil wins out over good in the individual person, and that each of us must face the potential for evil and nurture the hope for good that we possess within. The capacity for love and hate exists in a fragile balance in all individuals. We live constantly in the tension and energy of love and hate in our hearts. When we know and integrate the full potential for hate in ourselves, we also find the full potential for love, and then we can choose to live out of love. We need grace to accept ourselves and others, and courage to confront and set limits when love demands it. The meaning of Christian faith is that life in Christ requires diligence and courage.

Organization of Power in Families

Good and Evil are more than just motives in the human heart. They are also organized patterns of interaction and attachments between people. Niederland and Schatzman show us how abuse of power can be organized into the fabric of the family. In spite of their brilliant analysis, however, we still do not know much about the father and mother and the older brother and sister of Daniel Paul Schreber. We know that the father, Dr. Schreber, suffered a head injury and was deranged at the end of his life. We know that the other two children died of suicide and mental illness.[27] We know very little about the mother. We can assume from what we know of this family that every member suffered psychic pain. They all participated in a system that was more oriented toward death than life. The child-rearing philosophy of the father was systematically sadistic and cruel.

The behavioral patterns of the family were evil, and the consequences over a lifetime were evil. Yet this was a family of people who were deeply attached to one another and respected in their society. Even to the end of his life, Judge Schreber never criticized his father, to our knowledge, for the many cruelties he had suffered. The father's parenting methods worked to the extent that they were designed to create great respect and even affection in his son; that is, his legitimate anger was denied.

Whenever power is organized in any institution, there is potential for abuse of power. The family is an institution with great authority in our culture. Parents are entrusted with the nurture and socialization of the young. The family is one of the institutions of society that distribute resources and provide a setting for intimacy.

There are various ways that power can be abused in a family: systematic physical or sexual abuse, deprivation, erratic behavior such as that resulting from alcohol and drug abuse, narcissistic overinvolvement. In families where there is incest and other sexual violence, we see the abuse of power that is organized over many generations. Families seem to perpetuate their evil through the agency of individuals because the dynamics of repetition are so powerful. It is clear that families often serve to protect those who are abusive rather than those who need protection.

We suffer from a tremendous idealization of the family that prevents honest appraisal of family strengths and weaknesses. Many adults have had experiences of terror in childhood, which must be validated before they can mature in their ability to love. And yet they are deeply attached to the parents who mistreated them. The family has potential for good and evil, and our analysis of power must include a realistic understanding of both possibilities.

Organization of Power in Institutions

Analysis of institutional power is not well developed in the Schreber case commentaries. Judge Schreber testified that his physician and the hospital attendants were persecuting him. This has been interpreted as a displacement of his feelings about his childhood abuse. However, there is evidence that Schreber is telling the truth about real persecution. For example, Dr. Flechsig did misunderstand the cause of his suffering. The medical team labeled his condition "dementia paranoides," but they failed to understand the "exciting cause of the illness."[28] We know that his civil rights were curtailed during his hospitalization, because he engaged in complex lawsuits in order to get the freedom to publish his

Memoirs. We know that his physician had performed castration as a treatment for the offenses of other mental patients.[29] Schreber's fear of physical abuse may have been real. Certainly the use of drugs such as morphine and chloral hydrate were abusive in light of modern psychopharmacology.[30]

In an ideal world, institutions are centers of social power used to organize and improve society. The testimony of survivors and recovering perpetrators is that schools, courts, hospitals, workplaces, and all the rest conspire to deny the reality of their suffering and provide support for their abusers. Their silence is coerced by the way power is organized in social agencies. Whenever power is collected in an institution, the potential for evil is increased along with the potential for good. Adjusting to abuse by institutions is considered a part of the price we pay for the luxury of modern life. Seldom do we critically examine the consequences of institutional evil for our personal and corporate lives. We must learn to look critically at institutions in order to understand the full basis for sexual violence.

Organization of Power in Social Ideologies

Feminist scholars have uncovered severe distortions of the human spirit in the ideology of patriarchy and have shown some of its consequences for individuals. Sexism is sometimes misunderstood as a subtle phenomenon that requires high sensitivities to understand. But cases like Schreber's make the violence of patriarchy more tangible. Schreber was an infant whose rights to his body, his own feelings, his own will were stripped from him under the guise of science and love by a father who hated his son.

Survivors of sexual abuse are victims of social ideologies that devalue women and children. In chapter 7 we will explore how their suffering is sanctioned by ideologies about the family, sexuality, and the privileges of the powerful.

One of the roles of the church is to provide symbols that identify suffering and give permission for its expression. The way symbols are defined determines the structures of power in a community. There is a direct connection between individual suffering and social ideology that is hidden from those with power and privilege. Every social ideology and power structure is ambiguous, and its evil will flourish until it is acknowledged and faced.

Organization of Power in Theology

In Schreber's faith-system, the evil of his child abuse seemed to have religious sanction. His father was esteemed in the culture, and his books on rearing children went through forty printings. He was a leading expert on child-rearing philosophy, and even Freud suggested that it was not surprising that such a father would be transfigured "into a God in the affectionate memory of the son."[31]

There is more to this transfiguration than a young child's worship of a father figure. As Bregman suggests, such an image of the father matches traditional theology about God.

> Theologian Albrecht Ritschl summed up the official, public view: "The real analogy for the Kingdom of God should be sought, not in the national state, but in the family . . . the forgiveness of sin by God the Father finds no real standard of comparison in the right of pardon which belongs to the head of the state." But what of sins committed by the Father against His children? Can these be forgiven, or even mentioned? The head of state is—theoretically—subject to law (Schreber was a judge), but to what law must the Father be answerable? This, we believe, is the religious problem that faced Schreber's culture, and in another form, may be facing us still.[32]

When God is defined as a Father with absolute authority and absolute freedom, sanction is given to the omnipotent father of the nuclear family. There was a psychic connection for Schreber between his abusive father and God the Father. The Freudian analysis suggests that this connection in the patient's psyche was mistaken because religion is a delusion that is only the unconscious projection of the individual.

Many theologians would accept the Freudian analysis that the identification of one's human father with God the Father is mistaken, though for different reasons—because God the Father can never be identified with one's fallible human father. But Bregman is suggesting that there is a deeper continuity between Schreber's human father and the prevailing theology of God the Father. The two symbols are connected at a social, family, and individual point. What the church teaches about the nature of God influences how humans structure their relationships with one another. The question about the character of God is crucial for how human life is structured. Schreber's father did act with omnipotence and absolute freedom in a way that provided no space for his son to form an identity that had its own integrity.

We can dismiss this connection between father Schreber and God the Father as a distortion of intent, but symbols must be evaluated not only for their intent, but also for their impact. The symbol of God as an omnipotent Father who is perfectly free to love or abandon the creation functions to license earthly fathers to see themselves in the same way and interpret their controlling and abusive power as an expression of love that can only be judged by themselves. Schreber rejected such a view of God in favor of a God who included the principles of the "Order of the World," which means that God is obligated to interact in love with the creatures for the salvation of the world.

The genius of Bregman's article is that she is willing to listen to the distorted religious mysticism of the psychotic Schreber for insights about the character of God. And she has discovered there a God who risked God's own being in order to be connected to real human beings. Schreber believed that he had something (the nerves of his soul) attractive to God, and that the future of the creation depended on a partnership between God and humans that would bring forth a new generation of redeemed humanity. This was the testimony of one suffering human about the nature of God. This witness is important to us as we struggle with understanding ourselves as full partners in the ecosystem God has created.

Summary

The Schreber case gives insight into the individual, social, and religious grounds of child abuse and its long-term consequences. Judge Schreber grew up in a home where he was systematically abused in the name of love. This abuse created a personality structure that fit into a society that was abusive in regard to its family structure, its institutions, its ideologies, and its religion. He was considered well adjusted and was rewarded for being a conscientious and hard-working adult. However, the damage was profound and finally led to a severe mental illness at mid-life. In his crisis, he searched for answers denied in a culture where the abuse of power was a secret. He constructed an alternative vision that was considered psychotic by the scientists and leaders of his community. Scholars have discovered in his *Memoirs* a search for health that was present in his idiosyncratic witness. The search for truth in his life did not die because of taboos and secrecy. When truth is denied, the human spirit seeks other means for justice. As we listen today to witnesses to the abuse of power, we need to listen for the hidden truth about the family, about social institutions and ideologies, and about theology, and also discern the latent hope the resistance of witnesses reveals.

A METHOD FOR THE STUDY OF POWER

The Schreber case has demonstrated a method for studying power and abuse of power. First, witnesses search for a self of truth and integrity. Since important aspects of personal identity come through attachments in the family, the search for self is largely interpersonal. In chapter 4 we have examined the structure of the self and how the self is formed and deformed by interpersonal experiences.

Second, witnesses search for a community of justice and mercy. Abuse of power is made possible by institutions and ideologies that distort human experience according to some structure of dominance. Those who are privileged have the social sanction and the resources to abuse and deprive others. In our society, parents have power to abuse children, men have power to abuse women, whites have power to abuse blacks, dominant classes have power to abuse those who are marginal. The principle of justice demands that all persons be treated fairly and have adequate resources for quality life. Structures of dominance are violations of justice. In chapter 7 we will examine the dynamics of community and society to see how power is used and abused in hidden ways.

Third, witnesses search for a religious vision that expands human experience. Religion functions in an ambiguous way in relation to society. It often challenges the way power is organized in society according to a vision of what is good in some ultimate sense. But religion can also function to license questionable social behaviors. For example, religion tends to support the rights of parents to control and discipline their children without critical evaluation of the nature of good parenting. Religion often reinforces the subordinate status of women by elevating their maternal roles without critically assessing the social environment in which women as mothers are unjustly treated. Beyond this, the basic metaphors about God and God's relationship to the world sanction abuse of power unintentionally. In chapter 6 we examine images of God and how they function in relation to personal and social power.

CHAPTER SIX

THE SEARCH FOR SELF

In the testimonies we have heard, survivors of sexual abuse have reported a sense that something was wrong in the self, something was missing, or something did not seem to fit. There was an uneasiness that came from deep inside the self. Healing from sexual violence involved a search for a stronger sense of self.

Karen reports that one of her greatest struggles during her healing was with herself. When she became deathly ill after her graduate program, she had to face the fact that the secret of her experiences of sexual abuse was damaging to her self and protected perpetrators. When she confronted her family and the rapist, she had to face the fact that she was still looking to them to be benevolent after years of betrayal. When she went to church and saw the perpetrators held up as model Christians, she had to face the fact that after all these years she was still naive about the extent of human evil.

Abuse was not just a distant memory from Karen's past, but a reality that was structured into her patterns of living and relating to others. The fear, guilt, and shame she felt as a child while she was being molested were still present in her adult life in situations of conflict and stress. If she wanted to be strong in her new life, she had to face herself. She had to remember the painful truth of her suffering. She had to understand how the suffering of her abuse had been internalized into her self and controlled her future in unpredictable ways. She had to organize new patterns within her self to enable her to actualize her hopes for herself and her future.

Sam felt euphoric after he was arrested and started treatment. He believed he was going to get the help he needed. For the first time in his life he had the chance to stop being hurt and hurting others. He was not fighting in the streets or molesting his young son. His life was not controlled by obsessions with hurting others or using them for his own sexual gratification. He discovered that hope for himself had not been utterly destroyed.

But soon Sam was stuck. He had lost the symptoms that had kept him from going crazy inasmuch as he no longer acted out his rage and sexualized fantasies when he felt overwhelmed. But he had not found dependable new patterns for meeting his needs. He had to face himself and see how impoverished his life really was. He had to look at his family and see them for the fragile people they were. With no career that he was genuinely interested in, with a fragile marriage, and with no friends he could count on, he felt empty and depressed. He wanted to give up, and even suicide seemed attractive at times.

Sam's hope was fragile because he did not have the stamina for the hard work ahead. His suffering became more intense once he looked honestly at the mess of his life. He discovered that he did not have the inner resources for activating the hope he first felt and that his healing required more profound changes in his self than he had any way of recognizing. Much more than just behavior needed to be changed. He had to change his very self.

Abuse is not over when it is over. Abuse is not something that happens to a child and then is forgotten. Children internalize relationships with their abusers so that these experiences become a part of the very structure of the self. Unless these experiences are faced and dealt with, the consequences of abusive experiences are long-lasting. Islands of fear, hatred, and mistrust become organized and exert a controlling influence over the person over many decades. The damage done to the self interferes with survivors' ability to form lasting interpersonal relationships with peers, to rear their own children, and to enjoy the satisfaction of work.

Experiences of abuse are not just external events that must be endured by the self and can then be sloughed off later. The very experience of being abused, especially in situations of attachment to parents or other authority figures, actually constructs a defective self from the inside out. Somehow, in spite of the terror of their lives, many survivors do not give up all hope. Part of the puzzle of our research is the resilience of hope in the midst of extreme suffering caused by abuse.

In searching for self, Karen and Sam each struggled with the long-term consequences of sexual abuse. Karen suffered privately for decades until her repressed memory was recovered and she could begin her search for a new self. Sam projected his inner pain onto others in abusive ways and confronted himself only under the threat of prison. They had very different experiences because of abuse in their lives.

The different experiences of male and female victims raises the question of whether there are variations in the formation of the self because of gender. Most perpetrators of sexual violence are men.[1] Some literature suggests that women are more apt than men to assume a victim-identity and act in self-destructive ways. Men are more apt to project their inner pain by abusing others. This would fit the ideology of patriarchy in which men are socialized to be dominant and women to be submissive.[2] "When we understand why women do not sexually abuse children to the same extent as men do, we may reach some important conclusions about how to help prevent men from committing this kind of abuse."[3]

In this chapter we are interested in the following questions:

—What is the nature of the human self and how does this help us to understand the long-term consequences of abuse and the painful process of developing a new self?
—What are the differences in the way men and women experience and cope with abusive experiences?

To respond to these questions we explore the image of the relational, ambiguous self, an image that is more adequate than other conceptions of the self in explaining the long-term suffering of victims of sexual violence. It also explains more adequately the resilience of the hope of survivors.

The study of oppression and violence has led scholars and theologians to explore how we can answer these foundational questions about the nature of self. Feminist scholars who look at gender-related oppression and African-American scholars who look at the relationship of gender, race, and class are important guides in our exploration of the nature of the self.

> It is increasingly difficult and perhaps impossible for any given person to see him- or herself as autonomous, objective, rational and static. It is increasingly difficult and perhaps impossible for any of us to see ourselves as formed, completed, fully conscious selves in any significant way

> separable from each other, from our bodies, from our historical circumstances, from our ways of thought. This is what I mean by the breakdown of the autonomous and imperial self, which might be more constructively put as the recovery of the relational self.[4]

The image of a relational, ambiguous self is a response to the "breakdown of the autonomous and imperial self."

THE RELATIONAL SELF

The process of internalization is the way in which relationships make up the self. When a child is abused, the destructive relationship is internalized by the emerging self. Even when there is no memory of the abuse itself, the process of internalization ensures that the structure of the self is affected. Karen reports that she did not remember her abusive experiences for most of her life, but she felt empty and deficient in her ability to relate to others. The formative relationships of abuse from early life had become internal to her identity as a person and limited her ability to accomplish her goals in adulthood.

For process theology and psychoanalytic theory, internalization of relationships is central to understanding the nature of the self. The theory of internalization helps us understand how abuse becomes a part of the self and what kind of relationships can aid the building of a new, healthy sense of self.

The Relational Self in Process Theology

According to process theology, the self is constructed from its relationships. The interaction between self and others is the rhythm of life itself. We become selves through our relationships, and we give our selves to relationships. A human being is a sequence of moments of such receiving and giving. We come into being by our sensitivity to others, and we make our contribution to the future by our creative responses to others. Relationships are internal to the experience of the self. Alfred North Whitehead called this the "doctrine of internal relations."[5] The process of internalization by the self is a rhythm of sensitivity and creativity. "Human experience is a process of interaction characterized by sensitivity, that is, feeling the feelings of others, and by creativity, that is, responding to others with new feelings."[6]

Sensitivity of the Self The sensitivity of the human self means that relationships with other persons are internal to our experience.[7] This is evident in an infant who, from birth, focuses on the face of the parental caregiver and takes in that person with her eyes. In adulthood, our experience is largely determined by the relational environment in which we find ourselves. In one setting we conduct ourselves in a particular way; in another setting, we are quite different.[8] Part of our experience is a receptive mode that includes sensitivity to the feelings of others.

Sensitivity to others is greatly magnified in situations of attachment and unequal power. Children pay close attention to the moods of their parents, and abused children are hypervigilant because their survival depends on their alertness to danger.

According to Whitehead, *prehension* is the mechanism behind internalization of relationships. A prehension is a vector of energy connecting one person to another, or one situation to another. Prehensions are evaluated by the subject after they are received, but they must be felt in some way. He calls them "simple physical feelings" because they have a causal effect on the subject, and because they are felt by the whole person, including the body.[9]

Whitehead believed that a moment of experience is created when the many relationships of the past become one focus of feeling. The self has an identity because of what it makes out of the relationships it has been given. Others are internal to the very constitution of the self. The self cannot escape the causal influence of others on the interior of its life.

> The concept of the communal and relational self means, in short, that we are what and who we are largely because of what we have been given by others, including our past selves, and because of what we have absorbed from others. It means that we create each other, that we are quite literally derived from each other. Within this organismic process of mutual creation we feed upon each other psychologically, intellectually, and spiritually, much as we feed upon other organisms for our physical food.[10]

Creativity of the Self The creativity of the human self means that we contribute our selves to others through our responses to them. Each moment is a response of new feelings through interaction with others. Creativity is the source of our freedom and it gives us some limited ability to have an impact on our own future and the future of others. We have no choice about whether to be relational, but we do have a small measure of choice about how to value the relationships we have been given in a particular moment.[11]

Whitehead has elaborately described how individual creativity works in his theory of concrescence.[12] As soon as the relationships of a particular moment have been internalized, the self evaluates and reconfigures these relationships with an eye toward both continuity and change. In more creative moments, novelty is enhanced, but in some moments, a narrow range of repetition develops, which can be damaging to the self and to others.

This description of creativity matches aspects of the stories of our witnesses. They reported that their freedom of response was limited to a narrow range at certain points in their lives. Karen reports that in certain conflict situations, she felt caught between rage and helplessness, neither of which was appropriate to what was needed. She felt cut off from the creative response that would have enabled her to find the solution she wanted. She attributes this loss of creativity to the fears she developed as an abused child.

The Bi-polar Self Sensitivity and creativity come together in the bi-polar self.[13] The rhythm of interaction between receptive relationality (sensitivity) and assertive relationality (creativity) provides the basis for human experience. Relationships with others create the raw material that forms the basis of our experiences. That is, our relationships are internal to our experience.

> Whitehead describes our experience as a series of "concretions," that is, moments of new decisions, each with its relations to the past and to the social environment, and yet each with a novel addition from within the subjectivity of the person to the way in which experience takes shape for him.[14]

This rhythm of sensitivity and creativity provides part of the explanation for how abuse becomes internal to the self and how this evil can be overcome.

Sensitivity means that abuse has real consequences, especially in situations of unequal power such as that between parent and child. The child has no choice but to internalize the patterns of behavior and emotion received from the parents, and these patterns have long-term, cumulative consequences. The child who grows up in terror will struggle with fear for most of her life.

Sensitivity also provides a way by which some of the consequences of abuse can be overcome. As a person internalizes new relationships that are not abusive, healing is made possible. When new relationships characterized by love and support are internalized with enough strength, they counteract the previous trauma, leading to a new self. Our witnesses report that loving therapists, pastors, and support groups helped nurture confidence in them that they had not experienced before. New relational experiences created a new sense of self.

The creativity of the individual may be insufficient to overcome the oppression that is organized in family and society. Experiences of childhood abuse in a patriarchal culture mean that the range of choices for the individual may be diminished. Just as parents are seldom confronted when they abuse their children, so husbands in particular are not confronted when they abuse their wives and children.

But creativity also enables new patterns of relationships to take effect. By gradually seeking out new experiences in which to find healing, the person uses freedom to gradually devalue the abusive past and increase reliance on more healthful internalized values. One point of transformation came for our witnesses when they chose to turn away from the destructive persons in their past and sought to bring new and healthier relationships into their experience. Novelty entered their lives when they used their freedom to risk change.

According to Whitehead's theory of the self, an abused child has no choice but to internalize abusive patterns of interaction.[15] But over a lifetime, survivors strive for relationships and communities that are non-abusive, and this new setting gradually becomes a basis of power in the emerging self. Therefore the relational self provides a philosophical explanation for both the way abuse becomes internalized and the way its consequences can be overcome in the self.

The Relational Self in Psychoanalytic Literature

In psychoanalytic theory, the self emerges through the internalization of relationships to others and to society. Daniel Stern defines internalization as the process by which "actual happenings—that is, observable events . . . —become transformed into the subjective experiences that clinicians call intrapsychic."[16] Gertrude and Rubin Blanck define internalization as "the process whereby regulations which had taken place in interaction with the outside world are substituted by inner regulations."[17]

One interaction important to understanding internalization is that between parent and infant. Internalization occurs for the young child through emotional attachment to a parenting figure.[18] Through repetitive rhythms of interaction, internal images of self and other are built up.[19] If the relationships are benevolent, these images are primarily positive, with good and bad aspects integrated. For example, if the pain of hunger is followed in a reasonable time by the gratification of being fed and held, then positive images of self and other will gradually build up in a balanced way. But if physical pain from abuse or emotional isolation is extended beyond the ability of the infant to maintain homeostasis, then islands of pain and gratification will emerge in isolation from each other and will interfere with the holistic functioning of the child.[20]

The chart below attempts to diagram the outcome of the process of internalization for the healthy and the abused. It is a theoretical model and needs to be tested against the testimony of our witnesses, and against the reality of gender differences in the way abuse is experienced and internalized. There is vigorous discussion about the ways in which the psychoanalytic model itself is gender biased and assumes and perpetuates a patriarchal society. The following discussion seeks to explore the contributions and limitations of these theories for understanding how the process of internalization helps us to understand the personal and social aspects of sexual violence. In some ways psychoanalytic theory unmasks patriarchal assumptions and in other ways it perpetuates this evil structure.[21]

According to object relations theory,[22] there are five trajectories of development in the self as ascertained from clinical data: libido, aggression, narcissism, superego, and ego.[23] The function of libido is to regulate the attachment needs of the self and to balance the need to be alone and the need to be intimate with others.[24] The function of aggression is to regulate the need of the self to "seek and maintain separation and individuation" by pursuing creative tasks and protecting the self when it is in danger.[25] The function of narcissism is to regulate the self-esteem of the self by balancing the need for positive self-affirmation with the need for constructive self-criticism.[26] The function of the superego is to provide worthy ideals and ambitions for the self, and to limit the tendency toward destructive behaviors.[27] The function of the ego is to coordinate the various abilities of the self toward meeting instinctual needs and promoting a positive environment for self and others.[28]

In healthy development, the true self, or deepest self, is congruent with the structure of the self, and there is a sense of authenticity in the multiple interactions that make up a complex human life in modern society. In unhealthy development, the true self is repressed for protection, sometimes even to the extent of being inaccessible to consciousness.[29]

A positive sense of self is built up in an atmosphere of love and support through the internalization of interpersonal and communal interaction. If those with whom the child is positively attached are benevolent and attentive to the internal development of the child, all these aspects of the self develop through an ontogenetic plan according to the values and needs of a particular culture.[30] The emergent adult will reach his or her greatest potential to contribute to society when he or she gains an ability to sustain significant frustration and anxiety and an ability to nurture others.[31]

However, if a child grows up in an environment characterized by abuse and deprivation, the process of internalization will be destructive and development will be skewed. This creates the possibility of a distorted object world for the self.[32]

An aspect of skewed development that has appeared through our research into sexual violence is gender inequality. Nancy Chodorow suggests that the internal object worlds of men and women are very different because of gender inequality and because the primary attachment figures for most children are mothers rather than persons of both genders. A result of this asymmetry in the family, she suggests, is that boys tend to separate prematurely from their mothers in order to identify with the dominant father. As a consequence, men learn to be dominant in relation to women, but are deficient in their ability to sustain intimate relationships. Girls, on the other hand, identify strongly with their mothers and remain in the preoedipal stage of development much longer than boys. Thus, girls become experts at interpersonal relationships, but their identification with a woman leads to a sense of being devalued in a society that is oppressive toward women. Women tend to internalize the subordinate position socially defined for women, especially in relation to men. Thus patriarchy is not just a social phenomenon but is part of the structure of reality in the family and in the individual psyches of men and women.[33] As our analysis continues, we need to look for how gender identity is differently organized for men and women because of abusive experiences.

A Psychoanalytic Model of Internalization

A Model of Health

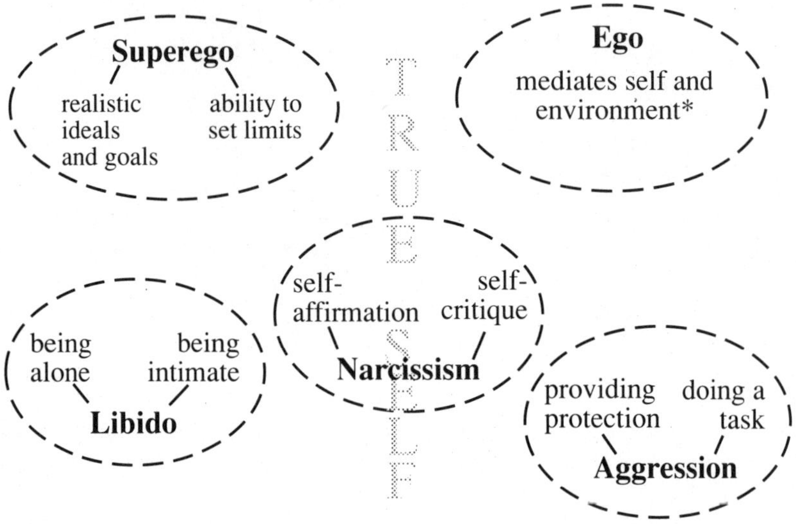

Possible Consequences of Abuse for the Self

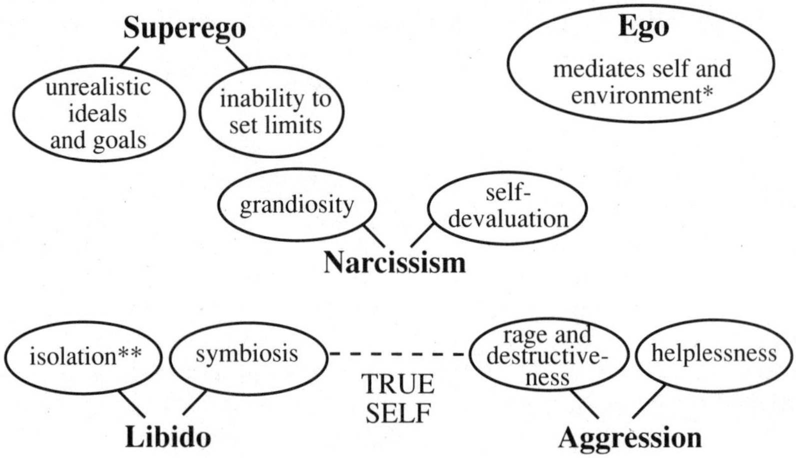

*Functions of the Ego: relation to reality, regulation of instincts, object relations. thought processes, defense functions, autonomous functions, synthetic functions. These functions may conflict or be conflict-free.[34]

** Islands of distorted internalized experiences such as "isolation" are called introjects by some writers.[35]

Long-term Consequences of Abuse Recent clinical research has focused on a group of persons whose development is fixated at a stage of distorted introjects. This research is based on the discovery of a group of patients whose development was uneven. They might be high achievers in one aspect of life, such as vocationally or artistically, and highly dysfunctional in another aspect, such as family life and intimate relationships. Therapists have found rigid and unintegrated islands of cognition and affect that cause massive problems when they appear. These introjects are often triggered in unhealthy ways by intense emotional attachments like those one finds in a family.[36] One survivor had succeeded in graduate study and performed well in her career, but she had divorced four times and her interpersonal life was unhappy. She could function well in the detached world of work, but was dysfunctional in the emotionally charged world of relationships. It is clear that child maltreatment is one of the principal causes of deficient development.[37] The severity of the consequences of any particular form of abuse depends on the circumstances and the process of internalization.

One of the chief defenses against fragmentation of the self is called splitting. In deficient development, islands of pain and need are internalized in isolation from one another.

> These contradictory ego states are alternately activated, and, so long as they can be kept separate from each other, anxiety related to these conflicts is prevented or controlled. However, these defenses, although they protect . . . patients from intrapsychic conflicts, do so at the cost of weakening the patients' ego functioning, thereby reducing their adaptive effectiveness.[38]

In Kernberg's definition, splitting is a defense designed to protect the self from internal fragmentation because of deficient development. The relevance of splitting to this discussion is that this defense is an important dynamic for victims of child sexual abuse. Experiences of terror and betrayal by trusted adults lead to introjects of fear, hatred, and mistrust, which are not integrated aspects of the self. In order to maintain balance, victims of sexual abuse must keep their introjects split from one another even though this creates massive problems. For example, some survivors report that they feel very little anger, even in highly threatening situations. This is a limitation because it exposes the ego to danger without adequate protection. The reason they must keep their anger repressed is that the internalized rage could become dominant if it were allowed to emerge. Unintegrated rage tends to function almost as a separate agency regardless of the consequences and in spite of the internal fragmentation of the self. Splitting protects the ego from internalized rage about one's history of sexual abuse.

In deficient development, each of the five trajectories has its particular configuration.

Libido In lay language, libido is related to the dependency needs of the person, that is, the need of persons to be firmly attached to significant trustworthy others. In situations of abuse, attachment is conflicted; libido tends to develop into the split introjects of symbiosis and isolation.[39] Symbiosis means that in the presence of emotional attachment, the self tends to lose its sense of boundaries and become absorbed into the other. The differentiation between self and other is so weak that any strong relationship can result in the loss of self. Isolation means that when there is an absence of the real object (person) the self tends to fragment. At this level of development, being with others is dangerous because the self can be absorbed into the other, and being alone is dangerous because the self can fragment into madness.[40]

A man who was abused as a child reports such an experience in relation to his father. In the presence of his father, he overidentified and tried to become whatever would make his father love him rather than abuse him. In his father's absence he survived by isolating himself in books until his father returned and the son could once again focus his behavior on pleasing him. This loss of self occurred because he was attached to an abusive father he could never please. Whether he was in his father's presence or away from his father, he did not have a cohesive self. He internalized deficient patterns for meeting his libidinal needs because of his attachment to a pathological object.

One of the distortions in development caused by gender inequality is that men tend to become isolated and women tend to become overinvolved in relationships. In their isolation men carry strong repressed needs for involvement with others. These needs tend to be sexualized and projected onto others. In deficient male development, sexualized dependency sometimes moves violently against the unprotected, namely, women and children. One of the reasons Sam became a molester was that he was deficient in forming and maintaining meaningful relationships. At a point of crisis, he sexualized his needs and projected them onto his son primarily because he had the power to be abusive and because it repeated his own childhood trauma.

In patriarchal society, women are socialized to connect their survival to their relationships with men, and they are often trapped in dangerous situations because the men they depend on are abusive.[41] In fact, men do have more resources for survival, and women face extreme needs if they find themselves alone, especially if they are responsible for children. Because of her fear and her need for support, one woman lived for many years in a situation where her husband was abusive to her and the children. When she discovered he had molested her sister, she saw that his problems were more serious than she had allowed herself to believe. Like a hostage who lives in constant fear for life, she had accommodated herself to his demands to the point where she nearly lost her sense of self. Her survival was jeopardized both because of her vulnerability in a patriarchal society and because of her attachment to an abusive husband. Symbiosis is a loss of the boundaries of the self in a dangerous situation.

To the extent that libido splits into isolation and symbiosis, this split corresponds to the social expectations for men and women under patriarchy. Men are socialized to be autonomous and dominant as a way of controlling others and denying their own dependence on others. From the dominant position, men have the power and control to abuse others to compensate for their deficiencies. Women are expected to be submissive and adaptive, even if the cost is a symbiotic loss of the boundaries of the self. From the submissive position, women are often trapped and unable to protect themselves from abuse.

Aggression Aggression in deficient development tends to split into rage and helplessness. The normal task of aggression is to "seek and maintain separation and individuation" by pursuing creative tasks and protecting the self when it is in danger.[42] In pathology, aggression becomes stuck in alternating polarized destructive and helpless phases. In its most dangerous form, this means a wish to destroy the attachment object whenever the self is frustrated, a state that Kohut calls narcissistic rage.[43] This danger is apparent in men who kill their estranged wives during separation. These men cannot tolerate the possibility that the other might have wishes different from the self. Aggression becomes distorted into a wish to control the other and even to destroy the object that is depriving the self of gratification.

The opposite tendency in distorted aggression is helplessness, or the tendency of the self to remain passive when something needs to be done. In normal development, aggression generates anger to protect the self when it is being abused. Anger is thus available when appropriate. Victims of abuse are often faced with a situation in which their anger is dangerous because it would be punished with even more violence. So their anger is suppressed into passivity. Adult-victims who decide to confront their abusers have to prepare carefully and often take along a support person.[44] The reason for this is that the feeling of helplessness in the presence of the abuser could become overwhelming and the self could fragment.[45]

One of the distortions in development due to gender oppression is that it is safe for men to express their rage, especially in the family, but anger makes things more dangerous for women. As children, both boys and girls are relatively helpless in the presence of the abuser. But as adults, men have safe outlets for their rage. Women are more likely to turn their rage inward against the self. Men and women tend to learn differently how to express their aggressive feelings.

In one family, both parents had eating disorders, which made them seriously overweight. Though both had self-destructive habits, the father was constantly angry and demanding. The family was financially dependent on him and had few choices. Confronting the father meant jeopardizing family security if he decided to leave. The mother tended to blame herself for his anger and for her own inability to protect herself and the children. She was ambivalently attached to her husband and did not have the support or resources to match the power of his anger added to his male privilege. It required many months of change in the family circumstances before she could begin to adequately protect herself and her children.

To the extent that aggression splits into rage and helplessness, this split corresponds to the social expectations for men and women under patriarchy. Because male rage is socially sanctioned, anger and abusive behaviors become the means whereby men enforce their control of women and their dominant position. Because women are trapped in subordinant positions, anger is dangerous because it is often used by men to justify violence against them. The vulnerability of women in society and the family often leads to an internalized sense of personal helplessness.

Narcissism In deficient development, narcissism tends to split into grandiosity and self-devaluation. The function of narcissism is to regulate the self-esteem of the self by balancing the need for positive self-affirmation with the need for constructive self-critique.[46] The deficient self often seriously overestimates or underestimates its ability to function in certain situations. A common testimony of survivors at certain points in the healing process is that they feel a lack of confidence to accomplish some normal adult tasks, such as handling interpersonal conflict. They feel devastated when confronted with a difference from the other, as if every difference is a competitive win-lose situation. This self-devaluation results from repetitive experiences in which the child-victim did lose to the omnipotent parent. The word *victim* itself often describes the self who is vulnerable in abusive situations.

The mirror image of self-devaluation is grandiosity, that is, the tendency of the self to overvalue its functioning and competence. This is just another aspect of the self damaged in its ability to make a realistic evaluation of its relation to others. Believing that one has the power or skills to handle an impossible situation results from development fixated on the grandiose self, which cannot fail. Therapists learn that whenever there is the presence of a devalued self, there is also an omnipotent self in hiding.[47] Many molesters are very cooperative in treatment and defer to anyone with authority. Yet they become enraged when their sense of entitlement to their children is questioned and limits are imposed. This coexistence of self-devaluation and grandiosity is typical of the distorted development of narcissism.

Another distortion in development due to gender oppression is that men have the social power to be grandiose and demand dominance over women. In contrast, women are devalued in family and society and adapt by internalizing the submissive role, which is required for survival. The testimony from some families in which abuse is common is that the father presents a sense of entitlement over every person in the family. He is often a petty tyrant who expects to be waited on and is intolerant of any desires that are not his own. In contrast, women in abusive families tend to accommodate in order to survive. Karen reports this pattern in her family. Her father was always right, in her mother's eyes, and she could not imagine her mother disagreeing with her father.

Parents sometimes reverse roles in the private domain of the family. In one family, the mother was dominant and grandiose, while the father was submissive and passive. However, when the father was alone with the son he initiated sexual abuse in the grandiose pattern. Although there is more than one pattern of narcissistic disorders in relation to gender, the often repeated pattern is the grandiose father and the devalued mother and children.

To the extent that narcissism splits into grandiosity and self-devaluation, and this split corresponds roughly to male and female, it is not surprising that men become perpetrators who control and devalue women in violent behaviors.

Superego The superego in deficient development tends to split into grandiose ideals and an inability to limit destructive behaviors.[48] The ability of the superego to set realistic goals and limits is damaged through child abuse. Often adult-victims engage in self-destructive behaviors, such as alcohol and drug addiction, eating disorders, suicidal ideation, sexual addictions, and other problems, as if the conscience is unable to function in a normal way.[49] The normal ability to set limits on destructive behaviors is distorted because the child was attached to adults who were deficient in their own superego development.

Abuse is a form of limit violation. Adult-victims often report that their parents were clearly emotionally different during abusive episodes, as if the child as a separate person became invisible. It is predictable that children who grow up in situations with adults who do not set appropriate limits on their own destructiveness and constantly violate the personal boundaries of their children will have trouble with limits in their own lives.

Likewise, in deficient development it is difficult to have a sense of realistic ambitions and goals. Some survivors form relationships with someone whose pathology renders him or her incapable of a mature relationship, and yet the survivor cannot relinquish an idealistic view of how such a relationship should work. Other survivors have reported severe problems with perfectionism. They feel a need to excel, yet they also feel that their attempts are nearly worthless. They have difficulty controlling their workaholic behaviors, even when their physical health is in jeopardy. These behaviors are signs of deficient superego development: an inability to set realistic goals and ambitions, and an inability to set limits on self-destructive behaviors.

A fourth distortion in development due to gender oppression is that men tend toward grandiose ideals and women tend toward self-destructive behaviors. In one family, an incestuous father was unable to keep a paying job. He would become frustrated after a few months and quit in a rage, then wait several months and repeat the same pattern. Part of the reason he could not work was because he had ambitions and ideals of being rich without working. He wanted to go hunting for deep-sea treasure or produce best-selling records; but he had no means to accomplish any of his goals and was unable to tolerate the frustration of work that he felt was beneath him. The mother, on the other hand, worked many years as a secretary, nearly the sole support of the family of three children. Overburdened by all the work, she felt unworthy of any better position. They were mirror images of the deficient superego, though the woman had many fewer choices about her own survival and that of her children.

To the extent that superego splits into grandiose ideals and an inability to set limits on destructive behaviors, and this split corresponds roughly to male and female, it is predictable that men will become perpetrators who act destructively toward women.

Ego In healthy development, the ego is that part of the self with responsibility for regulating the instinctual energy of the self and helping the self to relate to its environment. There are multiple ego functions that may or may not be caught up in the difficulties of a fragile self. In technical terms, these functions can become a part of the conflicts of the self, or they can be conflict-free.[50] For example, some adult-victims are gifted with intelligence, athletic ability, or artistic intuitions in ways that seem to be free of the damaged self.

Karen was a gifted person whose educational achievements provided significant satisfaction and probably enabled her to survive some of the most difficult times. However, in other persons, the ability to use intelligence becomes conflictual because it was once the focus of abuse; that is, the abuser humiliated the intellect of the abused as a way of enforcing cooperation and silence. Sam was unable to assess his gifts and locate himself in a career because his childhood was so chaotic. In some ways the ability of the ego to function effectively depends on which areas of the self were damaged in formative periods, as well as how severe the damage was. The relationship between ego functions and abuse deserves more discussion than can be given to it here.

Summary

This discussion shows how the relational self is formed in the abusive family. The human self is organized and becomes capable of complex interaction with others through a gradual process of development. In healthy development the self internalizes primarily positive aspects of relationships, and the self is balanced and has internal access to many resources for coping with the complexity of modern culture.

It is not going too far to say that the self is its relationships. When a person grows up and lives in a relational environment that is supportive and nurturing, the self becomes strong and able to withstand great frustration in the pursuit of worthy goals. When a person grows up in an abusive environment, the self is fragile and apt to be incapable of handling the normal stress of interpersonal life. The pain of the fragmented self may be hidden in secrecy for many years in compliance with the wishes of abusive parents and a society apathetic toward human suffering.

In children who are abused, the self internalizes isolated introjects, which lead to a fragmented and divided self. The defective self is in constant danger of splitting or acting destructively under the pressure of adult relationships and the expectations of modern culture.

This discussion gives clues to why men are the primary perpetrators of sexual violence. In development within a patriarchal society, men tend to distance themselves from mothers and identify with the dominant father, thereby internalizing characteristics that match the dominant male position in a patriarchal society—exaggerated masculine traits such as isolation, grandiosity, rage, and unrealistic ideals and ambitions. Within a male-dominant society, women survive by adopting stereotypical feminine traits such as symbiosis, self-devaluation, helplessness, and inability to set limits. Given these polarities in light of Chodorow's argument about how patriarchy influences the development of the individual's object world, it is not surprising that men are socially protected in and internally inclined toward sexual abuse. By sexualizing their needs and projecting them onto women and children, who lack the power of self-protection, some men become abusive because it is a socially sanctioned outlet for expressing their deficiencies.

Within process thought, the self is formed from its relationships through a process of sensitivity and creativity. Within psychoanalytic theory the self is formed through the process of internalization. The development of the self is distorted by experiences of sexual violence and by gender inequalities and patriarchy. Adults who were sexually violated as children suffer long-term injury to their ability to love and work. Men are more prone to become perpetrators of sexual violence because the introjects of isolation, rage, and grandiosity more nearly match the masculine stereotype in a patriarchal culture.

THE AMBIGUOUS SELF

A core issue in healing from sexual abuse is the ability to live in the midst of ambiguity. Ambiguity is a necessary component in forming a self that can flourish during the healing process. The ability to sustain the self in the midst of contradictions is crucial in order to sustain the higher values.

> The discipline demanded by the effort to sustain internal relationships is at least difficult. Its cost is large and sometimes enormous. The price to be exacted involves the expenditure of great energy in the form of an active patience, physical stamina, emotional and psychic strength, and a resilient trust and faith. Above all, the cost is measured in the coin of suffering. The capacity to endure a great suffering for the sake of a large purpose is one of the decisive marks of maturity. In the Christian tradition the adequate symbol of the cost of sustaining an internal relation is the cross.[51]

Bernard Loomer is writing here about voluntary suffering for a chosen value or purpose and not the involuntary suffering of victimization. Karen reports an increase in suffering because of her choice to face her past and begin to heal. When she lived in denial and amnesia, she was able to keep her balance and accomplish her work. When she started to remember her past suffering and mend her broken spirit, she went through agonizing pain. She was faced with the deep ambiguity of the possible dissolution of her self as she tried to find wholeness. Her ability to sustain her self in the midst of ambiguity was essential to her continuing search for a new self.

Ambiguity is a category necessary to explain the search for self among survivors of sexual violence. We need to know how the self sustains itself in the midst of the inner conflicts and contradictions of the healing process. What is the process by which the resilience of hope is enhanced and supported? There are three types of ambiguity that must be faced in order for the resilience of hope to be available: (1) the ambiguity of otherness in the self; (2) the ambiguous tension of transition-dissolution in the self; (3) the ambiguous tensions of good and evil, love and hate, life and death.

The Ambiguity of Otherness in the Self

The relational nature of the self means that there are many contradictory influences on the self from the past and from society. These influences cannot be easily integrated into the life of an individual, and many are felt as alien, as other. Otherness is more than just the presence of difference; it is the presence of difference that cannot be reduced or eliminated.

> Part of what theologians, philosophers and social theorists attend to with considerable care is the insistence by "the other" on being, still, the other. The term "other" in this technical sense, refers to that which is seen as different, strange, in need of definition, and often in need of control or domination. As deconstructionists put it, it refers to "difference," to what differs and what has been forced to defer to those with greater power. This is what I mean by the irruption of the other, which might also be put as the insistence by the other on the grace of speaking differently.[52]

Otherness refers to persons or groups who refuse to conform to the identity of one's own culture. Often, the other is found "within our own culture in the unruly presence of racial and ethnic minority groups who maintain their particular identity, of women who insist on defining their own identity, and the under classes and the homeless and the ill."[53] Projection of control and domination over different others is a typical form of social organization, as we shall see in chapter 7.

"The other is also within ourselves, in the equally unruly presence of the sub- and unconscious, in the presence of our bodies and our feelings."[54] Otherness is internal to the self. That is, there are parts of the individual self that are other in the sense of being virtually unknown to the conscious mind and being unmanageable. The body does what it needs to do without being under the conscious control of the self. Likewise, the unconscious introjects from our past continue to have power in our lives without our permission or appreciation.

> The unity of individuality often includes the presence of tension or incompatibility between the internalized causal influences. Each influence makes its claim and has its own appeal. In his composite unity an individual may be pulled in several directions. His motives may be mixed, causing him to be at odds with himself. His "decision" may embrace various indecisions and irresolutions. Possibilities may be ordered in their relevance for an individual (as Whitehead believes), but this hierarchical presentation may not be matched by a corresponding order of priorities within the subjective life of the individual.[55]

Part of the ambiguity of the human self in deficient development is the presence of repressed introjects. Because of abusive experiences, islands of fear, hatred, and mistrust emerge and are repressed. These introjects gain power through repression and return as otherness to confound the self. At one point Karen had to fight against a part of herself that wanted to die. She had internalized the abuse by her father as self-hatred. This pocket of powerful affect surfaced through her body in a severe illness. In order to survive, Karen had to confront her death-wish face-to-face and decide whether she wanted to live and whether she was willing to remember her childhood trauma in order to live. The otherness she faced was the enemy within.

> An individual cannot fully determine the quality of his life by himself, by a resolution of his will, however enlightened and decently motivated he may be. The confusions, prejudices, contradictions and brokenness of his society are present as shaping forces within him. He may mitigate their power, but he cannot be completely free from their influence until they are eliminated from his world.[56]

Because the self is relational, it also internalizes social attitudes. The dominance of men under patriarchy means that men are socialized to be abusers rather than victims. In psychoanalytic thought, men often have a sense of entitlement toward women and children and are enraged whenever this entitlement is challenged. In contrast, many men are taught to appear sensitive and caring. When entitlement and rage surface in such well-socialized men, they are confronted with otherness, that is, with impulses that seem incompatible with their conscious self-image.

In spite of Sam's childhood abuse and his history of street fighting, he was horrified that he was capable of molesting his five-year-old son. Unconscious introjects of sexualized dependency were strong in his life in spite of his conscious wish to be a good father. At a time of crisis, Sam was confronted with his own deep ambiguity. Regardless of his conscious intentions, he did molest his son. Many months of therapy and instruction were required to bring Sam to confront himself and accept that he was a molester who needed help.

In order to heal from sexual abuse, survivors must find the strength to confront parts of themselves that breed shame and self-hatred. This requires the ability to sustain long periods of ambiguity. Most painful, witnesses report that they find destructive attitudes within the self. That is, being abused by a trusted adult means that one identifies aspects of the self with the abuser. One survivor was horrified to discover that he hated his children as much as he loved them. He found the same attitudes in himself as he had experienced from his father.

The Ambiguous Tension of Transition-Dissolution in the Self

The therapeutic process of healing from the damage of sexual abuse includes many ups and downs. Karen reports that every time she felt as if she had reached a plateau where rest might be possible, she faced a challenge that was bigger than any preceding one. She found within herself a determination to keep growing and testing her limits, yet every time she made a gain she yearned for a respite from the struggle. At times the healing process seemed worth the struggle; at other times Karen was exhausted and she wished she had never started.

> The moment of success in any advance seems to create two contrasting impulses. On the one hand there is a restlessness to continue the advance to a more complex stage, even though this effort requires a finer and more demanding discipline. On the other hand there is an impulse to rest and to be content with the good that has been achieved. This leads to fixation and defensiveness.[57]

Sam was elated when he finally disclosed the pain he had been secretly holding for years. He wanted to leave the darkness and live in the light of honesty and truth. But within a few weeks, the truth he discovered about himself was almost more than he could bear. He became angry and accused his counselors of making things much harder than they needed to be. He did not realize that the ambiguity was within himself rather than others.

> The passion that compels us to search for truth is the same drive that leads to our neuroses and defensiveness when the truth (especially about ourselves) is more than we feel we can or want to bear.[58]

Judge Schreber was stuck because he did not find a supportive community that understood his pathology and could provide compassionate care. In his determination to survive and get well, he composed his memoirs, which he believed would be helpful to others as a religious vision. However, his judgment about himself and his contribution to the world was grandiose and idiosyncratic. His memoirs were dismissed by his generation as the crazy thoughts of a mental patient rather than the revelation of new truth. His drive toward health became a block to the communication he wished for.

> The strength that is poured into the formation of our virtues is the same strength that overplays itself and tempts us to think and act as though our virtues were more inclusive and adequate than they are: In this fashion our virtues become vices and our strengths, weaknesses.[59]

Our social state of affairs aggravates the ambiguity of transition for the self. Without knowing it, Sam was reenacting the propensity toward sexual violence that is latent in the masculine images in our culture. Even though he wanted to be a loving parent, he became abusive and violated the very ideals that were most dear to him.

> The relationships and institutions that bring us into being and shape us are the same forces that tend to restrict us to conformal patterns of thought and behavior and thereby to minimize our freedom.[60]

In psychoanalytic thought, transition is an important theme of the development of the self. Observing clients in therapy and children with their parents has resulted in several sophisticated understandings of how the self maintains its identity while it is changing dramatically.

Transition is a process full of ambiguity.[61] Before a period of transition, the self exists in a balanced state, called homeostasis. A person experiences little awareness of tension or need. Then something happens to create anxiety and a sense that things are not right. This uneasiness ushers in a period of transition characterized by lack of balance. Often the person feels divided and confused and fears the self will dissolve into nothingness. Finally, there is a resolution of the tension and a new sense of balance results. The self achieves a new organization and begins to feel normal and natural again. Anxiety lessens, and the challenges of the new situation are met.[62]

Transition of the self for survivors of sexual violence is fraught with ambiguity. Victims often repress large amounts of pain and other negative feelings in order to survive the trauma of abuse. They numb themselves to physical and emotional feelings for many years in order to resist being overwhelmed. They achieve balance through denial and dissociation of memory and feelings. There is little awareness of tension or need. There is little sense of ambiguity because negative experiences are banished from awareness.

Eventually this balance is disrupted because of some failure, and survivors are faced with trying to discover the reasons for the pain. For a survivor to discover a new sense of self, she must allow the defensive structure of denial and dissociation to fall apart so that the repressed introjects can emerge. When she let down her guard Karen reports that her memories were communicated first by her body. She became ill and discovered that she could not survive unless she faced the truth of her life, which threatened to break her spirit and lead her into death. She had to face waves of grief and suffering about her life, which often seemed more than she could bear. Her defenses collapsed and her usual way of living began to disappear.

A time of transition is a kind of psychic death. It means allowing oneself to enter into a fragmented state with no guarantee that the self will survive. The old self dissolves, and the new self is not yet formed. Paradoxically, transition requires a sense of hope and strength in order for it to become conscious, but it is a state with high anxiety and high risk.

Eventually, if healing occurs, there is an integration that creates the reality of a new balance. After Karen remembered that she was the victim of incest and had worked through that experience with therapist and friends, she began to accept her past victimization as a part of her identity. Now able to address large groups of people as a survivor of sexual violence, she has found a new balance in her life that includes memories of her experiences of abuse.

The process of healing entails the continuous work of disintegration and transformation in the self. As memories surface, and deficiencies become available for healing, there are small gains and some plateaus. A history of childhood abuse often means that transition seems endless. The ability to do the work of reintegration under this kind of pressure is a kind of ambiguity.

Sam maintained balance in his life by fighting in the streets to get rid of his unconscious rage about his childhood abuse. When his daughter died, he became severely depressed and began to molest his son to deal with his pain. His arrest became an opportunity for him to face what he had done, to face his own internal contradictions. He entered a prolonged period of transition in his life. His ability to stay in therapy depended on whether he could sustain himself in the midst of the ambiguity of this transition period. He had to face the horror of what he had done to his son. He had to face his memories of being a victim of childhood abuse. He had to sit in a group with other men and talk about his feelings and thoughts about himself. There were points of new balance as he began to accept the unacceptable aspects of himself. But it took years for the contours of a new self to take shape. In the meantime he had to live with the ambiguity of transition and the potential dissolution of the self.

Healing from sexual abuse requires the ability to sustain the self in the midst of the ambiguity of prolonged transitions. Living for months or years without a clear sense of who one is or where one is going is a deeply disturbing form of ambiguity.

The Ambiguous Tensions of Good and Evil, Love and Hate, Life and Death

The deeper levels of ambiguity come with the realization that good and evil cannot be separated in the human self and that evil cannot be eliminated from one's life. Survivors are painfully reminded of this reality. Many of them have spent years secretly coping with the overwhelming pain of their childhood abuse, determined to survive the trauma and get on with their lives. But what they discover is that to the extent that they repress the pain of their past, they also destroy their ability to be alive and creative in the present. Repression of suffering and its evil component of hatred and destructive impulses leads to diminished creativity and freedom.

At the base of human experience there is only one spirit, which cannot be divided. In order to be fully alive and creative, human beings must confront the full extent of evil in the self.

> The seamless actuality of the self houses the composite unity of the spirit of an individual. Within this unity of the spirit the inseparability of the capacities for good and evil is rooted. This means that the evil of a person cannot be exorcised without decimating his (her) capacity for achieving goodness. The evil proclivities of a person can be transmuted only by transforming his (her) essential spirit . . . the whole person must be accepted if the creative advance of life is to be enhanced.[63]

One of Freud's most controversial ideas was the death instinct. He believed that love and death were opposing forces in the self that could never be fully integrated. In his clinical work, Freud was impressed by the stubbornness of the destructive and self-destructive impulses in the self. Melanie Klein, who felt that the inborn urge to destroy the love object was strong and had to be respected throughout life, picked up this idea of a death instinct. Winnicott disagreed with Klein and suggested that the destructive impulse was a perversion of healthy aggression caused by abusive experiences in early childhood. The debate continues in psychoanalytic theory.[64] How can parents, who bring children into the world, systematically and sadistically attempt to destroy their children? How can men use the most helpless persons in a society as targets for their destructive rage?

The balance between good and evil, love and hate, life and death, is fragile. Reinhold Niebuhr thought that "every advance in goodness brings with it the possibility of greater evil."[65] Karen fought all her life to survive the abuse perpetrated by her father, and she survived, even though the abuse was costly to her happiness and creativity. She almost died when she fully realized what had happened to her as a child and how it had affected her adult life. She was determined not to let her father destroy her, but in seeking to survive the evil of her father, she also lost parts of her self. In order to control the consequences of the evil done to her, she nearly lost the good she sought for herself and her family. She had to face her own mixed feelings in order to discover her potential for good. Sam fought to survive. He was fighting against the destructive forces that had victimized him as a child, yet evil won out when he molested his own son. He had become the molester like those who had molested him. In order to find a source of good in his life and to gain access to that goodness, he had to face the full extent of his evil.

One of the deep ambiguities of life is the interpenetration of good and evil in the human self. The destructive and creative possibilities are inseparably intertwined. If we would be good, we must face the evil in ourselves.

JESUS AS A MODEL OF THE RELATIONAL, AMBIGUOUS SELF

For Christians, Jesus represents an image of the human self as God intends it. Jesus was fully human in a way that helps us understand the potential of the human self. In his ability to be relational, that is his "capacity to sustain a mutually internal relationship," Jesus reveals the human self.[66]

> Within the conception of power as relational, size is fundamentally determined by the range and intensity of internal relationships one can help create and sustain. The largest size is exemplified in those relationships whose range exhibits the greatest compatible contrasts, contrasts which border on chaos (Whitehead). The achievement of the apex of size involves sustaining a process of transforming incompatible contrasts or contradictions into compatible contrasts, and of bearing those contrasts within the integrity of one's individuality.[67]

Jesus was born into a nation oppressed by an imperial power and besieged by external and internal enemies. He emerged as a leader who challenged people to understand their identity differently. Throughout his ministry, Jesus sustained internal relationships with his friends and enemies without losing his integrity. A person of great stature, he has become a model of the relational self in his ability to confront his friends and challenge his enemies.

One of the most difficult things Karen did as a part of her healing was confronting her father and her rapist. She was faced with the problem of seeking justice and speaking the truth in relation to two men who were denying their evil. In talking with them, Karen exhibited great moral courage. She took responsibility for destroying the lies and deception of the past and creating new possibilities of liberation for herself and others. She also risked further denial and abuse by putting herself in relationship with them again. The fact that their denial continued was very painful for Karen because they rejected her courage and honesty and the chance for newness in their lives. They were too small to face the liberating truth that Karen represented in her soul. In this event, Karen was a liberating figure who acted to break the unjust abusive power in the relational web of which she was a part. Her decision to live in truth and justice was larger than their decisions to continue in deception and denial. The fact that her community continues to protect her abusers testifies to the evil that dominates society.

Jesus is also a model for the human self in his ability to sustain himself in the midst of ambiguity for the sake of qualitative richness.

> The suffering servant, in returning love for hate; and in attempting to sustain the relationship as internal and creative, must be psychically larger and stronger than those who unilaterally hate. Without this greater strength and larger size the suffering servant could not sustain the relationship.[68]

At the deepest level, the child who is sexually violated by a trusted adult is forced to internalize the terror of abuse and fight against the rage of the abuser. Because the child is vulnerable, its unprotected self is a receptacle for the unneutralized sexual aggression of the abusive adult. In speaking the truth about what happened and working through the effects with caring others, a survivor can gain freedom from the external abuser. In the process, the survivor is faced with a deep ambiguity, that is, the presence of the consequences of abuse within the self. This is, in essence, the presence of love and hate, good and evil, life and death at the foundation of the self.

Now we see why the ambiguity of abuse in the circumstances of a trusted relationship is so profound and why the process of healing is so belabored. In healing from abuse the survivor is seeking a spiritual stature that is greater than the abuser's. If there is an emotional attachment with the abuser, the abusive experience becomes internalized; the abuser becomes an internalized object, in psychoanalytic terms. The danger of this experience is that consequences of the smaller moral size of the abuser are reproduced in the victim. In order to find wholeness, the adult victim must attain enough moral strength to reconcile the contradictions of love and hate absorbed from the abuser.

To stand face-to-face with one's potential for good and evil and have the strength to choose the good is one of life's most difficult challenges. Survivors of sexual violence are pioneers in facing the depth of the human condition. Through solidarity with survivors we may see present-day analogies to Jesus' ability to face the possibility of good and evil in himself and to maintain his ability to love his enemies.

The image of Jesus who maintained his integrity in the midst of ambiguity is an important image for some. In other words, the ability to embrace ambiguity within the self is crucial to the process of healing and to fullness of life. The healing process leads one to the edge of chaos and fragmentation where the awareness of death and nothingness is fully present. In chapter 8 we will examine the reality of ambiguity in Jesus' life in more detail.

The testimony of adult survivors is that they have been faced with the choice of life and death. To live life with great risk, to face the internal contradictions of love and hate in oneself and in one's loved ones, is to live life the way God has created it. Living with ambiguity requires a strong network of support and patience to live with uncertainty. If this is true, then the adult victims who have the courage to face these deep ambiguities in themselves are revealers of Jesus for those who are willing to see.

CHAPTER SEVEN

THE SEARCH FOR COMMUNITY

Throughout their lives, survivors struggle to heal from the injuries they suffer from sexual violence. Their healing includes a search for loving community that can provide an environment for support and understanding. In their search for community they uncover the complicity of social institutions and ideologies in the abuse of power. Judge Schreber was upset at the medical system which misdiagnosed and mistreated his illness. Karen was betrayed by school and church leaders who silenced her expressions of suffering and denied her the resources needed for healing. Sam was abused by his own family, and his problems were mishandled by schools and courts.

In their own ways, survivors ask a compelling question: "Where is the loving community where I can be accepted and loved for my true self?" The search for community and betrayal by community are central themes in the testimonies we have heard. Abused children are betrayed by their parents and other adults, by the church and schools, and by the wider ideologies that determine how power and privilege are distributed. Analysis of social institutions and ideologies in recent feminist and African-American theologies uncovers the betrayal by community. Abuse does not occur in a vacuum. The testimony of our witnesses has disclosed how institutions and ideologies explicitly and implicitly sanction abuse of power.

The search for loving community sometimes varies according to gender. After years of secrecy and isolation, Karen sought out physicians, pastors, therapists, and friends to help her in her healing. Learning to trust them with her suffering was challenging. Karen had not abused others, but her secret suffering had led to isolation and fear.

Sam's hunger for community was disguised by a web of deceit that covered his destructive behaviors against others; he became an abuser as a way of avoiding his internal pain.[1] His search for community showed up in his attachment to his sick daughter and eventual trust of his wife and counselors during his recovery. The question of why men more often than women become perpetrators of sexual violence continues to be part of our research.

Our witnesses search for a community that is not characterized by the abuse of power, and they testify to the marks of such communities:

—Loving communities are *inclusive:* They value the interior experience of every person and create environments that embrace life in its fullness.
—Loving communities are *just:* They have the courage to confront abuse of power within the community and in the larger society.

BETRAYAL BY COMMUNITY

Central to the testimony of Judge Schreber was his perception that his physician was persecuting him. According to Freud's interpretation, this was a fantasy of paranoia based on Schreber's erotic transference to Dr. Flechsig. Freud thought that Judge Schreber had developed an attachment to his physician, which, because of homosexual panic, was converted into a fear and projected as an illusion of persecution. However, later study revealed that there was truth in Judge Schreber's perceptions. He had been drugged, physically restrained, and placed in isolation when he protested the interpretations his doctor put on his behavior. He had been misdiagnosed because his psychotic fantasies were never connected to the trauma of physical abuse by his father. He had been misunderstood and blamed for his condition by the mental health community, rather than accepted as a victim who was searching for understanding and truth. The inability of society to understand the traumatic consequences of his childhood abuse was a failure of community.[2]

During the time that Karen was being molested by her father, she remembers being taught at church to believe in the goodness of her parents.

> In a recent state of deep relaxation and trance, I found myself in the room where I went to Sunday School as a four- or five-year-old child. I stood in front of a poster on the wall which had all the names of my classmates listed. Beside our names were stickers, placed in a row after we had memorized certain Bible verses. I heard myself repeating "Honor thy Father and Mother." While sitting on the floor with my classmates, our teacher told us about the goodness of parents; they love us, feed, clothe, and protect us from ALL harm. I learned early, while being abused, that my parents kept me from harm. The church taught me to be grateful to my parents and to trust that they would always protect me. Again, when I was five, my young mind would not let me think that my father could be anything but good.

Similar experiences were repeated at school where the authority and goodness of parents were emphasized and children were taught to be obedient. Even when she developed somatic symptoms that required medical attention, no one asked her if she was being mistreated. Every intact, respectable family was assumed to be doing right for their children, and her suffering had to be borne in silence.

To protest his childhood terror, Sam turned to the streets. Even though he had a difficult time in school, he was identified as an adolescent who caused trouble rather than one who was abused. At one point he was involved with police, youth detention centers, counseling centers. None of these agencies heard the cries of pain he had turned into violent behaviors and rejection of society. Labeled a problem and punished, he was never given the real help he needed. He was betrayed by a society that defined him as delinquent rather than as a victim of child abuse.

To understand this betrayal by community and society, we must understand how families, churches, schools, and societies become organized so that their most vulnerable members experience extreme suffering. It is unjust that abused children are isolated from the resources of life and creativity. Power and privilege become organized in institutional forms that resist change, and these forms are protected by powerful ideologies that promote the power of some groups at the expense of others. Unjust ideologies create a state of affairs in which adults are privileged over children, men are privileged over women, whites are privileged over people of color, and rich are privileged over poor. We must know how society becomes organized in such an unfair manner, how it is maintained, and why the testimony of the victims of the abuse of power leads to so little change in institutions and attitudes.

THE NATURE OF COMMUNITY

In process-relational thought, community is a basic form of reality.[3] The building block of experience is the *actual occasion*, which is a momentary unit of experiencing. It comes into being as the many relationships of the past come together at a particular time and place (sensitivity). As the many become one, they are synthesized into a single complex feeling with its own particular character, which is then passed on as a cause for others (creativity). Occasions are "drops of experience . . . the many becoming one and increased by one."[4] An occasion is relational because the raw data of its experience is its sensitivity to others, and because it is a creative synthesis for others that come into being in the next moment.

One of the ways the relational nature of the actual occasion comes into human consciousness is through repeated patterns. Occasions repeat the essential forms of previous occasions so that the patterns over time become perceptible. For example, the color pink might be repeated for a time in a beautiful sunset. It is not exactly the momentary occasion that creates beauty, but the repeated pattern over many occasions. A series of occasions that repeats a particular pattern is called an *event*.

> Concretely the unity of an event constitutes a historic route of successive occasions, but the route itself is not an occasion. The abstract unity can be understood as a recurring structure that characterizes the enduring object in its persistence throughout the duration of the inclusive event.[5]

The event, or repeated pattern of occasions, is a structure binding many occasions together into a temporal community.

A collection of occasions with structured relationships is called a *nexus*. A sunset is a nexus of color and shape that endures over time. A pattern of distinguishing characteristics is what makes a collectivity of occasions into a nexus. A *society* is a nexus with enduring characteristics that are more unified. A tree is a living society with many subsystems—bark, capillaries, wood, leaves, and so forth. It does not have a center of consciousness, but it does have structured relationships that are predictable over time and coordinated within systems.

A human being is a living society with a presiding occasion that coordinates aspects of all its subsystems. A human being is a society of societies with a high level of sensitivity to experience and a high level of creativity for introducing novelty into relationships. In the terms of this chapter, a human being is a community of occasions. When Paul described the church as the body of Christ (I Corinthians 12), he was actually comparing two types of communities. The community that is a human being has a physical body and a consciousness with a particular character. A church is a community made up of many human beings with a shared consciousness about what it means to be a group in a particular time and place. Although a church community is somewhat more diffuse than a human being, they are both collections of occasions, events, nexus, and societies with common characteristics. Both human beings and churches are societies of societies with many subsystems and a center of consciousness that creates its identity and continuity.

In this section we are looking at those forms of community made of groups of human beings such as families, churches, nations, linguistic groups, and so on. This kind of community life is characterized by organized patterns of thought and behavior that have consistency over time and that bind the group together in varying forms of loyalty.

The enduring pattern of a community such as a church, a neighborhood, or a nation is a *culture*, or patterns of meaning and value that create its identity. Culture is the pattern of thought, behavior, language, and symbols that hold a people together. "It affects and shapes not only language, the mode of thinking and speaking, but sensibilities of thought, psychical orientation, and thus psychical expectations."[6] The following will serve as a working definition for this chapter.

> Community is a process of interaction that structures immediate experience into distinctive cultural myths within a historical and social framework.

The process-relational view suggests that the meaning of all human behavior is culturally constructed. Because the reality and significance of events of sexual violence have been denied and suppressed, their cultural meaning is difficult to explore. Sexual abuse of the vulnerable by the powerful, whether in families, schools, churches, or businesses, has been considered an unusual and insignificant event. In order to understand sexual violence in our society, we have to examine the cultural images of power and abuse of power within their historical and socio-political context.

Given the individualistic ways of thinking prevalent in the United States, the idea of corporate consciousness is hard to grasp. We most often think of community and culture as a collectivity of individual attitudes rather than a unified reality. The corporate reality of community, here defined as culture, does much to determine the consciousness of individual human beings.

> We are not . . . building up the behavior of the social group in terms of the behavior of the separate individuals composing it; rather, we are starting out with a given social whole of complex group activity, into which we analyze (as elements) the behavior of each of the separate individuals composing it.[7]

It is difficult to overcome our individualistic bias about the imperial, autonomous self in order to grasp how much the culture of community does to determine individual behavior and attitudes.[8] This section started with a philosophical explanation of community in order to encourage the cognitive structures necessary for a shift in thinking. We also need new metaphors of community.

Community as a Web of Relationships

The metaphor of a web helps us understand cultural reality as it affects our latent images of power and abuse of power.

> If we generalize the notion of causal relations we arrive at the conception of the world as an incredibly vast network of interlocked events. This network is the dynamic and relational web of life into which we are born and in which we live out our lives—for better or worse. This network obviously includes webs within webs, or societies within societies, in bewildering profusion. These societies vary enormously in spatial extensions, psychic intensity, complexity of shared defining characteristics, and depths of communications and mutuality of influence.[9]

As individuals we find ourselves at a particular time and place in the web of relationships. The web consists of relationships with past occasions, future directions, and social structures. We begin consciousness with awareness of the web. Our experience consists of our relationships to objects, to people, to language, to symbols of culture like art and the media. Even our private thought processes are internalizations of the "conversation of gestures" that we learn in human interaction.[10] When we act, we influence the shape and direction of the web to some extent.

> This larger and inclusive web is a given or primordial reality, whether we acknowledge its existence or not. We do not create it. That is, we do not create the relational character of existence. We are connected with all life, in varying degrees of direct and mediated forms of relationships. When we build our many societies (families, churches, clubs, nations) we exemplify the given relational character of existence. When we touch the web at any point, the consequences of our act reverberate throughout the network (again, in varying degrees of intensity and influence). This is the ecological premise, whether we refer to human life or to the world of nature and their interrelationship.[11]

The web is a metaphor not just for the collection of individuals that are bound together but for the whole pattern, which determines the context for the individual's life. Personal existence is a building block that makes up the fragile, temporal web of reality. Without the web, we cease to exist because the web is the totality of reality itself. The movement of life itself, the "Creative Passage," is organized into a web of relationships.[12] The web is the structure of existence that organizes process.

Culture is organized into patterns like a web.[13] Consider the activities that make up a huge international corporation like the news department of Columbia Broadcasting System (CBS News). Reporters are stationed around the world in places where important events are likely to happen, or where offices have been established in the past for historical reasons. (There are many more offices in Europe than in Africa, for example.) There is the common language of these reporters and their staffs, and the hookup of electronic equipment through satellites that enables instant communication. Money flows through the system, and information is collected and passed on to an audience. There are assumptions, stories from the past, expectations, lines of authority, future commitments. Everything that happens is defined by its location in this web of relationships. Every word is defined by its function in the web. The web has a history and every activity comes out of this history and becomes a part of it. The web has direction, and every event changes the future in some way. Everything that happens receives meaning and value because of its time and place in the relational web. The web shapes the individual, and the individual shapes the web. Everything exists in this "incredibly vast network of interlocked events."[14]

Sexual violence occurs within a web of relationships and meaning. We need to explore the ways in which the web of relationships creates sexual violence, and how the web must be changed so that the unjust suffering of vulnerable persons can be addressed. The testimony of survivors gives clues about the deficiencies of the web and about the resilient hope within the web that increases love and mercy.

In summary, we have defined the nature of community in process-relational terms as a society of actual occasions with a presiding order or culture that determines perception and human response. To overcome our individualistic and materialistic bias, we have used the metaphor of a web of relationships. This network of interconnected events is highly influential in human experience.

In the midst of church and society, children and adults have been suffering, yet their plight has not been identified and dealt with as reality. We need to turn our attention now to the culture of the United States, which forms our perceptions about sexual violence.

FEMINIST ANALYSIS OF CULTURE

Through careful listening to survivors of sexual violence, we have begun to see beyond the individual. Every event in human experience has its historical and socio-political context. The exact nature of the personal and cultural connection must be carefully explored. We need to know whether sexual violence is an aberration, with minimal cultural significance, or whether it is a highly symbolic expression of latent cultural values and norms.

There is a tradition of connecting individual difficulties with cultural critique. Several scholars who have explored this form of analysis in regard to women have shown how forms of madness historically attributed to women correspond to deficiencies in their culture that were denied or suppressed. One example is the way the illness of hysteria was related to the suppression of female sexuality in a patriarchal culture. Freud tried to apply science to the illnesses of women, but he colluded with his culture in attributing their maladies to individual pathology rather than to the patriarchal oppression of women.[15]

As recently as 1975, some leaders in the mental health community considered child sexual abuse an infrequent occurrence that had little if any significance as a mental health problem.[16] But recent research has shown that between one-third and one-half of all girls have had an abusive sexual experience before age 18,[17] and some estimates are that 5 to 10 percent of all boys have been sexually abused.[18]

One incisive analysis of the institutional and cultural basis of sexual violence is feminist analysis. In fact, sexual violence was "discovered" as a great problem when feminists began to make connections between it and the oppression of all women.[19] The cultural analysis of feminists and womanists[20] helps us thematize the testimony of the witnesses in this study, as (1) the ideology of the family; (2) devaluation of women and children; and (3) the confusion of sexuality and violence.[21]

Ideology of the Family

The idea of family privacy is one aspect of culture in the United States that contributes to sexual violence. Karen testifies that the wall surrounding the privacy of her family in certain matters was almost absolute. Since her parents were respectable and middle-class, no one considered that destructive violence was the core reality of the family. No one asked why Karen was so frequently ill, so quiet, so withdrawn emotionally. The boundary protecting the family hid the secret abuse of power so destructive in her life.

Historians and sociologists are discovering that the family was not always private in the modern sense. In previous times people tended to live more communally with many adults and children in regular contact. Although people were frequently mistreated, there were fewer secrets than in the modern incestuous family. Industrialization meant that adults began to work in factories and live in isolated nuclear units. This has meant fewer social controls on inequality and the corresponding abuse of power within the family.[22]

The privatization of the family has continued hierarchies of power that used to be part of the legal codes. One hundred fifty years ago women and children were the property of fathers, husbands, or other men. The Women's Rights Convention in 1848 in Seneca Falls, New York, passed a declaration of rights to protest the inequities of that time. Women were not allowed to vote or own property. They could not divorce abusive husbands, and if a husband sought a divorce or died, the woman could not even influence the decision as to what man would be given custody of the children. The temperance movement of that time received important impetus because abused women had no legal protection from alcoholic husbands.[23]

There have been gains over the official patriarchy of the nineteenth century, which disenfranchised women and children in the family. However, the isolation of the family combined with the stubborn inequality of men and women has made the family an increasingly dangerous institution for women and children. There is more sexual and physical violence, including homicide, in the family than in any other social location. For any particular person, the probability of rape, assault, or murder is greater in the family than in any other place.[24] Yet authorities are reluctant to intervene in the family and confront this violence. When police officers come to investigate a complaint of "domestic violence," they often leave without making an arrest. There are only a few states that give the police authority to arrest a man in the home without a complaint of the victim. Yet many victims have been threatened with additional violence if they tell the police anything. In many states, there are severe limits on child protective services for intervening in families to protect children in danger. Parents' rights organizations have increased the pressure on the state to limit family intervention.[25] We lack cultural understanding of the extent of violence in the family, and thus we fail to protect women and children who are victims. Although many of the legal barriers for women have changed in this century, inequality between women and men is now preserved by family privacy and economic inequality.

According to Richard Gelles and Murray Straus, three factors combine to make the family an increasingly violent institution, one in which women and children are seriously disadvantaged. First, there is cultural encouragement of violence as a legitimate form of interpersonal behavior. As long as violence is romanticized in the media as a way of handling interpersonal conflict, the physical strength of men is a source of danger for women and children. Second, the privacy of the family leads to a corresponding lack of social control over men who choose to be violent in the home. Since the family is considered a sacred institution whose boundaries cannot be crossed by agencies with authority to protect women and children, the violence of men continues to be a problem. Third, there is the stubborn inequality of women and children in relation to men. Although there has been significant change in the public rights and responsibilities of women in this century, women who are denied the right to support themselves and their children in the market economy are at a severe disadvantage. The alternative to abuse for women and children who are in danger is often poverty.[26]

The work of African-American scholars helps to put this historical and sociological analysis into a larger political and economic perspective.[27] The existence of a biased ideology of the family becomes clear when we see how the black family is mistreated in research and public policy. The isolated nuclear family, in which men are dominant over women and children, is normative in United States culture and is part of the social system that causes sexual violence. The African-American family is blamed because it does not conform to this ideal type.

During the last half of the nineteenth century, when white United States society was moving toward the private nuclear family, the African-American family was trying to survive in slavery. Under slavery the African-American family was illegal; that is, it was illegal for adults to marry, have children, and take care of their personal business as responsible citizens. In fact, slave policy was often directed toward disrupting emotional bonding between African-Americans. In spite of this severe oppression, bonds were formed and families maintained ties of loyalty. After African-Americans were freed from legal slavery, millions traveled at great risk to find beloved family members. The family has been an enduring institution among African-Americans.[28]

However, the norms for the African-American family have always been different from those of the stereotypical American nuclear family.[29] First, black families preserved some values of the African traditions of extended family. Because of their normative attitudes about human relationships, men, women, and children bonded together in extended kinship groups. Adoption of children and single adults into families was an expected pattern. Extended family units characterize the normative African-American family.

Second, because of the brutality of slavery and racism, the need for physical survival has shaped the norms of the African-American family. There has never been a time when the family unit has had freedom from terror. Men, women, and children bonded together in whatever functional units they could in order to cope with the oppression of daily life. Because slave masters considered emotional bonds between the slaves a danger to the desire for complete control, they often made decisions to sell or trade based on disruption of the family units. Since slavery, the use of Southern terror tactics and the brutality of Northern ghetto life has continued the pressure on the African-American family. Adaptability is a norm of the African-American family.

Third, the lack of an adequate economic base led to a norm of sharing resources for the African-American family. Unemployment and underemployment in an exploitative capitalist economy means that often the family lives under severe financial pressure. The welfare system often adds bureaucratic control to the difficulties of poverty. Sharing resources is a norm of African-American families.

In the midst of the historical and continuing oppression, a normative model of the family in the African-American community has emerged. This model is characterized by more flexible, equal relationships between men and women, the inclusive nature of families, which adopt adults and children, and the extended family concept, which binds persons together to share resources. Even though many African-American families cannot always live according to this normative model in the midst of a racist society, its very existence helps unmask the ideology of the nuclear family, which is a cover for sexual violence. The African-American church preserves the vision of such families through the structures of nurture and care like an extended family.[30]

In spite of the adaptive nature of the African-American family under nearly impossible conditions, there has been a constant attack on these families because they do not conform to the norm of the male-dominated nuclear family. The Moynihan report of 1968 blamed the African-American family for its own poverty. It suggested that the history of slavery and racism had created a matriarchal family in which men were prevented from functioning as "head of the family." This meant that children grew up in homes without male figures and with domineering women. The report further suggested that African-American women should be more passive so that their men could resume their rightful role in the family and the community.[31] This distorted view has been picked up by more recent conservative scholars, who blame the African-American family for crime and other problems of the ghetto. George Gilder has said, "In the welfare culture money becomes not something earned by men through hard work, but a right conferred on women by the state. Protest and complaint replace diligence and discipline as the sources of pay. Boys grow up seeking support from women, while they find manhood in the macho circles of the street and the bar or in the irresponsible fathering of random progeny."[32] Angela Davis says that this analysis completely overlooks the remarkable adaptive ability of the African-American family to survive nearly impossible conditions and that it blames the family rather than the capitalist system for ghetto poverty.

This section has reviewed some of the history of the African-American family in order to reveal the powerful ideology of the nuclear family in American culture. One contributing factor to sexual and physical violence in the family is the dominance of men over women and children, and this is preserved by family privacy and economic inequality. "The victims of violence in the home are disproportionately the smaller, the weaker, and the less powerful."[33] Because of the rigid boundaries protecting the sanctity of the home from social observation and control, and because women often face poverty if they leave the family, women and children are increasingly in danger. Society in the United States cannot see the amount of violence directed against women and children because of its need to protect the ideal family from criticism. As we begin to see the amount of destructive behavior in the family, we have to reconstruct our ideal images of the family. We need a reformulated family mythos in which equality between the sexes and the rights of children are established. Patriarchy has failed to provide a healthy family model in which all persons are treated with dignity and respect.

Karen's difficulties as a young child were not taken seriously by adults in church and school, because she came from such a nice family. Everyone assumed that parents take care of their children if anything is wrong. So outside adults made little of any problem they saw. The possibility that this young child was regularly sexually abused by her father was unthinkable.

Even though Sam's family was so dysfunctional that child protective services became involved, interventions were ineffective in protecting the children. They were more concerned with keeping the children within a family than understanding whether their basic needs for safety and nurture were being met.

The view of the family as necessarily good makes sexual violence unthinkable, and thus the suffering of many persons is suppressed. Most sexual violence occurs within the family, and victims are betrayed by society, which is willing to protect male privilege at the expense of women and children, whose lives are damaged by abuse of power. This injustice hinders the search for true community.

Devaluation of Women and Children

Sexual abuse is a form of devaluation. Instead of being nurtured, as a child has a right to expect from the caregiver, the child who is molested is used to gratify the selfish desires of the adult. Karen was expected to go to her bedroom in a large, isolated farm house without an adult to comfort her. Then later in the night when the "monster" visited her bedroom, her terror knew no comfort. Her father became her tormenter at an age when preschool children typically fear dangerous figures and need to be comforted. Her fragile life was severely damaged by these fears. She had to use all her resources to defend herself from being overwhelmed by evil. She was the victim of hatred.

Likewise, Sam became a monster in his son's life when he turned playful wrestling into sexual abuse. Many years of therapy were required before Sam could face the evil that he had done to his son. He had become a molester just like the ones who had terrorized him in his childhood. The hatred he felt all his life was projected onto his own son.

The hatred expressed in sexual violence is not only an attitude of individual men who are abusive, but it is also a culturally organized attitude. Although misogyny is defined as a prejudice against women, feminism is interested in the systemic forces that create such hatred and limit women's experience and opportunities. One expression of misogyny is the inequality of women, which can be documented by examining the economic position of women or by looking at the access women have to positions of power and influence in society.

> In 1987, women earned only 68 cents for every dollar men earned (N.Y. Times, 1987). . . . In general, if you are born female rather than male, the likelihood is twice as great that you will be below the poverty line at some time during your life. If you are born male, you are at greatest risk for being poor during childhood, when you are more likely to be financially dependent upon the earnings of a woman.[34]

Feminism has been especially interested in the psychic and cultural forces that keep women in a devalued position and how these patterns are related to sexual violence.

Toinette Eugene, an African-American womanist scholar, refers to two sets of dualisms behind misogyny and racism.

> *Sexist dualism* refers to the systematic subordination of women in church and society, within interpersonal relationships between males and females, as well as within linguistic patterns and thought formulations by which women are dominated. Hence the term "patriarchal dualism" may also be appropriate, or more simply, the contemporary designation of "sexism," may be used. *Spiritualistic dualism* has its roots in the body-spirit dichotomy abounding in white western philosophy and culture introduced at the beginning of the Christian era. Hence, the term "Hellenistic dualism" may also be appropriate.[35]

Misogyny should be understood in relation to two situations. The first situation is the subordination of women to men in institutions, relationships, and ideologies. The second situation is the unconscious identification of women with the physical body and nature as distinguished from mind and culture. Feminist theory has been intensely interested in both dualisms. One direction of research is to look at the psychoanalytic account of early childhood when gender identity is formed to see how the macro-system of asymmetry between the sexes becomes internalized into the personalities of boys and girls. Another direction is to look at the philosophical history of the body-mind or nature-culture distinction to see how women have been devalued. A brief look at each of these arguments can further clarify the structures of domination that lead to devaluation of women and children.

Sexist Dualism Nancy Chodorow, who has explored gender formation during early childhood, has found that in a patriarchal society boys have a different psychological formation from that of girls.[36] Both boys and girls are first attached to women because women are the primary caregivers of young children. Because the caregiving figure (mother) and the sexual identity figure (woman) are the same for girls, this attachment creates a strong identification. That is, a girl can be attached to the mothering figure out of need for nurture, and also as a way of understanding what it means to be female. In the absence of a responsible, caring male parent, girls tend to prolong their preoedipal state of development and develop an intrapsychic world that is more oriented to interpersonal relations. Even though there is considerable ambivalence toward the mother because of her devalued status in society, there is no need for internal division in the child's identity.

In contrast, boys have a built-in contradiction in their development. Even though their first attachment is to a woman, they become aware very early that this attachment is a danger to their sexual identity. In a world where inequality between men and women is so extreme, it is dangerous for males to overidentify with females. To be considered a girl is one of the biggest fears for many young boys because it leads to a loss of privilege.

Boys learn that they must identify with a male figure in order to avoid being mistreated and to obtain the privileges men expect in a patriarchal culture. This has several effects. One effect is that boys as young as three years old prematurely detach emotionally from their mothers in order to identify with a male figure. This shortens the time the boy has with his mother for development of his object world and often creates loneliness for boys if a father figure is unavailable. A second effect is that boys fear being dominated by a mother-woman who seems to be an overwhelming, dangerous figure. "A boy's struggle to free himself from his mother and become masculine generates 'the contempt felt by men for a sex which is lesser' (Freud)—'What we have come to consider the normal male contempt for women.'"[37] Philosophy and literature are filled with misogynous statements that reveal this male contempt for and ambivalence toward women. For example, Aristotle said, "And woman is, as it were, an impotent male, for it is through a certain incapacity that the female is female."[38]

> Dread of the mother is ambivalent, however. Although a boy fears her, he also finds her seductive and attractive. He cannot simply dismiss and ignore her. Boys and men develop psychological and cultural/ideological mechanisms to cope with their fears without giving up women altogether. They create folk legends, beliefs, and poems that ward off the dread by externalizing and objectifying women: "It is not . . . that I dread her; it is that she herself is malignant, capable of any crime, a beast of prey, a vampire, a witch, insatiable in her desires . . . the very personification of what is sinister." They deny dread at the expense of realistic views of women. On the one hand, they glorify and adore: "There is no need for me to dread a being so wonderful, so beautiful, nay, so saintly." On the other, they disparage: "It would be too ridiculous to dread a creature who, if you take her all around, is such a poor thing."[39]

Chodorow makes explicit that the hatred of women by men is not just psychological but also cultural-ideological. The right of men to be dominant over women, a characteristic of patriarchy, is reinforced with signals in the earliest experiences of boys and girls. Gender inequality is a part of family life down to the most intimate interaction between mother and child, between mother and father; it is institutionalized in the inequality of the wage structure, and romanticized in art and media.

When Eugene analyzes the psychological forms of misogyny from the perspective of the African-American community, the structure of sexist and racist domination stands out in bold relief.

> Sexist dualism, which has been organized along racial lines, refers to "schizophrenic" male attitudes toward women in general who are imaged as either the virgin or the whore—the polemical Mary or Eve archetype represented by the female gender. The prevailing model of beauty in the white, male-dominated American society has been the "long-haired

blond" with all that accompanies this mystique. . . . Sexist as well as racist dualisms have elevated the image of the white women in accordance with the requirements of a white worldview into becoming the respected symbol of femininity and purity, while the Black women must represent an animality which can be ruthlessly exploited for both sex and labor.[40]

While feminism has uncovered part of the structure of domination by showing the latent misogyny, the full impact of the devaluation of women within American culture becomes clear in the testimony of African-American women, who are "exploited for both sex and labor" because they do not fit the ideological ideal of the "long-haired blond." Some privilege is obtained for white women who can and do fit the stereotype of the female at the expense of persons of color. But all women are constantly faced with misogynist attitudes and institutional practices.

Hatred of women is so much a part of the very culture and language within which we live that abuse of women is often overlooked. The Sunday school teachers who taught Karen that parents are good were unwittingly providing protection for her abusive father. Whatever clues to Karen's suffering they might have seen were probably unselfconsciously dismissed as normal. Devaluation of women and children is often overlooked because women and children are considered less important, and their symptoms of suffering are considered a part of the normal course of life. The victims of sexual violence are betrayed by community when their suffering is hidden within the system of domination that devalues women and by extension their children.

Spiritualist Dualism Hester Eisenstein has summarized the feminist discussion about the correlation of gender with the distinction between culture and nature, what Eugene calls "spiritualist dualism."[41] The devaluation of women has a long history that is nearly universal across cultures.

Every society recognized a distinction between "culture" and "nature." . . . Culture, as expressed in ritual, was an expression of the need to regulate and control, "rather than passively move with and be moved by, the givens of natural existence."[42]

Over the generations of evolution, humankind has distinguished between nature as the source of life and death, and culture as the human power to ameliorate the capricious forces of nature. By making this cognitive distinction, the world of experience became dichotomized and was correlated with two socially constructed genders. Men became associated with culture, while women became associated with nature. Because women could bear young, they were identified with the home, and then with the danger associated with nature itself. To the extent that the power of nature was seen as a threat to human life, this fear was projected onto women. Women were hated because they represented the fear of dangerous and uncontrollable forces. The fact that men controlled the development of culture meant that these distinctions could be imposed by men without input from women.[43]

Eugene suggests that the dichotomy of nature-culture or body-mind and its corresponding identification with female-male is an important contributing factor in the devaluation of women and persons of color today.

> Bodily scapegoating implies a discomfort with our own bodies which leads us to discredit any human body-person which differs too much in appearance and similarity from our own. This scapegoating is particularly evident in racist, white-black relationships. But it is equally obvious in the revealing and discrediting attitudes of some men, white and black, about the assumed menstrual "uncleanliness" of women, or the intrinsic "repulsiveness" of the pregnant female form.
>
> Because blackness has long been understood as a symbol for filth as well as evil, a spiritualistic dualism prevalent in the worldview of many white persons has allowed them the racist option of projecting onto black persons any dirty or disgusting bodily feelings which they may harbor within themselves. Because of the fertility potential symbolized by the female menstrual and pregnancy cycles, a spiritualistic and sexist dualism has also been created and sustained by white and black males which has allowed them to act out their own latent anxieties and hostilities by sexually depreciating the value and worth of the black female person.[44]

African-American women scholars have shown how the nature-culture dichotomy contributes to the devaluation of women and persons of color. To the extent that communities have not faced their own unconscious feelings about their negative experience, including bodily experience, they will promote projection of these feelings onto those who are vulnerable in society.

This ambivalence toward nature and the physical body is a predominant feature in the perpetrators of child sexual violence. On the one hand, they idealize children's bodies as pure and full of life, and they have an obsessive attraction to them. Children seem to have something that these men lack in their own lives. They want to be close to children, to touch children, in order to be closer to the source of life and liveliness, especially in contrast to their own depression and distorted body image.[45] On the other hand, their hostility toward children is profound. How dare children have such life and liveliness when their own lives are so empty? They hate those who seem to be closer to the source of all life. So their behavior is designed to control "nature" and "body" by controlling children. Their neediness leads them to exploit children; their rage leads them to destroy children.

The dynamic of idealizing and hating children reveals the underlying dynamic of spiritualistic dualism. When one is separated from one's own physically embodied life, then one projects these distorted hopes and fears onto others for exploitation and destruction.

For our purposes this analysis shows that sexual violence is part of a much larger ideological and socio-political state of affairs. Idealized views in the public mind portray women and children as pure and vulnerable. But a careful analysis reveals attitudes and institutionalized practices that reflect latent hatred of women, children, and people of color. The testimonies of Karen and other survivors add voices to this analysis of the structures of domination. In patriarchal families children are endangered by men who are acting out, not just their individual pathology, but the cultural attitudes of devaluation. In a racist culture, the devaluation of racial groups becomes organized in ways that are destructive of men, women, and children of color. Men who have been sexually victimized as children sometimes become perpetrators who act out their rage toward women and children. In a culture that despises women it is no wonder that children frequently become victims of sexual abuse. They receive the abuse that is latently sanctioned by ideologies of patriarchy. To the extent that women, and by extension children, are devalued and hated in our culture, they are betrayed by community and become vulnerable to sexual violence. Their search for true community is prevented.

Confusion of Sexuality and Violence

Sexual confusion is common for children who are sexually abused. One survivor said, "I never had a positive experience with sex until I was married. I thought it was supposed to be a painful, ugly experience that had to be tolerated in order to get other things I wanted." Sexual activity between adults and children is a confusion of the purpose of sexuality.

The sexual exploitation of a child who cannot protect herself or even conceptualize what is being done to her by a trusted adult is a confusion of sexuality and violence.

The inability of our culture to devise a healthy sexual theory contributes greatly to the prevalence of sexual violence and to the inability of society to face the massive problem of sexual abuse. When women began talking about their own experiences of sexual violence, they discovered how many had been victimized by rape as children or as adults or both. Sexual activity can serve many purposes besides the expression of mutual respect and affection between two persons. Because there is inequality between men and women, and between men and children, sexuality can become a way of expressing control and power. Reports from many women that their sexual experiences with men are destructive has led to research to explain the prevalence of sexual violence.[46]

Throughout history rape has usually been understood as a violation of property rights of men rather than as a violation of the human rights of women.

> Punishment for rape was an action brought by one man against another for damage to his property. It was a form of compensation for the loss incurred through a daughter, or a wife, whose value, either for exchange in marriage or as a possession, had been thus reduced or destroyed.[47]

In some cultures, a man's punishment for rape was marriage to his victim, and thus responsibility for her future. The fact that this solution was a further violation of the woman's life was not considered important.

Rape functions as a form of social control over women by men. Historically, every "respectable" woman was the property of some man, and thus was protected from other men by property laws. Although laws that explicitly make women the property of men are no longer in legal effect in the United States, the myth that women need protection by men has become a part of the social mores. "Once 'discovered' by men, rape had been, and continued to be, used as a means to control women, both actually and potentially, by means of the fear that it inspired."[48] That is, after women were no longer the legal property of their husbands and could vote and own property, the fear of rape began to be used by men to keep women under control. According to the myth, a "loose" woman is likely to be raped because she does not have male protection. This is a means whereby men create pressure on women to live under the protection of a man in order to avoid being the target of rape by other men.

> Women alone were vulnerable and liable to be raped. They were in danger at all times, but especially on the streets at night. Therefore, a man could argue, a woman needed protection (by him) from every other man. . . . Each man could maintain his hold on "his" woman by threatening her with what could be done to her, in the absence of his protection, by the rest of the men. Each of these of course could make the same argument to "his" woman. By this primitive system, the law of the urban jungle, no woman could afford to be without her "protector." What the system omitted to make explicit, needless to say, was that often, a woman's "protector" could become her rapist as well.[49]

What has been previously defined as a sexual crime is actually a crime of power and control. Rape has very little to do with sex; it is primarily a crime of violence. But because it is *sexual* violence, certain forms of rape have been vastly underestimated and disregarded. For example, date rape and marital rape are only now beginning to attract legal attention and some state laws are being changed. Once a woman consents to come "under the protection" of a particular man, she has little legal recourse against his aggressive behaviors that may lead to rape or other forms of abuse.

Likewise, the sexual abuse of children has been disregarded for much of history because it is often perpetrated by the very men who are socially responsible for the protection of children. Most sexual abuse of children is perpetrated by adult men within the family or trusted male leaders in the community. When the sexual abuse of a child is disclosed, the community often rallies to defend the reputation of the man rather than the child. The notorious exception is the child who is raped by a stranger with no connection to the family. "Beware of strangers" is frequently taught children to caution them about the dangers of sexual abuse. Almost completely ignored are the fathers, step-fathers, grandfathers, brothers, and uncles who are more apt to be the perpetrators.[50] This shows that sexual violence as a form of control of women and children is latently supported in our culture. The lie that respectable men cannot be child rapists, that the only dangerous men are unattached strangers, actually serves to increase the danger to children by hiding from them the real danger within the family.

Patriarchy protects men as a group from suspicion of sexual violence. The patriarchal ideal of autonomy and individualism also enables the powerful to hide or be invisible.

A further development in feminist thinking about the confusion of sexuality and violence resulted from analysis of the nature of pornography. In sharing groups, women began to discuss and to critically examine the growing pornography industry. Indeed, there has been a dramatic increase in gross sales and an increase in the violent, sadistic content of pornography. With increasing frequency, pictures and videos portray violent sex, often combined with physical violence, even in some cases to the point of murder of women. The testimony of women who worked in the pornography industry also contributed to the concerns of feminists. Many women, who were vulnerable because of economic hardship or abusive childhoods, were being systematically exploited by the filmmakers.[51]

This evidence drew the attention of feminist scholars to try to understand the function of such pornography in a patriarchal culture. What surfaced in this research was another form of spiritualistic dualism.[52] Susan Griffin suggests that confusion of sexuality and violence is based on the "pornographic imagination," the latent personal and social attitudes toward women within the fantasies of men.

> The pornographer, like the church father, hates and denies a part of himself. He rejects his knowledge of the physical world and of his own materiality. He rejects knowledge of his own body. This is a part of his mind he would forget. But he cannot reject this knowledge entirely. It comes back to him through his own body: through desire. Just as he pushes away a part of himself, he desires it. What he hates and fears, what he would loathe, he desires. He is in a terrible conflict with himself. And instead he comes to imagine that he struggles with a woman. Onto her body he projects his fear and his desire. So the female body, like the whore of Babylon in church iconography, simultaneously lures the pornographer and incites his rage.[53]

The confusion of sexuality and violence is uncovered in an analysis of pornography. The split within male consciousness is laid bare. On the one hand, heterosexual male fantasy is preoccupied with the female body. There is an idealization of the value of nature that is, in fantasy, accessible through women. Thus there is a tremendous market for materials that uncover the female body. On the other hand, the fear and dread of the female body in the male imagination means that women must be humiliated and controlled. In its most extreme forms, pornography is a destruction of the female body as a way of killing the dread within the male mind. But even in its milder forms, the female body is presented as submissive and compliant to the wishes of the man. Nature is first idealized, then controlled, as a way of controlling the power and dread of woman.

Marie Fortune, a scholar who sharpens the ethical issues of sexual violence, asks:

> Why is most rape perpetrated by males against females? Why does a man choose to use his penis as a weapon to harm another person? Why are men "supposed" to be sexually aggressive and women sexually passive? Why is so much of the violence inflicted on women and children "sexual" in nature? Why do some people find violence erotic? Why does our society seem to be encouraging the eroticization of violence? . . . As long as erroneous beliefs about male sexuality go unchallenged, the confusion between sexual activity and sexual violence will remain a predominant reality in our society and will continue to support the conditions which encourage sexual violence.[54]

Rape and child sexual abuse is not primarily a sexual activity; it is primarily a form of control and violence. For the victim, it is an experience of terror that has long-term consequences for the development of trust and competence. For the perpetrator, it is an experience of controlling another for the expression of power and rage. As Karen said, "Incest and rape are not about sex. They are about power and control. It's about big people over little people, superior over subordinate."

Although the above analysis shows the relationship between sexual violence and the control and exploitation of women and children, it tends to obscure or ignore the use of sexual violence as a terroristic activity to enforce class and racial oppression. Angela Davis clearly reflects this analysis. First she discusses the continuing jeopardy of black women to experiences of rape.

> These particular manifestations of violence against women are situated on a larger continuum of socially inflicted violence which includes concerted, systematic violations to women's economic and political rights. As has been the case throughout history, these attacks most gravely affect women of color and their white working-class sisters. The dreadful rape epidemic of our times, which has become so widespread that one out of every three

> women in this country can expect to be raped at some point during her life, grimly mirrors the deteriorating economic and social status of women today. Indeed, as domestic racist violence mounts—and as global imperialist aggression becomes more widespread—so women can expect that individual men will be more prone to commit acts of sexual violence against the women around them.[55]

As rape and sexual violence become expressions of male attempts to keep women in submission, the consequences for women of color and white working-class women are more extreme. Rape is an instrument for the oppression of women. Rape and sexual violence are also interdependent with other forms of domination and control. Sexual violence is used as a weapon against women and others because it works. It is a weapon of terror against whatever group of persons needs to be controlled. Thus the oppression of women, of persons of color, and of lower classes is interrelated. Davis cautions her white sisters against an analysis of sexual violence that ignores the complex racial factors of our culture.

> During the early 1970's, when the antirape campaign was in its infancy, the presence of Afro-American women in that movement was a rarity. This no doubt was in part attributable to the underdeveloped awareness regarding the interconnectedness of racism and sexism in general among the white women who pioneered the women's liberation movement. At the same time, antirape activists failed to develop an understanding of the degree to which rape and the racist use of the fraudulent rape charge are historically inseparable. If, throughout our history in this country, the rape of Black women by white men has constituted a political weapon of terror, then the flip side of the coin has been the frame-up rape charge directed at Black men. Thousands of terroristic lynchings have been justified by conjuring up the myth of the Black rapist.[56]

The feminist and womanist analyses of rape and pornography unmask the confusion of sexuality and violence in a patriarchal culture. In a culture where the family is private and where women, children, and others are devalued, sexual violence has been used as a weapon of terror. Children who are sexually abused and raped learn of the danger posed to anyone who challenges male dominance. Women who are raped and whose injuries are ignored by hospitals and courts get the message that men are not accountable for their destructive acts under patriarchy. Persons of color who are victims of rape and of the false rape charge are terrorized into being submissive to the dominant white patriarchal culture. Sexual violence is not the isolated act of a few deranged men, but a pattern of exploitation and oppression directed against groups that are controlled for political and economic reasons: A submissive population of women and persons of color provides social control and a cheap labor force in a capitalist society.

Sexual violence directed against women, children, persons of color, and the lower classes is a norm rather than a forbidden activity. It is a weapon of power and control that keeps patriarchy intact. What at first appears to be the isolated and individual acts of a few mentally ill men turns out to be, through critical analysis, a pattern of violence that permeates the whole culture. Sexual violence is a shameful secret because it is normal for women and children to be treated in sexually violent ways. Accepted views of sexuality have strongly violent features so that within the public imagination there is scarcely a distinction between sexuality and abusive sexuality. It is typical of advertising and movies to portray physical and sexual violence against women as if it were a natural part of the sexual interaction between men and women. What is being hidden by the secrecy and denial surrounding sexual violence is patriarchy itself.

But feminist analysis shows that sexual violence cannot be normative in an ethical sense. Rather, sexual violence is perpetuated because it serves to keep women, children, and persons of color in subordination in a patriarchal culture. Women are submissive to men because of the real danger of being targets of male violence both within and outside the family. Until this connection between sexuality and violence is brought out into the light, the structures of domination and control will continue to function unimpeded. Victims of sexual violence have been betrayed by the community, which promises protection, but which allows the exploitation of those who are vulnerable by confusing sexuality and violence. The search for true community is hindered because of the ideological distortions about the nature of community itself.

Summary

In this section we have followed the analysis of feminist and womanist theories to understand the cultural basis for sexual violence. We have examined the privatization of the American family, the devaluation of women and persons of color, and the confusion of sexuality and violence.

We have discovered that sexual violence is a mirror of the structural violence inherent in patriarchal American culture. Men who molest and rape children and women are not an isolated or unusual phenomenon. In fact, a majority of girls and women and a significant percentage of boys are molested and raped in our culture. We are only beginning to uncover the astounding prevalence of this heinous crime, and we have barely begun to understand its significance.

The silence of the church on sexual violence is remarkable when one begins to understand the depth of evil we are discovering. Given that a majority of women in our society, including persons in the church, have been victims of sexual violence, how can we explain the almost unbroken silence of the church on this issue?

As hard as it is to accept, the silence of the church on the evil of sexual violence points to the complicity of the church in perpetuating the ideology of patriarchy and its contribution to making the suffering of women invisible. The church has practiced a historically all-male clergy, the subordination of women in leadership, authoritarian and moralistic preoccupation with sexual fidelity and heterosexuality, and an impotent critique of society that is sexist and racist. On the issue of sexual violence, there is scarcely a difference between church and society. The same ideologies we have criticized in this chapter can be applied to the church.

When Karen was a victim of incest in her family, her church was teaching her to respect her parents and be submissive to their authority. That was many years ago, before there was awareness of sexual violence. But today, the same congregation in which she was reared continues to honor the molesters and rapists as significant leaders, and Karen, the victim of their violence, has to leave the church to protect herself from further abuse.

Where is the church with the courage to begin to examine this evil in the midst of its life? Where is the church that is willing to critically examine its own complicity in this incredible evil directed against women, children, and persons who are vulnerable in society because of color, sexual orientation, or handicap? Our view of the church must change because of our analysis of the abuse of power.

THE NATURE OF LOVING COMMUNITIES

As a child, Karen yearned for a community in which her suffering could be addressed. She needed persons who could listen to the nonverbal messages of her body with its headaches and other ailments, who could talk to her about her fears of monsters, who could explore why she was so quiet and submissive to all adults. She needed adults who would not be fooled by her good grades and academic achievements, who would not be fooled by the pretense of her parents that everything was fine. She needed adults who were willing to get involved, who were not so defensive about the authority of parents and other adults, who were not blinded by the aura of respectability and church membership. She communicated her fears and suffering in the only ways she knew, but all her cries were denied and ignored in the culture's wish to assume that everything was fine.

Bob was not an active church person for most of his life. He attended chapel in the detention center a few times when he was fourteen. These experiences were entirely irrelevant to his inner struggle to survive the trauma and abuse he was experiencing. If Bob and his family had accidentally turned up in church, many church people would have been uncomfortable and secretly horrified because they were not middle-class. Church is not made for marginal people who are inadequately socialized and may question the values of the church. As a child, Bob needed a loving community where his suffering could be understood. As an adult, Bob needed a loving community where his abuse could be confronted and he could be given a chance for restitution and redemption.

Where is the community that can be sensitive to the abuse of power that is destroying the lives of so many children and women from the inside out? Our research leads us to describe the marks of loving community as revealed in the testimonies of survivors in dialogue with the Christian tradition.

Loving Communities Are *Inclusive*

They value the interior experience of every person and create environments that embrace life in its fullness. A loving community understands experience in such a way that the fullest reality of all persons is engaged. This requires a radical openness to otherness and difference whose incorporation constantly creates identity anew. In an inclusive community, perceptions are constantly transformed to correspond to the reality that makes up the concrete life of persons.[57]

When experience is defined within a narrow range that does not correspond to the rich variety available to individuals, then awareness is restricted and persons are made marginal. What is excluded from community awareness is defined as otherness and difference. To be able to engage what is perceived as alien and threatening is difficult, requiring a kind of courage that few individuals or groups can muster. Engaging experiences that threaten a group's identity and cohesiveness is a constant challenge facing any community.

When sexual violence occurs within an environment of taboo and silence, the experience of victims is excluded from the concern of the community. Victims are marginal as persons because the suffering of their lives has to be suppressed. Under patriarchy, whole groups of persons—women, children, and persons of color—are terrorized by sexual violence so that their existence is marginal.

Karen promised not to tell about her sexual abuse because she implicitly knew that her experience was taboo in her church and the larger community. The community did not help her face and integrate her pain and terror into the rest of her life. She was indirectly told to keep her silence. Public school teachers ignored her headaches and other physical symptoms. Sunday school teachers refused to see that her compliance and wish to please adults were exaggerated and were signs of trouble. Her family was honored with leadership in the community and held in great esteem. As she came into adulthood, there were few symbols or institutions to help her understand the hidden suffering of her life. To comply with her social setting and its ideologies, she did not tell her secret.

Only a special community could engage all of Karen's experience. First her physician, then her pastor and therapist, provided compassion and helped her give voice to her pain. They initially helped her find words, symbols, and a pattern of meaning for her suffering. When Karen selected a group of five persons to meet regularly with her, they became a counter-community to compensate for the deficiencies of her church and other social groups. This group agreed to be inclusive and compassionate toward the full range of Karen's experience, including her abuse. Because the larger church had no background in understanding victims of sexual violence, they could not be the loving community she required. Eventually she stopped attending worship because their ideas about life were not big enough to engage her suffering. The church had failed her. Her new community provided the inclusiveness she needed for survival and healing. She called this special community the true church.

Karen's father excluded from awareness his daughter's pain as well as acknowledgment of his own evil. He used his public image to support his denial that anything was wrong in his life. For him and other molesters, inclusive love would mean exposing and facing the violence in their lives. To understand their pain, perpetrators need an inclusive community that can confront them with their contradictions and offer them the accountability and support they need for healing. Unfortunately, many communities maintain their identities by denying that some men in leadership positions are molesters and abusers. Doing so excludes experiences of evil that need attention and redemption.

Inclusive love is challenging because of the basic human tendency to exclude whatever makes us uncomfortable and conflicts with our preferred perceptions. In the face of otherness and difference, we discover aspects of ourselves we don't like. Confronting the pain of others elicits the reservoir of repressed and denied pain that is part of all of us. We fear that our defenses will shatter and we will become nothing. Because our communities provide the surroundings for loving and working we fear our group identity will collapse if too much otherness and difference is engaged. Often we choose to live in a small world where pain is more moderate and our values are more easily supported. Communities that are inclusive of otherness are living deeply out of the relational nature of human existence itself and the ambiguity that is part and parcel of flesh and blood humanity.

In an inclusive community, victims are encouraged to give voice to their suffering so that it can be shared by others. Such openness gives reality to the experience of individual terror and provides protection from further abuse. In a setting of shared suffering, attention can be given to deficiencies that need correction. The community becomes a resource for the healing of those who have been damaged by the abuse of power.

In an inclusive community, there is no place for perpetrators to hide. Their attempts to avoid their problems through denial are fruitless, and their access to victims is destroyed. In such an environment, perpetrators have to face the inner pain hidden in their symptoms and choose whether to utilize the community resources that could lead to transformation. Inclusive community destroys the veil of secrecy that makes abuse of power possible.

Loving Communities Are *Just*

They have the courage to confront abuse of power within the community and in the larger society. Justice is the fair distribution of the resources necessary for full life by the institutions and ideologies that have power. All persons need supportive environments of physical and emotional resources in order to live. When power is fairly organized, all persons have access to the resources they need for survival and well-being.

Unjust communities organize power on the basis of privilege and dominance. Those who have power accumulate resources beyond what they need while others are made marginal and denied basic necessities.

Sexual violence is a form of injustice because it denies victims resources they need for life. Victims are abused for the gratification of someone more powerful, and the trauma creates fear, anger, and mistrust, which dominates their interior life. This interrupts their development and attention to their own perceptual world and whatever love and work they might have chosen for themselves. When sexual violence is repeated over a long period of time, its effects are profound, as we have seen. Injustice promotes silence and marginalization for many persons.

For much of her life Karen did not have a community of justice in her church. She heard only silence about her suffering. There was no accountability for her perpetrators. When she confronted them, their denial was sufficient to protect them because there was no other court of appeal. They had committed a crime that could not be publicly dealt with. She had to create resources for her own healing, and live with continuing abuse as her molesters were honored as ideal citizens.

In her smaller group, Karen did find some justice. The professionals and the support group believed her story and listened as she uncovered the truth about her life. They provided her with resources to compensate for what was missing in the larger community: listening, physical touch, tears, honest sharing, and so on.

Though Sam had contact with the police when he got into fights as a teenager and young adult, the full extent of his difficulties was not disclosed until he was arrested for molesting his son. In most communities, he would have been convicted and would have served time in jail without possibility of treatment. But here he was given the option of probation and treatment for his pathology. At first he was relieved not to be in jail, then he was resentful about the heavy requirements of therapy and therapy groups. But he was held accountable. He had to choose between jail and treatment, and any sexual misconduct would be dealt with harshly, which was the kind of accountability he needed in order to deal with his inner pain. If he wanted to stay out of jail and not lose his family, he had to look at himself in a different way.

The church has been very poor at placing accountability on those who abuse power. Male clergy who sexually abuse women and children through the power of their office have generally been protected or allowed to move to another congregation without appropriate consequences. Often victims have to leave the church because they are perceived to be disloyal and untrustworthy. A loving community of justice is not naive about how the powerful abuse the vulnerable, even when their power comes from ordination and church leadership.[58]

The practice of justice in a community is challenging because of the difficulty in facing our own ambiguity. We like to think of ourselves as fair and non-abusive in the way we conduct our lives, and we have faith that our communities function with justice toward all members. The disclosure of injustice within ourselves or our communities is frightening because it discloses aspects of ourselves that create shame and guilt. When sexual violence is disclosed in the church, there is often denial and dissociation: denial that such an evil could occur in our group, and dissociation of the facts from any serious consequences for ourselves. Often the victim is blamed for exaggeration or lying, and the perpetrator is protected to maintain the good name of the community.

A loving community is sensitive to the potential abuse of power and is careful to provide protection for its most vulnerable members. The discussion about whether or not abuse of power exists in a community cannot depend on the perception or honesty of the powerful because the powerful tend to justify themselves at the expense of others. Those who are vulnerable must be given authority to testify about their perceptions of abuse of power. There must be policies and procedures for hearing the testimony of potential victims and norms against which to judge whether abuse of power has occurred.

In a just community, victims are believed and are given the resources they need for protection and healing. The church needs trained counselors who know how to work with victims and link them to healing networks in the larger community. Karen said that her years of therapy and other healing experiences were costly. Such costs must be shared by the community. Most important, victims of sexual violence must not be made marginal because their difficulties are uncomfortable for others. We need new ways of thinking about sexual violence that do not repeat the trauma of victimization.

In a just community, perpetrators are held accountable. The traditional responses to sinners provide the basis for justice. First, there must be confession and full disclosure of acts of sexual violence against others. This breaks the cloak of secrecy that hides the acts in darkness and prevents support for the victim. Second, there must be repentance and acceptance of an adequately rigorous treatment program that offers real potential for healing. A sincere desire to face the pain and evil in one's life and turn in a new direction is the meaning of repentance. Third, there must be restitution to the victim and the community under conditions of full protection for those who are vulnerable. A just community will have the conceptual and procedural resources for facing instances of abuse of power by its members.

A just community will make a prophetic witness to the larger society in behalf of victims of sexual violence. The same structures of support and accountability within the community can be advocated for the larger community.

Jesus Formed a Community That Was *Inclusive* and *Just*

Jesus addressed the issues of sexual violence by talking about abuse of power. He scolded the disciples who tried to enhance their power in the coming kingdom (Matt. 20:20ff.). He was merciful toward the woman "caught in adultery" (John 8:3ff.) and inclusive of women in his ministry. He encouraged the prophetic tradition of favoring "the least of these" (Matt. 25:40, 45). He confronted the religious leaders of his day with their hypocrisy and abuse of power (Matt. 23:13ff.). Jesus was a person with enough stature to encompass the full experience of others in his experience, and who had an internal sense of power and strength so that he did not need to abuse others. He gave his followers a vision of an inclusive and just community that would use power to benefit all its members, with special attention for those most oppressed. And he called the leaders of the church to be the servants of all (Luke 22:26).

> It follows from all this that a christological figure such as Jesus, who is to be found at the bottom of the hierarchy of unilateral power, stands at the apex of life conceived in terms of relational power. . . . In the life of unilateral power the unfairness means that the stronger are able to control and dominate the weaker and thereby claim their disproportionate share of the world's goods and values. In the life of relational power, the unfairness means that those of larger size must undergo greater suffering and bear a greater burden in sustaining those relationships which hopefully may heal the brokenness of the seamless web of interdependence in which we all live. "Of whom much is given, much is expected."[59]

CHAPTER EIGHT

THE SEARCH FOR GOD

In their stories of healing, survivors have reported religious confusion. As they have struggled to make a positive life after years of abuse, they have searched for a God of love and power, but their search is difficult because so many of their images of God are negative.

For some victims, abusers used God to justify their behaviors. One perpetrator told his son that he was "beating the devil out of him," and said God would not accept a little boy who did not obey his father. Another perpetrator told his daughter that oral sex was her punishment for refusing to come in by curfew and that, "by God, I am your father." Judge Schreber's father believed that he had found the God-ordained plan for perfect child-rearing.

For others, abusers' allusions to God were indirect. Phrases such as, "I am your father. You should do it because I said so" or "This is something all fathers teach their children," implied that parental authority cannot be questioned. Since parents serve with god-like power in the lives of children, the implication, in the mind of a child, was that abuse was part of the order of things that included God.

Some witnesses report religious confusion because the church so strongly supported parental authority and made explicit analogies between God and fathers.

> I recognize my anger at church leaders who taught me to believe that whatever my parents did was right and good for me. What child can question the church? God, like parents, loves and protects us from harm. The message was clear. The church, then, as now, must accept responsibility for silencing those subject to abuse. (Karen)

Church and society give children many messages about the authority of parents. Survivors report that it is difficult to separate this early training from their images of God. To the extent that parents were abusive, abuse became a part of their images of God also.

Because of the connection of their abusive experiences to apparent sanction of that abuse by religion, our witnesses report difficulty in their own religious experience. Karen had a hard time in her prayer life because she could not find an image of God for her meditation. During some parts of her healing, religious faith was virtually impossible. At other times, she was able to find benevolent images, but they were very different from those given her by the church.

Many perpetrators are religious. They feel entitled to their possession of others, even sometimes to the point of identifying with the omnipotence of God. Their narcissistic disorder fits in well with a God of magic and power who has great privilege in relation to others. At other times, fearing the punitive wrath of God for their crimes, their devalued self feels like a victim of God's violence. At one time the perpetrator assumes the prerogatives of God; at another time he falls victim to God's wrath. God is not a stable figure in the interior life. The result of this confusion in recovering perpetrators is an inability to find a real relationship with God.

Schreber was explicit about his religious beliefs. He felt that he was a victim of God but that his suffering at God's hands would eventually improve the situation of humankind. As Lucy Bregman has said, Schreber's images seem to have been a critique of the classical God of omnipotent power and a vision of a relational God.[1] Schreber searched for a God who was not identified with oppression but with liberation.

These testimonies suggest confusion regarding God for at least three reasons:

1. Perpetrators made explicit and implicit references to God to rationalize their abusive behaviors.
2. The church and society supported the authority of parents over children and men over women and referred to images of father-God to sanction this authority.
3. The witnesses report confusion in their own prayer and meditation. They have trouble finding benevolent images of God, which would provide a stable reference point for their faith.

This testimony from the witnesses suggests a possible complicity of religion with sexual violence. Contemporary feminist scholars exploring biblical and theological materials to sort out this complicity have found that many images of God in the Bible and church history are patriarchal and racist and thus give sanction to the unjust use of power by men of power and privilege.[2]

The thesis of this chapter is that *abuse of power is a theological problem.* Sexual violence is not just a function of the pathological self or oppressive institutions and ideologies of society. It is also hidden in the images of God and the implicit ethical norms of theology. The theme of the violence of God in the Bible and in church beliefs under some conditions provides latent sanction for certain forms of human violence.

The method of biblical interpretation followed in this section is based on the impact of the text in its canonical form on readers today.[3] Although historical and literary critical studies are important as background material and are cited from time to time, the focus here is on understanding what is heard today rather than what historically happened or was intended by the author for the ancient audience.[4]

IMAGES OF GOD IN THE HEBREW BIBLE

In many important texts, the Hebrew Bible condemns violence against persons, especially widows, orphans, and strangers, that is, those who have the least protection in society (Jer. 22:3). The commandments against murder, stealing, adultery, and covetousness (Exodus 20) and the instruction to "love your neighbor as yourself" (Lev. 19:18) seem to exclude sexual violence against women and children. The Hebrew Bible teaches a basic respect for persons that precludes acts of violence against anyone.[5] There are many stories and other texts that survivors of sexual violence have found useful.[6]

However, there are certain biblical stories in which violence against women and children is uncritically portrayed as an aspect of patriarchal culture. The church needs to examine these stories more closely to see whether they implicitly sanction destructive patterns. Marie Fortune has listed the most important of these texts: the stories of Susanna (Daniel 13), the Levite and the Concubine (Judg. 19:11-30), the rape of Dinah (Genesis 34), the rape of Tamar (II Samuel 13), the Deuteronomic Laws (Deut. 22:23-29; Lev. 18:6-18). The story of Joseph and Potiphar's Wife (Gen. 39:1-23) encourages society to think that "the false rape charge" is perhaps more common than actual rape.[7] In these stories, violence against women is trivialized or overlooked, thus giving the message that violations of women are less important than the rights of men and the intrigue between nations.

> As Christians we need a clear and unflinching understanding of the ethical and theological dimensions of sexual violence to provide us with the foundation for both a pastoral and political/social response to the problem. . . . It is clear from the passages that the confusion about the nature of sexual violence was well-entrenched in the Hebrew and early Christian culture which produces these stories and laws. On the one hand, they treat crimes of sexual assault as property violations and as primarily sexual in nature; on the other hand, they compare it with murder. The message is inconsistent.[8]

In this section we examine two stories in the Hebrew Bible that give confused messages about abuse of power in relation to women and children and that contribute to our religious climate, which fosters confusion about sexual violence. We are looking for the images of God implied in them.[9]

The Rape of Tamar (II Samuel 13)

This story presents a detailed description of rape. Tamar is the daughter of David the king, the sister of Absalom, and the half-sister of Amnon. Her life on this day revolves around her relationships with these men.[10]

Amnon lusted for his sister Tamar and plotted with his uncle Jonadab to set up a situation where he could overpower and rape her. Pretending to be ill, he asked his father, King David, to send Tamar to him for comfort, then he sent out the servants and invited her into his bed. Tamar protested by appealing to the ethics of Israel where "such a thing is not done" and pointed out the shame they both would carry (II Sam. 13:12-13). "But he would not listen to her; and being stronger than she, he forced her and lay with her" (II Sam. 13:14). Afterward Amnon hated her and sent her away. When Tamar rent her gown and put ashes on her head to make her humiliation public, Absalom saw her and gave her protection in his home. David heard and was angry, but he did nothing, "because he loved [Amnon], for he was his firstborn" (II Sam. 13:21). Two years later, Absalom arranged a festival and had Amnon killed.

On one level this story shows the horror of rape and takes a clear ethical stand against it. However, further analysis reveals certain confusions that give mixed messages.

From Tamar's perspective, there are many problems. She lived in a world where men manipulated and coerced one another with their power. Amnon manipulated his father to gain access to Tamar and rape her. She was unable in this situation to protect herself, except to courageously state the ethical standard of her people. After the rape, she was desolate. In a patriarchal culture, losing her virginity, even through rape, made her into damaged goods; her value as property was destroyed. Her life in that society was ruined by this event, and she was never heard from again as a character in Israel. Because her life was circumscribed by male dominance, and after the incestuous rape, she had no place at all. She was protected by her brother and then disappeared from the stories of Israel.

Amnon was the rapist who nurtured a violent lust in his heart until he destroyed Tamar and lost his own humanity. Amnon's evil was that he turned his male power and privilege into destructiveness. He fantasied control over Tamar and used his power to take what he wanted by force. Amnon represents one option for what it means to be male even in society today.

In a patriarchal culture, men have the choice of being rapists, of using their power to destroy women and children. If secrecy can be enforced there will be no accountability. If the crime is disclosed, there may be a penalty. But often men are protected even if their crimes are disclosed. The abuse of male power is tolerated. Because of their social power, men have the potential to abuse others with only minimal risk.

David colluded with Amnon through his silence. He was angry that Tamar was raped, but he did not want to face the consequences of confronting his oldest son, heir to the throne. He had his plans for the future and he did not want them disturbed. Perhaps he did not want a repetition of his painful encounter with Nathan after he abused Bathsheba. So his own interests prevailed over his compassion for his daughter, and he withdrew into silence, leaving Tamar without any court of justice. He acted out of expediency rather than justice.

Within patriarchy, men are tempted to collude with one another at the expense of women. Even though men sometimes see the injustice done against women, they want to avoid the consequences for themselves of getting involved and confronting injustice. Men have the option of silence because they are not in danger from sexual violence as women are. Silence shares complicity in acts of sexual violence. Part of the reason sexual violence is so prevalent is that men protect one another rather than courageously confront the violence that their complicity perpetuates against women.

Absalom was a murderer in this story. He became so enraged at Amnon that he forgot about Tamar and became obsessed with revenge. His wish for revenge became more important than Tamar's need for a legitimate life in the community. Tamar was forgotten in the battle between the men. She was devalued not only by Amnon and David, but devalued again by Absalom's response.

A problem in many rapes is that the male relatives feel they are more offended than the victim; hence, the escalating anger and violence jeopardize the woman again. Revenge is much easier to indulge than sharing the pain of the sexual violence with the victim. In order to be empathetic with a woman who has been raped, one must imagine being in a vulnerable position of physical danger. Rather than face that pain, many men would rather imagine the active murder of the rapist than the passive position of the victim. Revenge becomes a repetition of abuse toward the woman, who needs companions in her suffering, not patronizing figures who unilaterally decide what she needs.

The latent message of this story is that sexual violence against women is not about the humanity of women but about power between men. The drama of the story is about the tension between the rapist, the silent colluder, and the murderer. Tamar is a figure for the exchange of power between men.[11]

Although this story does not explicitly mention the action of God, it does reveal something about the ethos of some parts of the Bible concerning the rights of women. The rape is avenged in the politics between men, but there is no restitution or justice for Tamar, the woman. She has no place in the community or future role in Israel. Such devaluation of women is part of the religious sanction that restricted the humanity and potential of women. The Bible has a patriarchal bias that has contributed to injustice under patriarchy in our own time. Stories such as Tamar's confirm the sense in our witnesses that their existence as children and women was devalued not only by the society, but also by the church and the general religious atmosphere.

The Story of a Biblical Family

The story from Genesis 12–22 is one of the church's paradigmatic stories about God's power and love in relation to human life. It is a story of women and children in danger because of the abuse of power, and it gives us a chance to examine images of God in relation to the theme of power. God is a character in the story who influences the dynamics and outcome of the family drama.

At the beginning of the story, Abraham and Sarah had married and had set up housekeeping.[12] They decided to leave home and set out for parts unknown. Their life was full of adventure and risk. They faced famine (Gen. 12:10), threats from enemies (Gen. 12:12), conflict with family (Gen. 13:8), and war (Genesis 14). But the biggest threat was the lack of a son. Given their culture and their religious convictions, the survival of the clan and their own future depended on having a child.[13] In Genesis 16, Abraham and Sarah came up with a plan to resolve the tension.

The traditions of their culture allowed Abraham to take another wife in order to get an heir and save the tribe. "Sarai, Abram's wife, took Hagar the Egyptian, her slave-girl, and gave her to her husband Abram as a wife" (Gen. 16:3). As soon as Hagar was pregnant, trouble started. Being with child elevated Hagar to a new status above that of a handmaid, and Sarah was faced with a serious threat to her own status in the tribe. With Abraham's permission, "Sarai dealt harshly with her, and she ran away from her" (Gen. 16:6).

Now we have a social justice issue, at least from a modern perspective. Even though the culture allowed an arrangement in which there were multiple wives and concubines with different rights and social status, there was no life outside the tribe. Sarah was condemning Hagar and her unborn child to death. Some interpreters have suggested that issues of race and social class were factors between Sarah and Hagar. Hagar, the Egyptian, was a woman from a different racial and social class that had few rights within the society.[14] As a character in the story, God intervened with Hagar and sent her back to Sarah for what would become further abuse: "Return to your mistress, and submit to her" (Gen. 16:9).

In chapter 17, God came to Abraham and Sarah and again promised a child. Abraham pointed to Ishmael as his son, but God said, "No, but your wife Sarah shall bear you a son, and you shall name him Isaac. . . . I will bless [Ishmael] . . . but my covenant I will establish with Isaac" (Gen. 17:19-21).

This is the story of a child whose presence had become a problem in the dynamics of this family and tribe. Ishmael was conceived out of Abraham and Sarah's fear that they would not have a child, and once

Ishmael was born, he was rejected. The figure of God intervened to protect Ishmael and created a space for Isaac. But the pressure on the tribe to survive was so strong that both children were actually in jeopardy. According to the culture, Ishmael was the heir, but Sarah had the social power to reject him. When Isaac was born, we discover that both children were in serious danger. There was a real possibility that neither of them would live to be adults.

In Genesis 21, the presence of Ishmael and Hagar became a more serious problem for Sarah and she asked Abraham to cast them out. God encouraged Abraham to support Sarah, and Abraham sent Hagar and Ishmael out into the desert with bread and water.

> [Hagar] wandered about in the wilderness of Beersheba. When the water in the skin was gone, she cast the child under one of the bushes. Then she went and sat down opposite him a good way off, about the distance of a bowshot; for she said, "Do not let me look on the death of the child." And as she sat opposite him, she lifted up her voice and wept. (Gen. 21:14-16)

According to this story, God heard her cry and opened her eyes and she nurtured her son into maturity. But we see the tension and danger that face children when the power of adults is abused. Because of the culture and values of this family, Hagar and Ishmael were in severe danger. Hagar was divorced from her family and cast out of respectable society without any means of support. In spite of the loyalty of his mother and the affection of his father, Ishmael was abandoned in the desert to die, what today we would call child abuse and neglect. The story implies that it was Hagar's loyalty and a miracle from God that saved Ishmael and gave him a place in the generations of humankind.

In the meantime, Isaac was also in danger. In a difficult passage, Isaac was nearly killed. Much has been made of the faith of Abraham, but seen from the perspective of Isaac, this is a terrifying story. Abraham took Isaac up on the mountain to make a sacrifice. He built an altar and arranged the wood. "He bound his son Isaac, and laid him on the altar, on top of the wood. Then Abraham reached out his hand and took the knife to kill his son" (Gen. 22:9-10).

What an awful story! God as presented here seems sadistic and cruel, and Abraham was willing to be the instrument of such a God. Perhaps the story challenged the practice of child sacrifice prevalent at that time.[15] But, still, the story is terrifying.[16] Isaac was within seconds of being murdered by his father, who "loved him." What kind of love is this? Abraham loved Ishmael and cast him into the desert. Abraham loved Isaac and nearly killed him. What are we to make of these stories? How is the violence of this family and society related to the image of God?

Power Struggles This was a family characterized by power struggles. In the patriarchal culture of that time, power was distributed according to gender and class. Abraham was the patriarch with most of the power. Sarah was his first wife and second in power among women, at least within the household. Hagar was a handmaid with little power except that she had a place within the tribe.[17]

The problem of having no son upset the prescribed power balance. The delicate power balance of power arrangements in a family is called "homeostasis," that is, the tendency of a system to maintain its current power structure against the threat of disintegration.[18] The system was homeostatic until it was upset by the pressure to find an heir to lead the tribe. Sarah tried to resolve this problem by giving Hagar to Abraham as his second wife. Sarah's barrenness was a threat to her status in the family, and when Hagar became pregnant, Sarah felt her vulnerability. Hagar was no longer just a handmaid; she was bearing Abraham's child. Hagar was the mother of the heir. In response, Sarah reasserted her power as the first wife and banished Hagar from the tribe. As a woman and a handmaid Hagar had no power to challenge this injustice. God intervened to bring Hagar back into the family, though in submission to Sarah, which eventually resulted in additional abuse. This established a new temporary homeostasis in the triangle of Abraham, Sarah, and Hagar, which had organized to scapegoat the most vulnerable member of the triad.

The power structure seemed to stabilize after this crisis. Even though there was significant injustice, all knew their places in the system. But when Isaac was born, the tensions flared again. The conflict of values and cultures arose when Sarah saw the two boys playing together and again insisted that Hagar be banished.[19] This time Abraham was distressed because he had a relationship with Ishmael, his son. But Sarah asserted her right as the first wife, and Abraham, with God's advice, went along. So again Hagar and Ishmael were banished and nearly perished. For them, the consequences of the power struggles were cruel. This family was willing to sacrifice its members in order to solve its power struggles, and the victims were those with insufficient social power to protect themselves.

The story about Isaac's near-sacrifice is also troubling. This is a story about a power struggle between God and Abraham over control of Isaac. One interpretation is that Abraham was overinvested in his son and needed to release him to do God's work. The fact that Abraham was willing to sacrifice his son was a sign that he gave Isaac up to God. The fight was over control of Isaac, and the method was willingness to commit murder.

There are often intense struggles between family members about relative power to control family identity. Many parents become locked in battle for control of their children. When these struggles become rigid and polarized, very destructive things can happen in families: suicide, murder, drug abuse, child abuse. The identity of the family is at stake. In this story, Abraham was trying to resolve the future of the family. But from the perspective of Isaac, this is a story of violent abuse.

What do we make of the image of God in this story? In the family of Abraham, Sarah, and Hagar, the lesson about God is mixed. In the story, God as a dramatic figure is implicated in some of the misuse and abuse of power. God sent Hagar and Ishmael back into an abusive situation. God rejected Ishmael as the heir and leader of the tribe, and encouraged Abraham to banish Hagar and Ishmael as Sarah had requested. God commanded Abraham to sacrifice Isaac. In these acts, God appears cruel and willing to use power against the vulnerable.

But God as a figure also rescued Hagar and Ishmael in the desert and restored Ishmael's place in the stream of the generations. God saved Isaac at the last moment from the sacrifice. God was deeply involved in the family struggles, and was even willing to become implicated in injustice in order to help the family grow in faith. In regard to the use and abuse of power, God's role was ambiguous.

Ambivalent Love This family was characterized by ambivalent love. Human attachments are strong feelings of dependency that can lead to a deep sense of belonging, or they can lead to feelings of betrayal and hatred.[20] In this story Abraham and Sarah were bonded to each other through marriage and through the trials they faced, such as those in the tribe. When their bonding did not produce a child, they reacted to this crisis by bringing Hagar into their relationship. For Hagar this represented a chance to build an identity of her own and become more than a handmaid. But Sarah's barrenness was a threat to her survival, and Hagar represented a threat to her bond with Abraham. So Sarah turned her aggressive rage against Hagar in order to protect her attachment to Abraham, and Hagar became the victim of betrayal. Hagar was brought into the center of the family, then banished when she was with child.

One of the touching aspects of this story is Abraham's attachment to Ishmael, the rejected child. Abraham and Ishmael were circumcised together (Gen. 17:26), and Abraham was "greatly distressed" when Sarah decided to banish Hagar and Ishmael for good (Gen. 21:11). But the betrayal of Hagar nearly led to death. The lack of a more healthy attachment between Abraham and Ishmael endangered the life of the child. Hagar and Ishmael were victims of failed attachment between Abraham and Sarah, who held the social power.[21]

The attachment to Isaac was also dangerous. The promise of a child for Abraham and Sarah was given in Genesis 15, but God returned twice more to repeat the promise. According to the text, Abraham was a hundred years old when Isaac was finally born (Gen. 21:5). What happens when so much parental expectation is concentrated on one child? One of the difficulties in this story seems to be the narcissistic overinvestment of the parents in their child. The attachment was so intense and so heavy that it was a danger to Isaac and the whole family. Perhaps this is one of the meanings of the sacrifice story—the willingness to give Isaac over to God was necessary in order to break the overinvolvement of the parents. It is dangerous for a child to have the full burden of filling the emptiness in his or her parents. In such a case the needs of the parents take precedence over the child's, and the child has no chance to form an identity and life of her or his own.[22]

What do we make of God's role in terms of attachment? In modern understandings of the family, Abraham and Sarah created a second marriage, a rejected child, and a divorced, impoverished single parent who could not provide for her family. The drama of the story was so compelling that there seems little possibility that Abraham and Sarah could have acted differently. Because they could not form appropriate attachments with Hagar and Ishmael, Abraham and Sarah could not act out of an even-handed love that took the needs of Hagar and Ishmael into account as real people. The lack of healthy bonding resulted in extreme danger. God as a character intervened to give a new set of circumstances in which Hagar and Ishmael could live but did not restore them to their family. God seemed to lack an even-handed attachment for Hagar and Ishmael and tended to side with the dominant power in the tribe, namely Abraham and Sarah. In this family there was a big gap between what happened and what Hagar and Ishmael needed.

In terms of Isaac, the attachment seems distorted in another way. Abraham and Sarah expected too much from Isaac, and God had to intervene to free the child from their expectations. The manner of God's intervention seems cruel by our standards, but was apparently effective in breaking the overwhelming dependency of these parents on their child. The difficulty from the perspective of abuse of power is that God's methods were abusive regardless of the outcome.

God is presented as an ambiguous character in this story in regard to bonding. The virtue of the story is that God did respond to every person. Within the limits of this family, God acted to take all persons seriously and relate to them as persons of worth. But God also seemed to prefer some characters to others, and God's attachment preferences contributed to the unjust structure of this family and community.

God's Ambivalence

Survivors of sexual violence seek images of God to support their search for justice in the midst of their religious confusion. They look for a God who is consistently just and loving. But in these biblical stories, we found the portrayal of an ambiguous God who could not always be counted on to respond with love and justice. If God is presented as not always just and loving in relation to the needs of humans, can there be any justice or love anywhere? Where is help for the victims of the abuse of power? Instead of the all-wise, all-loving figure, we found one who seemed to have an ambivalent love-hate relationship to humans. This study validates the testimony of our witnesses that they have witnessed a violent aspect in some images of God.

Our struggle to understand the violence of men toward women and children, especially within the family, has led to the possibility of violence in our understanding of the ultimate structure of the universe. Perhaps the terror and brutality that women and children experience is central to our images of ultimate reality. Now that the possibility of divine ambivalence toward creation has surfaced, other texts present themselves for study.

The Flood Story Ambivalence in the image of God appears in Genesis 6, where God looked at the wickedness of the creation and regretted having made everything, not only humans, but also animals.[23] So God responded with a great flood that destroyed almost all of the animal world including humans. The covenant with Noah and his family is often interpreted as the thread of God's compassion in the midst of terrible evil, and the creation is saved by this thread. But according to the text, God had regrets.

> I will never again curse the ground because of humankind, for the inclination of the human heart is evil from youth; nor will I ever again destroy every living creature as I have done. As long as the earth endures, seedtime and harvest, cold and heat, summer and winter, day and night, shall not cease. (Gen. 8:21-22)

The problem in this text is not just the evil of the creatures, but the destructive potential in the image of God. God has the power to create and the power to destroy. In this story, God was so enraged at the evil of the creatures that God's wrath was unleashed in a destructive act. God's rage was loosed and all life was destroyed, except for those saved on the ark. Horrified afterward by these impulses, God recognized that the destruction nearly severed the relationship with the creatures and was not effective in ridding the world of evil. This is a story about massive destruction followed by remorse and a promise never again to "destroy every living creature as I have done."

Hosea 11 Ambivalence in the image of God is also clear in Hosea 11, a poem about the mixed love and anger of a parent for a child who was disobedient.[24] "When Israel was a child, I loved him, and out of Egypt I called my son. The more I called them, the more they went from me" (Hos. 11:1-2).

God is presented as attached to Israel with memories of intimate times. Yet the child had behaved badly and deserved to be punished. At one point, God's rage became very dramatic. "They shall return to the land of Egypt, and Assyria shall be their king, because they have refused to return to me" (Hos. 11:5). It seems to be a repetition of the rage that caused the flood. But then the poem ends on another note.

> How can I give you up, Ephraim?
>   How can I hand you over, O Israel? . . .
> My heart recoils within me;
>   my compassion grows warm and tender.
> I will not execute my fierce anger;
>   I will not again destroy Ephraim;
> for I am God and no mortal,
>   the Holy One in your midst,
> and I will not come in wrath. (Hos. 11:8-9)

God is presented as a parent with mixed feelings toward a child. God taught Israel to walk, held the Hebrews close. How could God give up on Israel after such intimacy? Yet God was enraged about the evil of the children. Israel had been disloyal in their relationship with God and unjust with one another. God had fantasies of sending them back to slavery in Egypt or Assyria, of slaughtering their children. Then God recoiled at God's own wrath. God was horrified, not just at Israel's evil, but also at God's own impulses. The urge to destroy was intense.

Ambivalence characterized God's feelings toward the children. God loved Israel deeply, and yet God had the impulse to destroy. There are two problems: One is the evil of the creatures; the other is the violence of God, which was a constant threat to the creation.

Summary

The Hebrew Bible gives conflicting images of God for religious piety. On one hand, God is compassionate and just, protecting the vulnerable and seeking alternatives to the evil intentions of humans. But on the other hand, God is presented as insensitive to the vulnerable members of families and even destructive toward whole populations. In some ways this tension between love and hate in the image of God is unresolved. As in child abuse, where the parent acts out destructive impulses toward the helpless child, in some texts God functions as an omnipotent parent whose rage is destructive toward the children of creation. The Bible is replete with examples of God's wrath.[25] Although the evil of creation is part of the manifest plot of the Bible, rage in God as portrayed in some texts is a latent plot. Within history, human evil is a constant threat to the future of humanity. But within the cosmic drama, the violence of God is a danger. What role do these violent impulses play in our images of God? Within the Bible, God frequently repents of evil and struggles to overcome the temptation to become violent.[26] These texts can be crucial to our attempt to understand human violence and evil. Perhaps texts such as Genesis 6, Genesis 12ff., II Samuel 13, and Hosea 11 will give us new images of a God who faces the violent potential in the universe directly and maintains the struggle for justice.

IMAGES OF GOD IN THE NEW TESTAMENT

On one level, the New Testament condemns human violence forcefully. There are many passages about the use of violence: Turn the other cheek (Matt. 5:39), repay no one evil for evil, vengeance is mine, says the Lord (Rom. 12:19), love your neighbor as yourself (Matt. 22:39), love your enemies (Matt. 5:44). The ethic of love is one of the predominant themes in the New Testament, and has been well developed in historical and modern theology.[27] Christian love should eliminate the possibility of sexual violence against women and children.

Jesus said in the Sermon on the Mount, "Everyone who looks at a woman with lust has already committed adultery with her in his heart" (Matt. 5:28). The word for lust, *epithumeo* has a mixed meaning. Sometimes it seems to be a neutral term for desire, such as hunger or sexual feelings, having no negative connotation. In some traditions, such as Stoicism, desire per se is evil; thus, sexual desire is condemned. But sometimes *epithumeo* picks up the ambiguity of desire with potential for violence. "[*Thuo-*] originally denotes a violent movement of air, water, the ground, animals, or men. From the sense of 'to well up,' there seems to have developed that of 'to smoke,' and then 'to cause to go up in smoke.'"[28] *Epithumeo* can mean desire that is violent, that wells up, that goes up in smoke, therefore desire that could become destructive.

This text, therefore, may speak directly to a culture in which sexual desire and sexual abuse are confused. Jesus was saying that sexual desire includes the temptation to engage in abuse of others. Every desire has abusive potential. It is better to lose an eye or cut off a hand than to engage in destruction of another.

Other New Testament texts can be used as principles for ministry to victims of sexual violence.

> We can look to Jesus' parable of the Good Samaritan for a model of how to respond to the victim if we regard the act of sexual violence as an act of assault and aggression that results in injury. In addition, the Gospels consistently regard women as persons in their own right rather than treating them as property. Jesus' ministry was most unusual and puzzling to his followers in that he treated women as persons. Because of this sensitivity we can assume that victims of sexual violence were not doubly victimized by Jesus' response to them. However, there is no evidence that the confusion of sexual activity with sexual violence had diminished in its influence on the attitudes and practices of the period.[29]

In spite of the clear emphasis on love, there are ambiguities in the New Testament attitudes that create danger for women and children. As we saw in the Hebrew Bible, the confusion about sexual violence is often implicit rather than explicit. There is much study of the patriarchal structure of the New Testament and its resulting oppression of women. Women may have had important leadership roles in some communities during Jesus' time and the first decades of the early church, but some texts encourage women to be submissive to their husbands, to be quiet in church, and to defer to men in many matters.[30] There is little indication of sensitivity to the problems of patriarchy as they affect women and children.

Survivors of sexual violence are searching for non-abusive images of God. They search for a God of love and power who is not like the men who abused them. Christians look to Jesus for compassion for suffering, and as a model for handling oppression. Jesus reached out to the marginal. He confronted the powerful men of his day. But some survivors have mixed feelings about Jesus. They say that the victimization of Jesus in the crucifixion seems to give implicit sanction to the victimization of women. By patterning their lives on that of Jesus, women are encouraged to accept their suffering as a sign of virtue rather than press their complaints toward justice and restitution. They ask what kind of God would base salvation on the suffering, torture, and death of an innocent person who did not protest his mistreatment. To some this masochistic image of virtue ignores the evil of patriarchal violence and must be challenged.[31] Since witnesses have questioned abusive images of God, the crucifixion must be examined to see to what extent an abusive image of God is behind Jesus' death by crucifixion.

Theories about the crucifixion are called theories of atonement, that is, how the crucifixion accomplished reconciliation between God and humans. One theory suggests that it resolved the cosmic competition between God and Satan and destroyed the power of evil. Another, that it satisfied the wrath of God against the evil creation and offered salvation for believers. And another argues that it exposed the violent potential of humans and demonstrated the full power of God's love.[32]

Theories of Atonement

In Christianity a central event of the Christian faith, especially for Western Protestants, is the violent death of Jesus followed by his resurrection. This has been taught to many as the supreme example of God's unconditional and sacrificial love for the creation. Jesus' death on the cross was the revelation of how much God loves us, and it gives an example of how we should love one another. "No one has greater love than this, to lay down one's life for one's friends" (John 15:13).

In this characterization of the divine-human drama, God was the father of Jesus, and humans are the children of the promises made to and by Jesus. The quality of the relationship between God the parent and Jesus the child is central for our faith. Jesus reveals the perfect faith of a believer toward the creator of the universe. But if the relationship between God and Jesus was so ideal, then why did the son of God die on the cross? The idea that there is any justification for a parent to sacrifice a child is difficult to accept in the light of testimonies of victims of abuse. Given this perspective, we need to ask whether the image of God in the crucifixion is abusive.

The Theory of Substitutionary Atonement Substitutionary atonement is closest to what Brown and Bohn call the "satisfaction tradition" of Anselm[33] and what Williams calls "the Latin theory, stated most adequately in Anselm, in which Jesus . . . pays the penalty incurred by sin, a sufficient payment since he is the Son of God."[34] In this theory Jesus was the substitute sacrifice for humans, who deserved to die for their sin and evil. Through Jesus' perfect sacrifice, humans have access to the divine grace of God's forgiveness.

The underlying structure of this theory is the contrast between the perfect parent and the sin of the children. Because humans are evil, God's plan for the future is jeopardized. Throughout history, God attempted through various plans to correct human sin: the Exodus, the Law, the Babylonian captivity, the restoration of Jerusalem. But things only got worse. Finally God had to do something drastic to prevent the destruction of creation. God designed a plan for Jesus to come down as a human, to live and to die as a sinless sacrifice to save humanity from its own evil. Jesus' sacrificial death means that humans do not have to pay the full penalty for sin, but can be reconciled with God. Now, through the blood of Jesus, those who believe can be saved from the evil world. Those who do not confess Jesus will be destroyed in an apocalypse as they deserve. One of the texts for substitutionary atonement is I Timothy 2:5: "There is one God; there is also one mediator between God and humankind, Christ Jesus, himself human, who gave himself a ransom for all."

> Atonement christologies contain some notion of original sin, in which humanity is believed to be born with a tragic flaw. Therefore we must be

> dependent upon the perfect father to show us the way to a restored relationship with him and each other. The punishment of one perfect child has to occur before the father can forgive the rest of his children and love them. . . . The sacrifice of this perfect son is the way to new life with the father for all those, who in their freedom, choose to believe someone else's suffering can atone for our flawed nature.[35]

The structure of this theory is the patriarchal family. The father is all-loving and all-powerful; the children are guilty. There is nothing the children can do to earn mercy and no moral basis on which to make appeal to the love of the Father because their sin and guilt is so overwhelming. The Father's rage is justified because of the disobedience and disloyalty of the children. No matter how they are treated by the Father, it is their own fault, and they must carry the blame for whatever the Father decides to do with them.

The guilt of the children is made worse by the existence of a perfect child who gave up his life for his siblings. He proves that the Father is just after all. If the guilty children repent of their sins, pledge complete obedience to the reborn sibling, and agree to become submissive to the all-knowing Father, then there is a chance they will not have to die a violent death like their brother. The Father and the Son are all-powerful and perfect, and they hold the keys to salvation for humankind.

In terms of the dynamics of sexual violence, this theory has serious problems. The powerful figure is always right, and the vulnerable ones are always wrong. The rage of the Father is caused by the children, and they deserve whatever punishment they get. In terms of our analysis of abuse of power, God in the theory of substitutionary atonement is like an abuser. God's rage at the sin of creation is a large problem. If God acts on this rage, there will be an apocalypse of destruction; some in fact predict such an armageddon. Those who reject the father's plan of salvation will spend eternity in hell. Those who confess Jesus as Lord will be saved from this destruction.[36]

The problem with the theory of substitutionary atonement in relation to the issue of sexual violence is the image of the abusive God against which the children of creation have no power or moral claim. The omnipotence and perfection of God create a unilateral relationship in which humans are in constant danger from an enraged God. The only protection is for the children to be submissive and obedient to God by praising the father and the son and living sanctified lives.

This family structure gets played out in many families. In many abusing families, the father is a petty tyrant who cannot see his wife and children as separate persons with any moral claims on his power. He interprets his own motives as all good and those of the rest of the family as all bad. He considers any extreme behaviors on his part as responses to the sins of others and justifies his own sadistic behaviors as generous and necessary for the health of the family. He rules as an omnipotent figure and demands complete submission as a price for sustenance and harmony.

Substitutionary atonement is based on the wrath of God. Many biblical texts point to a divine rage that is a threat to creation: the destruction of the flood, the killing of the first-born of the Egyptians, the slaughter of Israel's neighbors. These texts point to the reality of destructive violence in God. This view is testimony that there may be a tendency toward abuse of power within the nature of things. We have seen how violent abuse of power is well organized in the personalities of many persons and how it is organized into institutions and ideologies in our culture. The view of God in the theory of substitutionary atonement is that abuse of power is not just a human problem, but a cosmic problem. God has the power of life and death over creation, and how God chooses to use this power determines the fate of humankind. We will return to this issue later when we discuss the nature of God's power.

The Theory of Incarnational Atonement In this theory, the wrathful image of God is replaced by an emphasis on God's mercy and love toward the creation. God voluntarily suffers on behalf of the children of creation. The problem in human history is not the wrath of God, but the self-destructive nature of sin and evil.

In their prideful arrogance humans try to be gods by creating institutions of great power. But because they do not acknowledge the sovereignty of God, these human creations become destructive, causing great suffering for everyone. Without the intervention of God's power and love, the creation is doomed to annihilation, and the signs of this possibility are ever present for those who have eyes to see.

God is not angry, but saddened, by the evil of humanity. God sees that human sin is destructive. Eventually everything will be destroyed. In this theory, God is not directly abusive but is more like the non-offending parent, the one who cannot stop the violence because divine action would curtail human freedom. So God faces a dilemma. How can God respond to the evil of humans without being destructive?

The answer, in this theory, is the incarnation, which takes several forms, according to Daniel Day Williams. One is Abelard's "moral influence theory," which "interprets Christ's suffering as divine instruction about love."[37] Jesus becomes a model for humans of how suffering overcomes violence and the power of death. A variation of this is Williams' theory in which reconciliation is the heart of atonement based on the suffering of God.

> We come to the deepest mystery when we see in the suffering of Jesus a disclosure of the suffering of God. . . . What Jesus reveals on the cross surely is not that human love suffers while the divine love does not. What he reveals is the love which does not shirk suffering, and that love is God himself at work. . . . The cause of Jesus' suffering is sin and the human predicament. He meets that situation by bearing what has to be borne that the work of love may get done. God in Jesus Christ suffers with his world, not meaninglessly but redemptively. He has inaugurated a new history by an action which restores the possibility of loyalty in this broken, suffering, yet still hopeful human community.[38]

In the incarnation God comes to earth in human form. In Jesus, who came as a baby and grew into a powerful healer and preacher, God communicates a message of love. By loving the outcasts and confronting those in power, Jesus models a form of power that is not destructive, but redemptive. Those who perceive and follow Jesus are those who can love as he loves.

However, the climax of the story comes when Jesus is faced with the organized principalities and powers of the world and has to decide how to respond. At this point God in the form of Jesus chooses suffering over violence and goes to the cross in order to reveal that love is more powerful than hate. "In Christ God was reconciling the world to himself, not counting their trespasses against them, and entrusting the message of reconciliation to us. So we are ambassadors for Christ" (II Cor. 5:19-20).

The witness of Jesus is made even more powerful by the fact that God's presence among humans is absolutely voluntary. There was no compulsion or obligation on God's part to make such a sacrifice to save humanity. Rather, in God's complete freedom, God chose to suffer with the creation in order to bring salvation. For the children who recognize the reality of God in Jesus, there is new life and new power to practice love in history. For those children who remain stubborn in their prideful sin, self-destructive consequences follow, and the tragedy of history continues.

The theory of incarnational atonement seems designed to deal explicitly with the problem of the abusive God. By turning from an emphasis on wrath and sacrifice to an emphasis on suffering and imitation, God is presented as compassionate, and love is seen as more powerful than violence.

However, in light of what we are learning from survivors of sexual violence, this theory also has problems. Although a benevolent parent is preferable to one who is abusive, the patriarchal structure of the relationship is fully intact. God is the perfect parent who intervenes in history to save the disloyal and disobedient children. God has the power to give and take life, and God unilaterally decides to institute the incarnation as the revelation of divine reality. The children are helpless until they are rescued by the omnipotent God. The children are morally corrupt until they are saved by the perfect God. The unilateral power relationship between God and humans is fully maintained. God has the power to be abusive, but God freely chooses instead to suffer in response to the evil of creation.

In addition, the emphasis on the suffering God is highly problematic for many survivors of sexual violence. Through this theology they feel they have been encouraged by the church to suffer abuse in silence without seeking justice for their mistreatment. While women and children are suffering in silence, male perpetrators of sexual violence are leaders in society and the church without accountability for their crimes. There is something wrong with an omnipotent God who encourages victims to suffer in silence for the evil of others. There is something wrong with an innocent Jesus who suffers because of the evil of the leaders of his society. Such a view ignores the cries for justice from those who do not have the power to protect themselves, while the powerful maintain their privilege and abusive behaviors.[39]

The value of the theory of incarnational atonement is its emphasis on the search for a relational God who is fully involved in human suffering. Survivors of sexual violence yearn for a God who is not abusive like the men who violated them, but is compassionate and accessible during the healing process. The issue is: How can we discover a God of love and power who is not patriarchal and does not encourage victims to suffer?

A REVISED IMAGE OF GOD

In response to the religious testimonies of survivors of sexual violence, we seek revised understandings of God. In the theories of atonement we have reviewed, God is a powerful figure who has the freedom to be wrathful or compassionate without considering the moral claims of the creation. In this view God's relationship is characterized by lack of mutuality and accountability, which is typical of the abusive relationships we have studied. Like the perpetrator of sexual violence, such images of God assume prerogatives of unilateral power over those who are unprotected. Such a God may not hear the silenced voices of victims and feel their suffering and hope.

What would it mean to devise an image of God who lives within the relational web as a fully active and inter-dependent partner with creation? Bernard Loomer describes a God of relational power whose existence includes the suffering and hope of all the creatures.

> In terms of this analysis, God as a wholeness is to be identified with the concrete, interconnected totality of this struggling, imperfect, unfinished, and evolving societal web. . . . God is expressed as the organic restlessness of the whole body of creation, as this drive is unequally exemplified in the several parts of this societal web. This discontent, which is an expression of the essential "spirit" of any creature, may exemplify itself as an expansive urge toward greater good. It may also become a passion for greater evil that, however disguised or rationalized as a greater good, also has its attractiveness . . . God is not only the ultimate end for which all things exist; God is also the shape and stuff of existence.[40]

In this paragraph, Loomer has suggested a radical alternative which could change our conception of power. Although many theologians believe in a relational God who feels the hurt of creation, most are not willing to accept the moral ambiguity of a relational God whose destiny is identified with creation. This image of a fully relational God would be ambiguous in terms of good and evil because the creation itself is ambiguous. Loomer suggests that "an ambiguous God is of greater stature than an unambiguous deity" because such a God includes the full reality of creation as a part of ultimate reality.[41] A relational God is one who is fully interdependent with the ambiguities of human life. It seems worth exploring whether such a God contains some of the elements of love and power that respond to the religious needs of survivors.

Where Is the Love of God?

In the conception of a relational, ambiguous God, the love of God is measured by the suffering required by inclusive relationality, that is, the complete inclusion of all the contradictions of human life into the experience of God. The love of a relational God knows no bounds in regard to inclusiveness. Everything that exists is included in God's experience. Through the suffering of such inclusiveness, the contradictions of good and evil are transformed into compatible contrasts and the relational web moves beyond self-destruction to re-creation.

This means that the victims of sexual violence are included in the experience of God. God has experienced the full depths of suffering throughout history: the crucifixion of Jesus, the genocide of peoples, the holocausts of slavery and destruction of the Jews, the assault of chemicals and waste on the environment, the stockpiling of nuclear weapons. The history of the suffering creation is the history of God's experience. The suffering humanity has become fully a part of God's experience in ways that enable the relational web to resist its own demise. In the midst of the worst evil, God's love is resilient and overcomes its destructive potential. The silent suffering of victims of sexual violence is fully a part of God's life and victims are the means whereby this suffering is connected with ultimate reality. There is nothing that can separate us from the love of God (Rom. 8:35-39).

For the perpetrators of sexual violence, there is no place to hide from God's justice and love. No matter how strong the denial, no matter how good the rationalizations, God knows the truth about evil and its destructive reality. Even though human evil leads to fear of God's presence, there is nothing that can shock God. As revealed in Jesus, God knows the same impulses as humans, even the inner temptation to do evil (Matthew 4). But in God these impulses toward evil have been integrated into God's character so that human impulses are no threat. When perpetrators decide to face the truth about themselves, they may find the compassionate limits of God. Their suppressed reality is already a part of God's experience. Even if we live in hell, God is there (Ps. 139:8).

There may be gender differences in the ways men and women experience the love of God. For women God's love may mean that the secret suffering of women is identified and the patriarchal abuse of power is confronted. Suffering demands justice for women in a patriarchal culture. For men, God's love may mean a new awareness of the suffering of others and a relinquishment of patriarchal power in favor of mutuality.

The love of God means that all the suffering of all creation is fully a part of God's experience. When Karen imagines a figure with open arms who accepts her completely, she is imagining the true God. Even though her parents rejected her as a preschool child and forced her to sleep alone in a dark, dangerous house, God accepts her with open arms and includes all of her fears and rages. All of Karen's experience is a part of God. When Sam abused his son, God knew the secret agony of his evil and the suffering of his son and family. And when he went off for a week to "think about whether I want to live," God shared his suffering and fear. There is nowhere he can go where God is not a companion and a resource to help him renounce evil and find a new center for his life.

The theory of incarnational atonement strives for the truth of God's radical identification with the world. Its image of a God who suffers with the world in the death of Jesus is that of a relational God. In many stories Jesus shows his ability to include the experiences of others. When he met the victims of oppression and illness, he provided resources and challenges in a way that enabled them to find power to change their lives. When the woman with the flow of blood touched Jesus' garment and was healed, Jesus said, "Daughter, your faith has made you well; go in peace, and be healed of your disease" (Mark 5:34). He was bound in a relationship of mutuality, and power flowed between them in a way that changed the structure of her suffering. Her suffering was transformed through this new connection with the heart of the relational web, and she experienced healing.

When Jesus met the oppressors of his day, he ate and talked with them and challenged them to change their abusive habits and serve the God of justice. He had no fear of their power, because he understood, though they did not, the contradictions in their lives. He knew the temptation to abuse power, but he also knew that power does not have to be abused and that liberation can come through relinquishment. Human impulses to evil can be neutralized without destroying the ones who are enslaved to evil. God's suffering love extends to the perpetrators of evil and transforms their experiences into safe limits that protect all in the web from destruction.

When he faced the crowds and the leaders who had authority to take his life, Jesus was fully present. He did not exclude their hatred and ignorance. Even at the point of death, Jesus maintained integrity and compassion for himself and for others, at no time pretending that his murder was a just cause. He showed that even though there are times when the power of evil is overwhelming, we can trust in the One whose love is not limited, even in death. When the power of evil was fully organized against him, Jesus knew who he was. By his example we can live, even in the knowledge of our own evil and death, without betraying the life God has given us.

The relational God loves us wholly and fully. This image has been picked up forcefully by Jacquelyn Grant:

> In the experiences of Black people, Jesus was "all things." Chief among these however, was the belief in Jesus as the divine co-sufferer, who empowers them in situations of oppression. For Christian Black women in the past, Jesus was their central frame of reference. They identified with Jesus because they believed that Jesus identified with them. As Jesus was persecuted and made to suffer undeservedly, so were they. His suffering culminated in the crucifixion. Their crucifixion included rape, and babies being sold. But Jesus' suffering was not the suffering of a mere human, for Jesus was understood to be God incarnate.[42]

In Jesus, God suffered for the sake of inclusive relationality, and empowered humans in situations of oppression, according to the testimony from those who suffer oppression. This is not suffering for its own sake, or suffering for the gratification of oppressors, but the shared suffering of love that saves the relational web and binds people together into relationships that bring liberation from oppression.

The image of Jesus who suffers the injustice of his own death may not be helpful for all victims of sexual violence in our time. The glorification of suffering in some Christian piety may actually increase the silent suffering of those who feel their experience is being suppressed.[43] For some oppressed groups, however, the suffering of Jesus' death is an inspiration to continue to struggle toward liberation. This tension will be with us for some time as we struggle with the meaning of God's love in an evil world.

Where Is the Power of God?

In the conception of a relational, ambiguous God, the power of God is measured by resilient hope for justice in the midst of ambiguity. Since power as intended in God's creative act is synonymous with life itself, God's power is the restlessness for abundant life. It is characterized by a passion for the more—more richness, more depth and breadth, more beauty. This passion enables the web to transcend itself and grow into new forms of creativity. But it also risks the fragmentation and eventual destruction of the web.

God's power includes the power of death and the power of evil. The creation itself lives on the razor edge between creativity and destruction, between life and death. The violent potential of God as witnessed in the Bible is real. Whether the relational web maintains its balance in this tension of good and evil depends on the concrete decisions of individuals within the web. The revelation of God in Jesus Christ is that God's love and justice are resilient in the face of evil, but its concrete actuality depends on the partnership of all in the web. God's stature is measured by an ability to embrace the ambiguity of both justice and injustice in the integrity of God's being while maintaining resilient hope for justice in the midst of this ambiguity.

> The suffering servant is rather one who can sustain a relationship involving great contrast, in [the crucifixion] the incompatibility between love and hate. In absorbing the hate or indifference derived from the other, while attempting to sustain the relationships by responding with love for the other, the extreme of contrasts is exemplified. This contrast is an incompatibility, in fact, an emotional contradiction. But by having the size to absorb this contradiction within the integrity of his own being, and in having the strength to sustain the relationship, the incompatibility has been transformed into a compatible contrast.[44]

God is present in survivors' resilient hope for justice. What is astounding about our study of sexual violence is the resilience of hope in those whose lives have included so much suffering and terror. Before they had identity, they were victims of destructive impulses perpetrated by the very adults they trusted completely with their lives. Yet in the midst of their overwhelming suffering, hope did not die. In their healing, survivors have reported that they must be able to incorporate great ambiguity in their lives. They must experience cognitive and affective memory of their suffering. Some must contain the presence of tendencies toward abuse because of their identification with the abuser. They must face the indifference toward and denial of their suffering by the larger community. They have suffered the wish to die, to kill, to live shallow lives, to escape in any way they could. They must face all of these forms of ambiguity and yet maintain resolve and commitment to their own future. In order to be the persons the restless God calls them to be, they must be able to turn the power of their resilient hope into forceful patterns of health in the midst of great ambiguity. Their resilience testifies to the resilient power of God.

God's power is present in the surprising hope of transformation in some recovering perpetrators. In order to heal, perpetrators have to face the suffering of their childhood and also the destructive behaviors they have dealt on others. They must be able to accept their own tendencies toward abuse, while at the same time containing these tendencies in the hope of new possibilities for themselves in the future. They must be able to stay in relationships of healing even when they cannot see the outcome for themselves. Whether there is enough resilient hope toward justice in God in a world of nuclear weapons may be revealed by whether recovering perpetrators can find new life.

There may be gender differences in the way men and women experience the power of God. For women, God's power may mean living out of resilient hope through resistance to continuing oppression and finding new connections at the margins of patriarchy that enable life to continue. For men, God's power may require a critical examination of complicity in the evil of patriarchy. Facing ambiguity is more likely a matter of confession, repentance, and restitution for the abuse of power, which causes so much suffering for women, children, and the relational web.

The truth for which the theory of substitutionary atonement strives is an image of the awful power of God confronting evil. Angry about injustice and evil in the world, God is tempted to use the power of life and death for evil, as we have seen in the biblical stories. God's power is seen in the willingness to risk ambiguity for the sake of inclusive relationality, but whose resilient justice perseveres in the face of suffering and evil. But the possibility that violence will eventually destroy the relational web is ever present and must be constantly resisted by those whose consciousness of evil is sharpened by oppression.

Though he did not hold office or rank, Jesus was a person with great authority. He was recognized by the crowds as someone who had resources needed for abundant life. He was feared by the leaders as a threat to their oppressive power. In the crucifixion, the power of the world was organized to murder Jesus. Even in that moment, Jesus was powerful—Do you not think that I cannot appeal to God to send down more than twelve legions of angels? (Matt. 26:53). In that ambiguity Jesus faced not only the power of evil organized against him, but also the temptation to use evil power himself. As God, in Hosea 11:9, tried to control his destructive impulses toward Israel, so Jesus faced the inner struggle of his own ambiguity. In Jesus' death, God is revealed as one who identifies completely with human life in all its ambiguity. But in the midst of that ambiguity, God's hope for love and justice is resilient. Despite its brutality, the crucifixion is not the end of the story. God's resilience reappears in the resurrection of Jesus, and in the resurrected church, which testifies, in its inadequate way, to Jesus as the sign of God's love and power.

Humans have power to nurture or abuse others. In order for evil to be overcome, we each must face the tendency in ourselves and in others to use power in evil ways. When we face the depth of our own ambiguity, we will discover the resilient hope that power can be used with justice. Only as we confess the abuse of power in our own lives, confront the abuse of power in others, repent of its evil, and commit ourselves anew to justice and righteousness will the possibility of evil be contained.

Walter Wink, examining the end of evil in Revelation, was surprised to find that Satan, the embodiment of evil, was not finally destroyed in this vision but was condemned to live "in the presence of the holy angels and in the presence of the Lamb" (Rev. 14:10). Wink concludes:

> Transformation comes not through the denial and repression of our evil, but by naming it, owning it, and lifting it up to God. . . . There is a residue of evil that can neither be cured nor integrated nor humanized. *That* we can only bring before God to be burned forever (for it never burns up altogether; it is in fact a kind of fuel), trusting God to transform even our irredeemable evil into fiery light.[45]

God's power is seen both in firm commitment to justice in the world and also in an ability to embrace great amounts of ambiguity in the search for justice. This image of God is summarized by Jacquelyn Grant as she shares the testimony of Sojourner Truth:

> "Praise, praise, praise to the Lord! An' I begun to feel such a love in my soul as I never felt before—love to all creatures. An' then, all of a sudden, it stopped, an' I said, Dar's de white folks that have abused you, an' beat you, an' abused your people—think o' them! But then there came another rush of love through my soul, an' I cried out loud—'Lord, I can love *even de white folks*.'"
>
> This love was not a sentimental, passive love. It was a tough, active love that empowered her to fight more fiercely for the freedom of her people. For the rest of her life she continued speaking at abolition and women's rights gatherings, condemning the horrors of oppression.[46]

A God We Can Worship

Survivors with whom I have worked witnessed concerning their religious experience. From their perspective, we looked at some scriptures in a fresh way, especially texts that included images of an abusive God. From this research we devised the image of a relational, ambiguous God of love and power. God's love is measured by the suffering required for inclusive relationality. God's power is measured by the resilient hope for justice in the midst of ambiguity.

Is it possible to worship a relational, ambiguous God? The answer to this question depends on the worship life and praxis of the church. Whether such a God can be worshiped will be based on the courage of Christians honestly to face themselves and their own suffering and to find symbols that can inspire resilient hope.

As we confront the evil of patriarchy, it may be that women and men will be inspired by different images of God. During their healing, survivors of sexual violence face the struggle of integrating painful memories of terror into their conscious experience. They face destructive impulses that come from identification with their abuser. In the healing process, they seek connections with others who do not fear their own suffering, and with those who acknowledge their own destructive impulses. When victims and caregivers come together with a mutual commitment to honest, inclusive love, and resilient hope for justice, the possibility of intimate community exists. Karen reported that the group of persons she chose for her healing became a source of support and comfort for every member, not just for her.

In my own religious experience, I have been comforted and challenged by the image of a relational, ambiguous God. As God is revealed in Jesus Christ, I see One who did not exclude any part of experience. Jesus did not shrink from those with taboo diseases, from outcasts, or from publicans and sinners. Nor did he avoid the evil leaders of his day. Jesus embraced concrete experience fully, even the most ugly and awful things. In his crucifixion, he experienced fully the sadism and brutality of human hatred and violence. Jesus was fully relational.

This God of inclusive relationality gives me hope that I need not fear my own experience. As a white man I carry the fear of my own suffering and of disclosing my history of abusing patriarchal power. For most of my life I have denied my pain and complicity. But believing in the God of love is believing that nothing in my past or my social situation can shock God. There is no depth of suffering in my past or present life too terrifying for God, no evil intent that is beyond God's understanding. With God's love, I can have the courage to accept my own suffering and the suffering of others in the knowledge that God will sustain me. Everything that I am, without exclusion, is received into the experience of God.

In Jesus I see a God who can embrace the full ambiguity of good and evil without losing integrity. The images of a perfect Jesus without sin have blinded me in the past to Jesus' own interior spiritual struggles. He was tempted to use his power from God for unholy purposes (Matt. 4:1-11). Accusing the Syrophoenician woman of being a dog, he was corrected by her and she expanded his understanding of faith (Mark 7:24-30). Jesus asked for the crucifixion to be postponed (Matt. 26:39), then had to resist the temptation to use angels against the crowd and leaders who threatened him (Matt. 26:53). In death, Jesus felt abandoned by God (Matt. 27:46). Surprisingly, the emphasis on God's ambiguity has opened up a depth of understanding of the scriptures, one that reveals God's sympathy with the terrible ambiguity of being human.

As a white man I have tried to avoid awareness of my ambiguity. Assuming that my use of power is just and creative, I have denied the impact of my abuse of power on others. The concept of an ambiguous God of power means that there is no potential or actual evil in my life that God has not already faced. My personal and corporate responsibility for increasing evil in the world can be contained by God's stature. In the midst of my ambiguity there is a resilient hope in the justice of God. The mess of my life does not end my struggle to seek what is right and good for myself and others. Even when evil seems to penetrate everything in my sight, still there is hope in a God who strives for beauty and justice. I do not need a perfect God to rescue me from the mess of this concrete life. Rather I need a God whose power is sufficient to sustain resilient hope for justice in the midst of ambiguity.

My testimony, based on work with survivors and on my inner search for God in the midst of great evil, is that the love and power of the relational, ambiguous God is sufficient. I can worship a God who knows the full experience of human life with all its good and evil, its justice and injustice, and yet a God who is restless—for more beauty, for more justice, for larger selves and communities who can live with resilient hope in the midst of great suffering.

CHAPTER NINE

MINISTRY PRACTICE AND PRACTICAL THEOLOGY

Another book could be written about the implications of our research on sexual violence and abuse of power for the ministry of the church. Fortunately much good material is already available that gives practical guidelines for responding to the crisis of sexual violence. This chapter summarizes several principles from our research that can provide the basis for more effective ministry. Then it briefly discusses some implications for the discipline of practical theology.

PRINCIPLES FOR MINISTRY PRACTICE

1. Church and society must be reorganized so that victims have adequate resources for prevention and healing from sexual violence.[1] Many victims of sexual violence have been silenced and isolated because their suffering is taboo.

a. Victims of sexual abuse must have access to counseling, education, support groups, and other resources for healing. As the issues of sexual violence have been identified in recent years, there has been a dramatic increase in victims seeking help and protection. Yet they do not begin to have affordable counseling and other services that are required.

b. There must be more effective procedures for crisis intervention when sexual abuse is disclosed. Recent research has shown that early intervention is important because it provides protection from further abuse and interrupts the tendency of victims to blame themselves and internalize the abuse. Children who disclose their suffering and get help are more likely to ameliorate the consequences of their trauma. Women who receive needed resources after sexual trauma suffer fewer long-term symptoms.

c. There must be great emphasis placed on teaching and other preventive programs to increase protection for those who are vulnerable to sexual violence. One of the principal reasons for the prevalence of sexual violence is the secrecy and ignorance of the public about this problem. Everyone needs to know that sexual violence is common and preventable.

2. *Church and society must devise more effective accountability to challenge the ways men use and abuse power.*[2]

a. Methods for handling disclosures of sexual violence must improve so that men are confronted with their abuses. Courts and other authorities need to be more sophisticated at detecting denial and rationalization in perpetrators so that they cannot escape accountability. There must be clear consequences that enforce limits to abuse of power and sexual misconduct.

b. When power is effectively limited so that victims are protected, society should consider the needs of perpetrators and provide opportunities for healing their spirits. Sexual violence will not be completely stopped until we understand how to correct the deficiencies in men that lead to such destructive behaviors.

c. Our examination of sexual violence has alerted us to other forms of abuse of power that need further research. Many persons are abused in professional relationships. Groups are kept in poverty because of abuse of economic power. Groups are excluded from participation through manipulating sexual fears. Persons of color are denied access to resources through stereotyping and scapegoating. These abuses must be further studied and confronted.

3. *Church and society must revise their institutional policies and procedures to prevent abuse of power and sexual violence.*[3] Men in power are too often protected when they abuse their power. We need to examine why this is true and make revisions necessary to correct this injustice.

a. We need methods of investigation that take seriously the prevalence and destructiveness of sexual violence. Those with authority to investigate must be able to move quickly to protect vulnerable persons.

b. We need clear ethical norms for sexual misconduct that emphasize its destructive nature and do not confuse violence with sexual activity.
c. In investigations and restitution we need to give priority to protecting victims.
d. We need fair appeal processes for those occasions when the charges are unsubstantiated. Wherever power is organized, there is potential abuse of power.

4. *Church and society must examine assumptions about the family, about the devaluation of women, and about sexuality and violence.*[4] We have seen that these assumptions provide the social sanction for sexual violence.

a. The family can be a dangerous institution for women and children. We need reformulated understandings of the family that present a balance between its value and its danger and that provide procedures for intervention when persons are in serious danger.
b. Women are devalued in a patriarchal culture in ways that lead to sexual violence. The inequities that women face in church and society must be addressed and corrected before justice can be delivered. This means rethinking our images of male and female.
c. We live in a society that confuses sexuality and violence. Sexual violence has been interpreted as sexual activity rather than as violence. We need to reformulate our views of both sexuality and violence so that they are no longer confused.

5. *The church must reformulate the images of God that sometimes give latent sanction to abusive patterns in families and interpersonal relationships.*[5] Theological assumptions about the relation of God and humankind need to be examined and revised. This requires new methods of Bible study, preaching and worship, and education and pastoral care.

a. We need to study the Bible critically in order to sort out its systematic distortions about the nature of God. This requires methods of historical and literary criticism that would retrieve and criticize the abusive and redemptive stories in the Bible. God as a relational, ambiguous figure of love and power becomes unhidden only as we wrestle with the Bible with courage and honesty.
b. Our changing images of God will require new imagination in our preaching and worship. God as a benevolent father who must be

served by the faithful is no longer adequate for proclaiming the whole word of truth and salvation. Bringing all human experience before a God who is identified with the suffering world will challenge some of our imperial images of worship. The theories of atonement that inform the celebration of the eucharist need to be examined to see if they implicitly sanction unjust suffering.

c. The patterns of dominance and abuse in education and pastoral care must be exposed and new forms of ministry that are liberating for all God's people devised. Too often ministries of teaching and care are based on perpetuating dominant values and maintaining boundaries that exclude marginal experiences and groups. Teaching children to obey Jesus can reinforce their silence about secret suffering. Pastoral care and counseling practices often give sanction to male privilege and dominance over women. Outreach programs to the poor and oppressed can be paternalistic and abusive.

These principles from our research on sexual violence require revisions of the ministry practice of the church.

PRACTICAL THEOLOGY

This project has been an exercise in practical theology, that is, theological reflection on the relation of God and humankind that arises out of the practice of ministry. In another work I helped devise the following definition and method for practical theology:

> Practical theology is critical and constructive reflection within a living community about human experience and interaction, involving a correlation of the Christian story and other perspectives, leading to an interpretation of meaning and value, and resulting in everyday guidelines and skills for the formation of persons and communities.[6]
>
> The essential components of practical theology . . .
>
> 1. Description of lived experience
> 2. Critical awareness of perspectives and interests
> 3. Correlation of perspectives from culture and the Christian tradition
> 4. Interpretation of meaning and value

5. Critique of interpretation
6. Guidelines and specific plans for a particular community.[7]

Based on the research in this project, I have formulated a new definition of practical theology:

> Practical theology is theological interpretation of the unheard voices of personal and community life for the purpose of continual transformation of faith in the true God of love and power toward renewed ministry practice.

The essential components of practical theology are:

1. *Reflection begins with the presence of difference and otherness in experience.* Difference provokes thought. When persons or communities become aware of some desire that contrasts with identity, the potential contradiction requires reflection. Self-conscious lived experience is filled with the tension of similarity and difference, and identity becomes stronger as these tensions are faced and worked through. This means that otherness must be preserved as a window into the depths of ultimate reality. Without difference and contrast, there can be no self-conscious experience.[8]

In our research, the depth of experience was unlocked through reflection on the contrast between evil and suffering on the one hand and hope on the other. As long as a survivor's life is characterized by private suffering, she is blocked from the depth of her own experience. But when, by talking with others about her suffering, she acts on the latent hope in her spirit, her life can be changed. In my work with survivors, it is not evil and suffering that are compelling, but the contrast between their pain and a resilient hope that will not die. This contrast begins to unlock the depth of experience for our participation and research. The *depth of human experience* is the data for practical theology, and experience is disclosed by seeking the contrast between human suffering and experiences of hope.

2. *Reflection leads to awareness of tensions within the self.* Perception of otherness and difference in experience enables one to see that the self is a fragile construction that needs continual transformation. Previous assumptions about this balance are challenged, and hidden desires of the heart are made manifest. Reflection requires a reformulation of

one's personal identity, and eventually of one's *theological anthropology* or theology of humankind.

There is a search for a self of integrity and justice in the human spirit. We have found courage and hope in unlikely places, among the survivors and recovering perpetrators of child sexual abuse. If hope can be found there, perhaps it exists in other places where evil seems predominant. The truth of a survivor's life can be remembered by the physical body for many years when the conscious mind has forgotten. The search for an integrated self is resilient and can be a source for attachments that move toward redemption. The self is relational, that is, the intrapsychic experience of the self is formed by internalization of others through emotional cathexis. Evil enters a survivor's life through the internalization of family and social interaction. In the healing process, survivors reach out to others who can stand the truth and maintain supportive relationships.

3. Reflection leads to awareness of tension between oppression and liberation in the institutions and ideologies of community. Communities include some parts of experience and exclude other parts. Communities extend power to some persons and withhold it from others. The oppression of community becomes evident in reflection on the depths of experience. Previous assumptions about community life are challenged. Reflection requires a reformulation of corporate identity, and eventually of *ecclesiology,* or theology of community.

There is a search for community in the human spirit, which is more than face-to-face interpersonal relationships. By community, we mean those institutions and ideologies that shape and control the course of human lives. Women grow up in a society where male privilege is dominant. The ideology of patriarchy gives men permission to abuse women, and patriarchy protects them from accountability for their behaviors. Survivors' resilient hope for community appears dramatically in their initiative to form counter-communities for healing.

4. Reflection leads to one's ultimate horizon, one's understanding of truth or God, and questions whether these metaphors and images are abusive or redemptive. Parts of our inherited and constructed religious vision are abusive, and parts are redemptive. When we see the complicity of religious ideas in abuse, previous assumptions about basic reality and the nature of God are challenged. Reflection requires a reformulation of faith, and eventually of the *doctrine of God.*

The resilient human spirit sustains its search for a God of love and justice in spite of the dominance of evil. The goal of practical theology is constructive statements about God's relation to human experience that lead to strategies of liberating action. One starts with how evil and suffering contrast with experiences of hope. This leads to the analysis of experience and culture through the use of critical theories.[9] Then there is the moment of constructive religious interpretation. Given our research, what generalization can we make about the nature of truth, that is, the nature of God?[10]

Truth has a narrative structure. Every person and group forms identity through story. But stories tend to give only an official version of the past. Stories partially distort identity in favor of the ideological restrictions of those who are dominant. Persons cannot report the latent structure in most cases. This is one reason why the voices of oppressed groups must be heard. They are often the carriers of the stories that must be heard for the full identity of a community to be known.

In theological terms, God is the story of stories. There are deeper narratives of which we are all a part, and to which our stories relate. The human soul hopes that its own self-conscious stories will be congruent with the great stories of divine life. We want our stories to be true rather than false. But we fear that the deeper truth of our lives will destroy the pseudo-stories we have created in order to defend ourselves against non-being. One way to know God is to deconstruct and reconstruct our individual and collective narratives.

Truth is a relational web. The discovery of the radical interdependence of all things is a basic paradigm shift from the world of the imperial self and the isolated object. Everything exists in a web of interdependence. Our experience is experience of the web of reality, and our individual response to the web is our contribution to its quality in the future. The web includes the interpersonal world of persons we interact with on a daily basis, institutions of power that set limits on behavior and action, the structure of language and the ideologies that determine perception and identity. God is radically identified with the relational web, that is, the totality of everything that exists at a particular time. To the extent that we are in the web and the web is in us, our experience is the incarnation of God. The principle of empiricism means attending to the web, which is God.[11] One way to know God is to reflect on the relationships within which our lives are embedded.

Truth is a process of immediacy. At the heart of experience is the process that Bernard Meland refers to as "vital immediacy."[12] Analysis of the process of immediacy means attending to the movement of God in the moment. The creative urge of the human soul is the divine urge. There is the flow of energy from entity to entity. There is a moment of receptivity through which relationships become internal to the individual (sensitivity). There is a moment of freedom, of novelty by which life is passed on to the future (creativity).[13] Because of trauma, survivors are often hindered in their ability to attend to the vital immediacy of their lives. They need the secure and compassionate presence of others. As nurturing relationships gain power, survivors gain strength to trust the flow of their own experience. God is the process of vital immediacy. Within the internal movement of our own spiritual experiences, our memories of the past, and our interactions with other persons and communities, God is present. One way to know God is to reflect on the vital immediacy of our experience.

5. *The final step in the hermeneutics of practical theology is reflection on the tension between faithful and unfaithful ministry practice.* As we see more clearly the truth that difference and otherness brings to experience, to the self, to community, and to God, we find that ministry practice must be changed. Previous assumptions are challenged. Reflection requires a reformulation of one's professional identity and eventually of one's *definition of ministry.*

My own practice of ministry was transformed by this research in sexual violence. My new focus includes:

—seeking justice with survivors of sexual violence,
—confronting perpetrators who abuse their power,
—challenging my communities to be liberating rather than oppressive,
—passionately serving and worshiping the relational, ambiguous God of love and power.

In conclusion, practical theology is based on an empirical and personal epistemology. We know the truth by attending to the empirical depth of experience and by honestly reflecting on our personal relationship to truth within the relational web. My own life is being transformed as I have witnessed the resilient hope of those whose lives have been more controlled by evil than good. I have found glimpses of faith in a God of love and power. This God is so completely identified with the world that our normal distinctions about good and evil do not apply to such a God. Whatever is evil is as much a part of God as whatever is good. Yet in the midst of this radical ambiguity there is resilient hope, a restlessness toward beauty that cannot be suppressed. In the midst of the worst evil, God's resilient hope is ceaselessly at work. This is why the witness of slaves, holocaust survivors, and victims of child abuse is so important. They know the truth about good and evil. They know there is a hope at the center of reality that cannot be destroyed by evil. Those of us with social privilege, who are oversocialized and anesthetized against our own evil and suffering, discover such hope only with great difficulty. We must attach ourselves in solidarity with those who have been to the bottom and have found there the source of good itself. The task of practical theology is to hear the silenced voices of truth, to hear them against the destructive force of ideology and religion. This is the work of justice in practical theology.

NOTES

CHAPTER 1:
HEARING THE SILENCED VOICES

1. "38 in 100 girls in most high schools have had at least one experience of sexual abuse. Other studies indicate that 10-20% of boys may have been sexually victimized as children." James Poling, "Social and Ethical Issues of Child Sexual Abuse," *American Baptist Quarterly,* 8-4: 257-66. On child sexual abuse, *see* the following: Diana Russell, *The Secret Trauma: Incest in the Lives of Girls and Women* (New York: Basic Books, 1986); David Finkelhor, *Child Sexual Abuse* (New York: Free Press, 1984); Dante Cicchetti and Vicki Carlson, eds., *Child Maltreatment: Theory and Research on the Causes and Consequences of Child Abuse and Neglect* (New York: Cambridge University Press, 1989) (*see* esp. chap. 4, "Sexual Abuse of Children: Causes and Consequences," Carol Hartman and Ann Burgess). On incidence of rape of women, *see* Diana Russell, *Sexual Exploitation, Rape, Child Sexual Abuse, and Workplace Harassment* (Beverly Hills: Sage Publications, 1984) and Susan Griffin, *Rape: The Politics of Consciousness* (New York: Harper and Row, 1986).
2. Russell, *Secret Trauma,* p. 79: "Figure 5-2 shows that with the exception of the youngest cohort of women, the older the cohort the less incestuous abuse was reported." Griffin, *Rape,* p. 141: "[In the Russell study] of women who were between the ages of 50 and 59, 33.9% had been raped. Of those between 40 and 49, 46.2% had been raped; of those between 30 and 39, 58.7% had been raped; and, most alarmingly, between the ages of 18 and 29, 53.2% had already been raped."
3. Russell, *Secret Trauma,* pp. 81ff.; Richard Gelles and Murray Straus, *Intimate Violence* (New York: Simon and Schuster, 1988), pp. 17ff.
4. Russell, *Secret Trauma,* pp. 81ff.; Cicchetti and Carlson, *Child Maltreatment* (*see* esp. Part I, "History and Definition"); Lloyd de Mause, *The History of Childhood* (New York: Psychohistory Press, 1974); John Boswell, *The Kindness of Strangers: The Abandonment of Children in Western Europe from Late Antiquity to the Renaissance* (New York: Pantheon Books, 1988); Philippe Aries, *Centuries of Childhood: A Social History of Family Life* (New York: Vintage, 1962).
5. Susan Griffin, *Pornography and Silence: Culture's Revenge Against Nature* (New York: Harper and Row, 1981); Andrea Dworkin, *Pornography: Men Possessing Women* (New York: Perigee/Putnam, 1981); Susan Brownmiller, *Against Our Will: Men, Women, and Rape* (New York: Simon and Schuster, 1975).
6. There are some excellent autobiographies and anthologies of the stories of survivors of sexual violence. Charlotte Vale Allen, *Daddy's Girl* (New York: Wyndham Books, 1980); Maya Angelou, *I Know Why the Caged Bird Sings*

(New York: Random House, 1970); Ellen Bass and Laura Davis, eds., *The Courage to Heal: A Guide for Women Survivors* (New York: Harper and Row, 1988); Ellen Bass and Louise Thornton, *I Never Told Anyone: Writings by Women Survivors of Child Sexual Abuse* (New York: Harper and Row, 1983).

7. Finkelhor, *Child Sexual Abuse,* pp. 11-12: "After reviewing all the studies, Diana Russell and I conclude in Chapter 11 that men constitute about 95% of the perpetrators in cases of abuse of girls and 80% in cases of abuse of boys."
8. I am indebted to Rob van Kessel for insight into the dynamic tension of suffering and hope in theology. *Zes Kruiken Water: Enkele Theologische Bijdragen Voor Kerkopbouw* (Netherlands: Gool and Sticht, 1989).
9. The focus in this book is based primarily on the testimony of adult women who were abused as children and perpetrators who have been convicted of sexual violence. Research is just beginning with adult men who were molested as children, and their testimony will be important in the continuing work in this field. *See* Mike Lew, *Victims No Longer: Men Recovering from Incest and Other Sexual Child Abuse* (New York: Nevraumont, 1988).
10. Rita Brock, *Journeys by Heart* (New York: Crossroad, 1988), pp. 26-27. *See also* the following for discussions of this principle in liberation theology: Barbara Andolsen, et al., eds., *Women's Consciousness, Women's Conscience* (New York: Harper and Row, 1985); G. Wilmore and J. Cone, eds., *Black Theology: A Documentary History, 1966-1979* (Maryknoll, New York: Orbis Books, 1979); Cornwall Collective, *Your Daughters Shall Prophesy: Feminist Alternatives in Theological Education* (New York: Pilgrim Press, 1979).
11. My experience is similar to the one reported by Peter Rutter, *Sex in the Forbidden Zone: How Therapists, Doctors, Clergy, Teachers, and Other Men in Power Betray Women's Trust* (Los Angeles: Jeremy Tarcher, 1989), p. 8: "Betrayal By My Mentor: The second episode that led me to write this book was the painful and disturbing discovery that a mentor who had seemed to represent all the best qualities of a teacher and healer had been repeatedly . . . having sexual relations with many of his female patients." *See also* Marie Fortune, *Is Nothing Sacred? When Sex Invades the Pastoral Relationship* (New York: Harper and Row, 1989).
12. Finkelhor, *Child Sexual Abuse,* p. 47.
13. For more on the methods of practical theology, *see* James Poling and Donald Miller, *Foundations for a Practical Theology of Ministry* (Nashville: Abingdon Press, 1985); Lewis Mudge and James Poling, eds., *Formation and Reflection: The Promise of Practical Theology* (Philadelphia: Fortress Press, 1987); Don S. Browning, ed., *Practical Theology: The Emerging Field in Theology, Church, and World* (New York: Harper and Row, 1983).
14. For a complete bibliography of Bernard Loomer's written material, *see* William Dean and Larry Axel, *The Size of God* (Macon, Ga.: Mercer University Press, 1987), pp. 18-19.

CHAPTER 2:
POWER AND ABUSE OF POWER

1. Marie Fortune, *Sexual Violence* (New York: Pilgrim Press, 1983), pp. 102ff. *See also* Diana Russell, *The Secret Trauma* (New York: Basic Books, 1986), esp. chap. 3, "Can Incest Be Nonabusive?"
2. *See* Mary Pellauer, Barbara Chester, and Jane Boyajian, eds., *Sexual Assault and Abuse: A Handbook for Clergy and Religious Professionals* (New York: Harper and Row, 1987). *See* esp. chap. 3, "If She Says No, Then It's Rape," by Ellen Goodman, pp. 17ff.
3. Fortune, *Sexual Violence*, pp. 105ff. *See also* Marie Fortune, *Is Nothing Sacred: When Sex Invades the Pastoral Relationship* (New York: Harper and Row, 1989); Peter Rutter, *Sex in the Forbidden Zone: When Men in Power—Therapists, Doctors, Clergy, Teachers, and Others—Betray Women's Trust* (Los Angeles: Jeremy Tarcher, 1989); Diana Russell, *Sexual Exploitation: Rape, Child Sexual Abuse, and Workplace Harassment* (Beverly Hills: Sage Publications, 1984).
4. Toinette Eugene, "When Love Is Unfashionable," in Barbara Andolsen, et al., eds., *Women's Consciousness, Women's Conscience* (New York: Harper and Row, 1985), pp. 121ff.; and Angela Davis, *Women, Race, and Class* (New York: Vintage, 1983), pp. 172ff.
5. Bernard Loomer, "Two Conceptions of Power," *Criterion* 15 (1976), p. 12.
6. Personal communication from Marie Fortune, Seattle, Wash., November 1990.
7. B. Meland, *Essays in Constructive Theology: A Process Perspective* (Chicago: Exploration Press, 1988), p. 5.
8. Loomer, "On Committing Yourself to a Relationship," *Process Studies* 16-4 (Winter 1987): 257.
9. Rita Brock, *Journeys by Heart* (New York: Crossroad, 1988), p. 41.
10. Loomer, *Two Conceptions*, pp. 20, 23, 25.
11. Brock, *Journeys*, pp. 26, 37, 39.
12. Walter Wink, *Unmasking the Powers: The Invisible Forces That Determine Human Existence* (Philadelphia: Fortress Press, 1986), p. 4.
13. Paraphrased from James N. Poling, "A Theological Integration of the Social and Personal in Pastoral Care and Counseling: A Process View" (Unpublished dissertation, School of Theology, Claremont, Calif., 1979), p. 60.
14. Daniel Day Williams, *The Spirit and the Forms of Love* (New York: Harper and Row, 1968), p. 153.
15. Ibid.
16. Ibid.
17. Loomer, *Two Conceptions*, p. 16.
18. Several summaries of the ideology of families are: Mary Lystad, ed., *Violence in the Home: Interdisciplinary Perspectives* (New York: Brunner/Mazel, 1986); Hester Eisenstein, *Contemporary Feminist Thought* (Boston: Hall, 1983);

Marianne Walters, et al., eds., *The Invisible Web: Gender Patterns in Family Relationships* (New York: Guilford, 1988). We will examine this issue more closely in chap. 7.

19. Brock, *Journeys,* pp. 30-33.
20. The Cornwall Collective, *Your Daughters Shall Prophesy* (New York: Pilgrim Press, 1980), p. 39.
21. Paraphrased from Poling, "A Theological Integration," pp. 95, 97.
22. Williams, *Spirit and Forms,* p. 130 (Adapted).
23. Ellen Wondra, "The Dialogue Which We Are" (unpublished essay), p. 4.

CHAPTER 4: STORIES OF RECOVERING PERPETRATORS

1. My previous research in child sexual abuse has been published in several articles: "Child Sexual Abuse: A Rich Context for Thinking About God, Community, and Ministry," *Journal of Pastoral Care* 42-1 (Spring 1988): 58-61; "Issues in the Psychotherapy of Child Molesters," *Journal of Pastoral Care* 43-1 (Spring 1989): 25-32; "Social and Ethical Issues of Child Sexual Abuse," *American Baptist Quarterly* 8-4 (December 1989): 257-67, rprtd. in *Watchword* (National Ministries, ABC/USA, Valley Forge, Pa.) 14-2 (May-June): 3-6.
2. I also engaged in systematic study of the literature about child molesters. Some helpful books are the following: Nicholas Groth, *Men Who Rape* (New York: Plenum Press, 1979); David Finkelhor, *Child Sexual Abuse* (New York: Free Press, 1984); Mary Lystad, ed., *Violence in the Home* (New York: Brunner/Mazel, 1986); Richard Gelles and Murray Straus, *Intimate Violence* (New York: Simon & Schuster, 1988); George Barnard, et al., *The Child Molester* (New York: Brunner/Mazel, 1989); Mike Lew, *Victims No Longer: Men Recovering from Incest and Other Sexual Child Abuse* (New York: Nevraumont, 1988); Mic Hunter, *Abused Boys: The Neglected Victims of Sexual Abuse* (Lexington, Mass.: Lexington Books, 1990).
3. Diana Russell, *The Secret Trauma: Incest in the Lives of Girls and Women* (New York: Basic Books, 1986), p. 86.
4. I am a fellow in the American Association of Pastoral Counselors, and a clinical member of the American Association of Marital and Family Therapists. I have been a professor of pastoral counseling in seminary for twelve years.
5. Finkelhor, *Child Sexual Abuse,* p. 47.
6. This argument is presented most forcefully in the works of Alice Miller. *See* esp. *For Your Own Good* (New York: Farrar, Straus & Giroux, 1983). Dr. Miller reviews case histories of known murderers in light of their childhood trauma.

CHANHASSEN DINNER THEATRES

Tbl#732 ... 10/09 ... 8:09 #4007

---

2 HOUSE .00
STEAK-D MED WEL .00 11.00 Prepaid
STEAK-D MED WEL .00 11.00 Prepaid
SILK TUX CHEESE 6.75
HOT FUDGE SUNDA 6.25

TOTAL VALUE: 29.00
less prepaid: -22.00

Sub-Total: 7.00

7. Finkelhor, *Child Sexual Abuse,* p. 47.
8. *See* the summary of this discussion in Finkelhor, *Child Sexual Abuse,* pp. 33ff.; Russell, *The Secret Trauma,* pp. 215ff.; and Groth, *Men Who Rape,* p. 151.
9. Again, I do not wish to leave the impression that all perpetrators have been victims of child sexual abuse. The issue of the relation between being a victim of sexual abuse and becoming a perpetrator of sexual abuse is complex. According to Finkelhor, those child molesters who have been studied do seem to have experienced higher rates of child sexual abuse themselves than normal adults, but there are many molesters who have not been sexually abused (Finkelhor, *Child Sexual Abuse,* p. 47). Studies of child molesters are incomplete because of the secrecy and denial about these problems within the male population.
10. For information on the consequences of sexual abuse for boys and men, *see* Lew, *Victims No Longer;* Hunter, *Abused Boys.*
11. Finkelhor, *Child Sexual Abuse,* p. 47. His summary of other studies suggests that as many as two-thirds of child molesters were not molested as children.
12. Ibid., p. 12.
13. Ibid., p. 54.
14. Gertrude and Rubin Blanck, *Ego Psychology II: Psychoanalytic Developmental Psychology* (New York: Columbia University Press, 1979), pp. 31ff.
15. Finkelhor, *Child Sexual Abuse,* pp. 39ff.; Alice Miller, *Thou Shalt Not Be Aware* (New York: Farrar, Straus & Giroux, 1984), p. 123.
16. Finkelhor, *Child Sexual Abuse,* p. 47; Miller, *Thou Shalt Not Be Aware,* pp. 162ff.
17. Miller, *For Your Own Good,* p. 229.
18. Nancy Chodorow, *The Reproduction of Mothering* (Berkeley: University of California Press, 1978), pp. 173ff.
19. Larry Baron and Murray Straus, *Four Theories of Rape in American Society* (New Haven, Conn.: Yale University Press, 1989), p. 6.
20. Heinz Kohut, *The Restoration of the Self* (New York: International Universities Press, 1977), pp. 111ff.; D. W. Winnicott, *Deprivation and Delinquency* (London: Tavistock, 1984), pp. 81ff.
21. Blanck and Blanck, *Ego Psychology II,* pp. 43ff. "Identification with the aggressor" is a term introduced by Anna Freud and elaborated by Rene Spitz.
22. Ruth Lax, et al., eds., *Rapprochement: The Critical Phase of Separation Individuation* (New York: Jason Aronson, 1980), pp. 439-56.
23. Miller, *Thou Shalt Not Be Aware,* p. 163.
24. Marie Fortune, *Sexual Violence* (New York: Pilgrim Press, 1983), p. 5.
25. Blanck and Blanck, *Ego Psychology II,* pp. 31ff.
26. Blanck and Blanck, *Ego Psychology II,* pp. 176ff.; Otto Kernberg, *Internal World and External Reality* (New York: Jason Aronson, 1980), pp. 135ff.; Kohut, *The Restoration of the Self,* pp. 63ff.

27. Heinz Kohut, *How Does Analysis Cure?* (Chicago: University of Chicago Press, 1984), pp. 192ff.
28. Barnard, *The Child Molester*, pp. 43ff.
29. This section is a revised excerpt from "Issues in Psychotherapy with Child Molesters," in *Journal of Pastoral Care* 8-1 (Spring 1989): 25-32.

CHAPTER 5: THE SCHREBER CASE: METHODS OF ANALYSIS

1. Daniel Paul Schreber, *Memoirs of My Mental Illness,* trans. Ida Macalpine and Richard Hunter (London: Wm. Dawson & Sons, 1955). The book first appeared as *Denkwurdigkeiten eines Nervenkranken* (Leipzig: O. Mutze, 1903).
2. I want to acknowledge my indebtedness to Dr. Carl Schneider of Atlanta, Ga., for introducing me to the Schreber case and its significance for pastoral theology.
3. William Niederland, *The Schreber Case: Psychoanalytic Profile of a Paranoid Personality* (London: Analytic Press, 1984).
4. I am especially indebted to Lucy Bregman for her summary of the commentary on the Schreber case, in "Religion and Madness: Schreber's Memoirs as Personal Myth," *Journal of Religion and Health* 16-2 (1977): 119-34.
5. Schreber, *Memoirs,* pp. 61-62.
6. Ibid., pp. 45-46.
7. Ibid., p. 214.
8. Sigmund Freud, "Psychoanalytic Notes upon an Autobiographical Account of a Case of Paranoia (Dementia Paranoides) (1911)," in *Three Case Histories* (New York: Collier Books, 1963), pp. 103-86.
9. Macalpine and Hunter, "Introduction," in Schreber, *Memoirs,* pp. 8-9.
10. Freud, "Case of Paranoia," p. 112.
11. Ibid., p. 114.
12. Ibid.
13. Ibid., pp. 147-48.
14. Niederland, *Schreber Case,* p. 50.
15. Morton Schatzman, *Soul Murder: Persecution in the Family* (New York: New American Library, 1973).
16. Niederland, *Schreber Case,* p. 54.
17. I hold that at least four writers take an essentially "feminist" position: Macalpine and Hunter, "Introduction" in Schreber, *Memoirs;* Bregman, "Religion and Madness"; Louis Breger, "Daniel Paul Schreber: From Male into Female," *Journal of the American Academy of Psychoanalysis* 16-2 (1977):

119-34; and Anthony Wilden, *System and Structure: Essays in Communication and Exchange* (London: Tavistock, 1972), pp. 278-300.
18. Wilden, *System and Structure,* p. 299.
19. Bregman, "Religion and Madness," 129.
20. Breger, "From Male into Female," 140.
21. Wilden, *System and Structure,* p. 301.
22. Bregman, "Religion and Madness," 131.
23. Ibid., 131-32.
24. Ibid., 132.
25. Ibid., 131-32.
26. Sigmund Freud, "Beyond the Pleasure Principle," *Standard Edition of the Complete Psychological Works of Sigmund Freud,* vol. 18 (London: Hogarth Press, 1955), pp. 3-64. *See* discussions in H. Kohut, *The Restoration of the Self* (New York: International Universities Press, 1977), pp. 111ff., 123; Otto Kernberg, *Internal World and External Reality* (New York: Aronson, 1980), pp. 19ff.
27. Niederland, *Schreber Case,* p. 58.
28. Freud, "Case of Paranoia," p. 147.
29. Niederland, *Schreber Case,* pp. 101ff.
30. Schreber, *Memoirs,* pp. 64ff.
31. Freud, "Case of Paranoia," p. 151.
32. Bregman, "Religion and Madness," 132.

CHAPTER 6: THE SEARCH FOR SELF

1. David Finkelhor, *Child Sexual Abuse* (New York: Free Press, 1984), pp. 11-12.
2. Hester Eisenstein, *Contemporary Feminist Thought* (Boston: G. K. Hall, 1983), pp. 37ff.
3. Finkelhor, *Child Sexual Abuse,* p. 12.
4. Ellen K. Wondra, "Theology in a Postmodern Key," *Plumbline: A Journal of Ministry in Higher Education* (December 1989), 5.
5. Alfred North Whitehead, *Process and Reality,* ed. D. R. Griffin and D. W. Sherburne (New York: Free Press, 1929, 1978), p. 59.
6. James N. Poling, "A Theological Integration of the Social and Personal in Pastoral Care and Counseling: A Process View" (Ph.D. dissertation, School of Theology at Claremont, Calif., May 1980), p. 36.
7. Ibid., pp. 39-46.
8. George Herbert Mead, *Mind, Self, and Society,* ed. Charles W. Morris (Chicago: University of Chicago Press, 1934, 1962).
9. Whitehead, *Process and Reality,* p. 238.

10. Bernard Loomer, "The Free and Relational Self," in *Belief and Ethics,* ed. W. W. Schroeder and Gibson Winter (Chicago: Center for the Scientific Study of Religion, 1978), p. 71.
11. Poling, "A Theological Integration," pp. 46-53.
12. Whitehead, *Process and Reality. See* esp. pp. 249-66.
13. Ibid., p. 45.
14. Daniel Day Williams, *The Minister and the Care of Souls* (New York: Harper and Row, 1961), pp. 98-99.
15. Whitehead, *Process and Reality,* p. 59.
16. Daniel Stern, *The Interpersonal World of the Infant* (New York: Basic Books, 1985), p. 18.
17. Gertrude and Rubin Blanck, *Ego Psychology: Theory and Practice* (New York: Columbia University Press, 1974), p. 67.
18. The Theory of attachment is a central concept in psychoanalytic theory and is basic to the argument in this book. For good summaries of attachment theory, *see* Althea Horner, *Object Relations and the Developing Ego in Therapy* (New York: Jason Aronson, 1984); Stern, *Interpersonal World of the Infant;* Robert Kegan, *The Evolving Self* (Cambridge, Mass.: Harvard University Press, 1982).
19. Stern, *Interpersonal World of the Infant,* pp. 97ff. Stern refers to internalized patterns as "Representations of Interactions that have been Generalized (RIGs)." Object relations theory refers to them as self and object representations (Blanck and Blanck, *Ego Psychology: Theory and Practice,* pp. 35ff.).
20. These internalized experiences are called "objects" or "introjects" in object relations theory. *See* Horner, *Object Relations,* and Rubin and Gertrude Blanck, *Beyond Ego Psychology: Developmental Object Relations Theory* (New York: Columbia University Press, 1986). The process of internalization as described here is closely related to that of Jean Piaget, *The Construction of Reality in the Child* (New York: Basic Books, 1954) and George Herbert Mead, *Mind, Self, and Society* (Chicago: University of Chicago Press, 1962). *See* summary in Kegan, *Evolving Self.*
21. For more detailed feminist critique of the metatheory of psychoanalytic thought, *see* Eisenstein, *Contemporary Feminist Thought;* Jane Gallop, *The Daughter's Seduction: Feminism and Psychoanalysis* (New York: Cornell University Press, 1982); Jean Baker Miller, *Psychoanalysis and Women* (New York: Penguin Books, 1973); Nancy Chodorow, *The Reproduction of Mothering* (Berkeley, Calif.: University of California Press, 1978).
22. Object relations theory is one stream of interpretation of psychoanalytic theory. It is represented in this discussion by Otto Kernberg, Heinz Kohut, Althea Horner, Gertrude and Rubin Blanck, W. W. Meissner, and others. One of the best summaries is found in Horner, *Object Relations:* "The term *object relations* refers to specific intrapsychic structures, to an aspect of ego

organization, and not to external interpersonal relationships. However, these intrapsychic structures, the mental representations of self and other (the object), do become manifest in the interpersonal situation. That is, 'the inner world of object relations determines in a fundamental way the individual's relations with people in the external world. This world . . . is basically the residue of the individual's relations with people upon whom he was dependent for the satisfaction of primitive needs in infancy and during the early stages of maturation' (Phillipson, 1955, p. 7)," p. 3.

23. The theory elaborated here is my own summary, but similar views are argued in some of the following sources: Horner *Object Relations;* Heinz Kohut, *The Restoration of the Self* (New York: International Universities Press, 1977); W. W. Meissner, *Internalization in Psychoanalysis* (New York: International Universities Press, 1981).
24. Gertrude and Rubin Blanck, *Ego Psychology II: Psychoanalytic Developmental Psychology* (New York: Columbia University Press, 1979), pp. 31ff.; Kohut, *Restoration of the Self,* pp. 85ff.; Kegan, *Evolving Self,* pp. 107ff.
25. Blanck and Blanck, *Ego Psychology II,* p. 39. *See also* Kohut, *Restoration of the Self,* pp. 111ff.; Kegan, *Evolving Self,* pp. 107ff.
26. Kohut, *Restoration of the Self,* pp. 83ff.; Blanck and Blanck, *Ego Psychology II,* pp. 57ff.
27. Heinz Kohut, *How Does Analysis Cure?* (Chicago: University of Chicago Press, 1984), p. 192; Otto Kernberg, *Internal World and External Reality* (New York: Jason Aronson, 1980), pp. 98ff.
28. Horner, *Object Relations,* p. 5.
29. D. W. Winnicott, *Deprivation and Delinquency* (London: Tavistock, 1984), pp. 112, 198; Alice Miller, *Thou Shalt Not Be Aware* (New York: Farrar, Straus & Giroux, 1984), pp. 192ff.; Stern, *Interpersonal World of the Infant,* p. 227.
30. Erik Erikson, *Childhood and Society* (New York: W. W. Norton & Co., 1963).
31. Kohut, *How Does Analysis Cure?*
32. Splitting as a defense against the fragmentation of the self is important in modern object relations theory. *See* Kohut, *How Does Analysis Cure?*; Kernberg, *Internal World and External Reality;* Meissner, *Internalization in Psychoanalysis.*
33. Chodorow, *Reproduction of Mothering,* pp. 173ff.
34. Horner, *Object Relations,* p. 5.
35. *See* Meissner, *Internalization in Psychoanalysis.*
36. *See Diagnostic and Statistical Manual of Mental Disorders* (3rd, rev. ed.) (American Psychiatric Association, 1987), pp. 346-47. For summaries of research on the Borderline Personality Disorder, *see* W. W. Meissner, *The Borderline Spectrum: Differential Diagnosis and Developmental Issues* (New York: Jason Aronson, 1984) and *Treatment of Patients in the Borderline Spectrum* (New York: Jason Aronson, 1988); Otto Kernberg, *Borderline Conditions and Pathological Narcissism* (New York: Jason Aronson, 1975) and *Severe*

Personality Disorders: Psychotherapeutic Strategies (New Haven, Conn.: Yale University Press, 1984).

37. Dante Cicchetti and Vicki Carlson, eds., *Child Maltreatment: Theory and Research on the Causes and Consequences of Child Abuse and Neglect* (New York: Cambridge University Press, 1989).
38. Kernberg, *Internal World and External Reality,* p. 6. There is some controversy about the process of splitting. D. W. Winnicott gives a different definition in *Deprivation and Delinquency:* "If we deprive a child of the transitional objects and disturb the established transitional phenomena, then the child has only one way out, which is a split in the personality, with one half related to a subjective world and the other reacting on a compliance basis to the world which impinges. When this split is formed and the bridges between the subjective and the objective are destroyed, or have never been well formed, the child is unable to operate as a total human being," pp. 187-88. *See also* the critique of Kernberg by Meissner, *Internalization in Psychoanalysis,* pp. 106ff., and by Stern, *Interpersonal World of the Infant,* pp. 248ff. Whatever the outcome of this debate, there does seem to be a lack of integration of experiences in the victims of child sexual abuse, which results in introjects of cognition and affect.
39. Meissner, *Internalization in Psychoanalysis.*
40. Kohut, *How Does Analysis Cure?*
41. Chodorow, *Reproduction of Mothering,* pp. 183ff.
42. Blanck and Blanck, *Ego Psychology II,* p. 39. *See also* Kohut, *Restoration of the Self,* pp. 111ff.; Kegan, *Evolving Self,* pp. 107ff.
43. Kohut, *Restoration of the Self,* pp. 111-31. Kohut argues that narcissistic rage is the response of the self to chronic injury and will not be alleviated until the person recovers a sense of self.
44. "Adult-victims" is a term that refers to adults who were victims of sexual abuse as children and continue to experience the consequences of their victimization as adults.
45. Kernberg, *Internal World and External Reality,* pp. 20-38, 135-53.
46. Kohut, *Restoration of the Self,* pp. 83ff.; Blanck and Blanck, *Ego Psychology II,* pp. 57ff.
47. Meissner, *Internalization in Psychoanalysis.*
48. Kohut, *How Does Analysis Cure?,* p. 192; Kernberg, *Internal World and External Reality,* pp. 98ff.
49. For summaries of the long-term symptoms of child abuse, *see* Cicchetti and Carlson, eds., *Child Maltreatment;* Finkelhor, *Child Sexual Abuse;* Murray Straus, et al., *Behind Closed Doors: Violence in the American Family* (Garden City, New York: Anchor, 1980); Diana Russell, *The Secret Trauma: Incest in the Lives of Girls and Women* (New York: Basic Books, 1986).
50. Blanck and Blanck, *Ego Psychology: Theory and Practice; Ego Psychology II; Beyond Ego Psychology.*
51. Bernard Loomer, "Two Conceptions of Power," *Criterion* 15 (1976), p. 28.

52. Wondra, "Theology in a Postmodern Key," 5.
53. Ibid.
54. Ibid.
55. Loomer, "Size of God" in Dean and Axel, *The Size of God, The Theology of Bernard Loomer in Context* (Macon, Ga.: Mercer University Press, 1987), p. 45.
56. Ibid.
57. Ibid., p. 46.
58. Ibid.
59. Ibid.
60. Ibid., p. 45.
61. I am indebted for my insight into the process of change to Lauree Hersch Meyer, theologian in Lombard, Illinois.
62. *See* summaries in the following: Kegan, *Evolving Self*, p. 95 (he uses the terms *embeddedness, alienation, new balance*); Stern, *Interpersonal World of the Infant*, p. 29; Blanck and Blanck, *Ego Psychology: Theory and Practice*, p. 38 (they suggest the following names for the three stages I am discussing: primary narcissism, need gratification, and object constancy).
63. Loomer, "Size of God," p. 47.
64. *See* summaries of this discussion in Kernberg, *Internal World and External Reality*, pp. 19ff.; Blanck and Blanck, *Ego Psychology II*, pp. 31ff. *See also* Winnicott, *Deprivation and Delinquency*, pp. 81ff.
65. Loomer, "Size of God," p. 46.
66. Loomer, "Two Conceptions of Power," p. 23.
67. Ibid., p. 28.
68. Ibid.

CHAPTER 7: THE SEARCH FOR COMMUNITY

1. D. W. Winnicott, *Deprivation and Delinquency* (London: Tavistock, 1984). Winnicott discusses how destructive behavior can be interpreted as a distorted search for significant others who can set limits without losing compassion.
2. Daniel Paul Schreber, *Memoirs of My Nervous Illness* (London: Wm. Dawson & Sons, 1955), pp. 61ff.
3. For summaries of the nature of individuals and communities, *see* John Cobb and David Griffin, *Process Theology: An Introductory Exposition* (Philadelphia: Westminster Press, 1976); William Dean and Larry Axel, *The Size of God: The Theology of Bernard Loomer in Context* (Macon, Ga.: Mercer University Press, 1987), pp. 40ff.; Bernard Meland, *Essays in Constructive Theology: A Process Perspective* (Chicago: Exploration Press, 1988), pp. 1ff.; John Cobb, *A Christian Natural Theology* (Philadelphia: Westminster Press, 1965), pp. 47ff.; Bernard Loomer, "Two Conceptions of Power," *Process Studies* 6 (1976):

5-32; Bernard Loomer, "The Free and Relational Self," in *Belief and Ethics*, ed. W. W. Schroeder (Chicago: Center for the Scientific Study of Religion, 1978), pp. 69-86.

4. Alfred North Whitehead, *Process and Reality*, ed. David Griffin and Donald Sherburne (New York: Free Press, 1978), pp. 18, 21.
5. Bernard Loomer, "The Size of God," in Dean and Axel, *The Size of God*, p. 40.
6. Meland, *Essays in Constructive Theology*, p. 5.
7. George Herbert Mead, *Mind, Self, and Society*, ed. Charles Morris (Chicago: University of Chicago Press, 1934, 1962), p. 7.
8. Ellen Wondra, "Theology in a Postmodern Key," *Plumbline* (December 1989), p. 5.
9. Bernard Loomer, "On Committing Yourself to a Relationship," *Process Studies* 16-4 (1987): 257.
10. Mead, *Mind, Self, and Society*, pp. 42ff.
11. Loomer, "On Committing Yourself to a Relationship," 257.
12. Meland, *Essays in Constructive Theology*, p. 5.
13. *See* Meland, *Essays in Constructive Theology*, pp. 5ff., for a discussion of the structure of relationships as a culture.
14. Loomer, "On Committing Yourself to a Relationship," 257.
15. Phyllis Chesler, *Women and Madness* (New York: Doubleday & Co., 1972). A detailed discussion of this same phenomenon can be found in Charles Bernheimer and Clair Kahane, eds., *Dora: Freud, Women, and Hysteria* (New York: Columbia University Press, 1985). *See also* the discussion of "consciousness-raising" in Hester Eisenstein, *Contemporary Feminist Thought* (Boston: Hall, 1983), pp. 37ff.
16. Diana Russell, *The Secret Trauma: Incest in the Lives of Girls and Women* (New York: Basic Books, 1986), pp. 1-9.
17. Ibid., p. 70.
18. David Finkelhor, *Child Sexual Abuse* (New York: Free Press, 1984), p. 166.
19. Eisenstein, *Contemporary Feminist Thought*, p. 37.
20. "Womanist" is a term preferred by many African-American women who explore sexism and racism as interlocking forms of domination. *See* Toinette Eugene, "A Hermeneutical Challenge for Womanists: The Interrelation Between the Text and Our Experience," in Gayle Koontz and Willard Swartley, eds., *Perspectives on Feminist Hermeneutics* (Elkhart, Ind.: Institute of Mennonite Studies, 1989), p. 26.
21. One of the important references for this section is the summary by Eisenstein in *Contemporary Feminist Thought*.
22. For summaries of the history of the family and child-rearing practices, *see* Philippe Aries, *Centuries of Childhood: A Social History of Family Life* (New York: Vintage, 1962); Dante Cicchetti and Vicki Carlson, *Child Maltreatment* (New York: Cambridge University Press, 1989); Lloyd de Mause, *The History of*

Childhood (New York: Psychohistory Press, 1974); Linda Pollock, *Forgotten Children: Parent-Child Relations from 1500-1900* (New York: Cambridge University Press, 1983); Angela Davis, *Women, Race, and Class* (New York: Vintage, 1983); Alice Miller, *For Your Own Good: Hidden Cruelty in Child-rearing and the Roots of Violence* (New York: Farrar, Straus & Giroux, 1983).

23. For the history of how nineteenth-century oppression of women was encouraged through family law, *see* Nancy Hewitt, *Women's Activism and Social Change: Rochester, NY, 1822-1872* (New York: Cornell University Press, 1984); Miriam Gurko, *The Ladies of Seneca Falls: The Birth of the Woman's Rights Movement* (New York: Schocken Books, 1976); Elizabeth Cady Stanton, *Eighty Years and More, Reminiscences, 1815-1897* (New York: Schocken Books, 1971); Ellen Carol DuBois, ed., *Elizabeth Cady Stanton, Susan B. Anthony: Correspondence, Writings, Speeches* (New York: Schocken Books, 1981).
24. Mary Lystad, ed., *Violence in the Home: Interdisciplinary Perspectives* (New York: Brunner/Mazel, 1986).
25. "The Unique Death of Eli Creekmore" (Videotape produced by KCTS, Seattle, Wash., 1987).
26. Richard Gelles and Murray Straus, *Intimate Violence* (New York: Simon and Schuster, 1988), pp. 28ff.
27. For history of the African-American family, *see* Herbert Gutman, *The Black Family in Slavery and Freedom: 1750-1925* (New York: Vintage, 1976); Mary Helen Washington, *Invented Lives: Narratives of Black Women 1860-1960* (New York: Doubleday & Co., 1987); Davis, *Women, Race, and Class;* Eugene Genovese, ed., *The Slave Economy of the Old South: Selected Essays in Economic and Social History* (Baton Rouge, La.: Louisiana State University Press, 1968).
28. Toni Morrison, *Beloved* (New York: New American Library, 1987). This is a novel about the struggle of families to survive in the post–Civil War period. *See also* Gutman, *The Black Family in Slavery and Freedom: 1750-1925,* pp. 361ff.
29. I am indebted for this material to Angela Davis, *Women, Culture, Politics* (New York: Vintage, 1990), pp. 73ff. *See also* Wallace Smith, *The Church in the Life of the Black Family* (Valley Forge, Pa.: Judson Press, 1985), pp. 34ff. *See also* Toinette Eugene, "Moral Values and Black Womanists," *Journal of Religious Thought* (Spring 1988).
30. Smith, *The Church in the Life of the Black Family,* pp. 29ff.
31. Daniel P. Moynihan, *The Negro Family: The Case for National Action* (U.S. Dept. of Labor, 1965).
32. Quoted in Davis, *Women, Culture, Politics,* p. 77.
33. Gelles and Straus, *Intimate Violence,* p. 32.
34. Monica McGoldrick, Carol Anderson, and Froma Walsh, eds., *Women in Families: A Framework for Family Therapy* (W. W. Norton & Co., 1989), p. 360.
35. Toinette Eugene, "While Love Is Unfashionable: An Exploration of Black Spirituality and Sexuality," in Andolsen, et al., *Women's Consciousness,*

Women's Conscience (New York: Harper and Row, 1985), pp. 128-29. Dr. Eugene gives credit for the structure of these ideas to James Nelson, *Embodiment: An Approach to Sexuality and Christian Theology* (New York: Pilgrim Press, 1976).

36. Nancy Chodorow, *The Reproduction of Mothering,* pp. 92ff. *See also* discussion in chap. 6 of this work.
37. Chodorow, *Reproduction of Mothering,* p. 182.
38. Juliet Mitchell, *The Longest Revolution* (New York: Pantheon Books, 1984), p. 64.
39. Chodorow, *Reproduction of Mothering,* p. 183.
40. Eugene, "While Love Is Unfashionable," p. 129.
41. Eisenstein, *Contemporary Feminist Thought,* p. 22.
42. Ibid. Eisenstein is quoting from Sherry Ortner, *Woman, Culture, and Society,* ed. Rosaldo and Lamphase, pp. 67-87.
43. Eisenstein, *Contemporary Feminist Thought,* p. 23.
44. Eugene, "While Love Is Unfashionable," pp. 130-31.
45. Alice Miller, *Thou Shalt Not Be Aware* (New York: Farrar, Straus & Giroux, 1984), p. 123.
46. Eisenstein, *Contemporary Feminist Thought,* pp. 37ff.
47. Ibid., pp. 27-28; *See also* Susan Brownmiller, *Against Our Will: Men, Women, and Rape* (New York: Simon and Schuster, 1975).
48. Eisenstein, *Contemporary Feminist Thought,* p. 29.
49. Ibid., p. 31. Susan Griffin has three books on rape and pornography: *Women and Nature: The Roaring Inside Her* (New York: Harper and Row, 1978); *Rape: The Power of Consciousness* (New York: Harper and Row, 1979); *Pornography and Silence: Culture's Revenge Against Nature* (New York: Harper and Row, 1981).
50. Russell, *Secret Trauma,* p. 216.
51. Griffin, *Pornography and Silence;* Laura Lederer, ed., *Take Back the Night: Women on Pornography* (New York: Wm. Morrow & Co., 1980).
52. Toinette Eugene, in Andolsen, *Women's Consciousness, Women's Conscience,* pp. 128-29.
53. Griffin, *Pornography and Silence,* p. 20.
54. Marie Fortune, *Sexual Violence* (New York: Pilgrim Press, 1983), pp. 16, 21.
55. Davis, *Women, Culture, Politics,* p. 38.
56. Ibid., pp. 43-44.
57. Charles Winquist, *Practical Hermeneutics: A Revised Agenda for Ministry* (Chico, Calif.: Scholars Press, 1980). Winquist suggests that the depth of experience becomes available when one attends to the cracks and fissures in language and perception.
58. Marie Fortune, *Is Nothing Sacred? When Sex Invades the Pastoral Relationship* (New York: Harper and Row, 1989).
59. Bernard Loomer, "Two Conceptions of Power," p. 28. *Criterion,* 15 (1976).

CHAPTER 8:
THE SEARCH FOR GOD

1. Lucy Bregman, "Religion and Madness: Schreber's Memoirs as Personal Myth," *Journal of Religion and Health* 16-2 (1977): 119-34.
2. One of the first commentaries was Mary Daly's *Beyond God the Father* (Boston: Beacon Press, 1973). In this chapter we will examine other feminist and womanist theological reflection on religion and sexual violence.
3. All biblical quotations are from the New Revised Standard Version of the Bible, copyright © 1989, by the Division of Christian Education of the National Council of the Churches of Christ in the United States of America.
4. These biblical expositions are written from the perspective of practical theology rather than biblical exegesis. Though I have tried to be conversant with historical and literary critical discussions of these texts, I am primarily interested in how the text in its final form has impact on the reader of today, that is, in hermeneutics rather than exegesis. I have looked at how the gaps in the text can be interpreted by the present-day reader in a way that is allowed by biblical criticism. The texts examined have frequently been interpreted in a way that promotes certain values about power and the family. My exposition uses somewhat untraditional methods as a way of deconstructing the effects of the texts' impact on the modern reader. For example, the role of women, namely, Tamar, Sarah, and Hagar, has been trivialized in these stories in ways that hide violence toward women. This exposition approaches the text specifically with questions about sexual violence and with methods of the psychology of families. Out of this new ethical context, we may discover that the texts do not so clearly support some traditional interpretations.

   One version of this method of interpretation is summarized by Walter Brueggemann: "It is the purpose of this exposition to consider the texts as they address the community of faith in its present context. In that regard, this commentary does not seek to do what critical commentaries have done, though it relies on them. . . . Though our exposition depends on careful exegesis, it does not seek either to reiterate that fund of learning nor to advance the frontiers of exegetical method. . . . By and large, historical questions have not been given major attention in this commentary. . . . In a similar way, literary questions have been treated sparsely. . . . Throughout the commentary, we have used the phrase, 'the listening community.' By that, we refer to the community to whom the text and the exposition are addressed. In the first instance, this means the church. But derivatively, it refers to any person or group seriously engaged with the text" (*Genesis: A Bible Commentary for Teaching and Preaching,* Atlanta, Ga.: John Knox Press, 1982, pp. 5-8).

   A similar method is described by Nelle Morton: "I have taken my stance among the masses and listened with the common woman's ear to that which patriarchal religious institutions must begin to accept responsibility for. No longer can they hide behind: 'But the real intention is . . . ,' 'In the original language it says . . . ,' 'The real truth is . . .' when the world is hearing something else again as it continues to bow hopelessly under poverty, threat of nuclear war, and discrimination. Not accepting responsibility for how what one says is heard is only a step from the refusal to care about and accept responsibility for the world" (*The Journey Is Home,* Boston: Beacon Press, 1985, p. xxii).

See also Brevard Childs, *Old Testament Theology in a Canonical Context* (Philadelphia: Fortress Press, 1985); James Sanders, *Canon and Community* (Philadelphia: Fortress Press, 1984).

5. *See* David R. Blumenthal, *God at the Center: Meditations on Jewish Spirituality* (New York: Harper and Row, 1988) for more discussion of the positive images of God's love and power in the Hebrew Bible.
6. E.g., the rejection of blaming the victim in Job, the texts about justice in the prophets, the compassion between women in Ruth, and many psalms about God's relationship with victims of violence.
7. Marie Fortune, *Sexual Violence,* pp. 44-56. Several of these texts have been examined more closely by Phyllis Trible, *Texts of Terror* (Philadelphia: Fortress Press, 1984), and other feminist scholars.
8. Fortune, *Sexual Violence,* pp. 43, 45.
9. I agree with Sallie McFague that all talk about God is interpretation and metaphor. Throughout this section, I am trying to interpret the impact of certain images of God on the community of faith and to search for new images that "will bring the reality of God's love into the imaginations of the women and men of today." This is "a post-modern, highly skeptical, heuristic enterprise" that, in spite of its presumption to speak about God at all, is a modest attempt at reconstruction of the human imagination about God (*Models of God,* Philadelphia: Fortress Press, 1987, p. xii).
10. I am relying especially on the exegetical work of Trible, *Texts of Terror,* pp. 37ff.
11. Claude Levi-Strauss, *The Elementary Structures of Kinship* (Boston: Beacon Press, 1969), pp. 115ff. *See also* the discussion in Gerda Lerner, *The Creation of Patriarchy* (New York: Oxford University Press, 1986), pp. 46ff.
12. I have been especially informed by the following commentaries on this story: Trible, *Texts of Terror,* pp. 9ff.; Breuggemann, *Genesis;* Renita Weems, *Just a Sister Away: A Womanist Vision of Women's Relationships in the Bible* (San Diego, Calif.: LuraMedia, 1988); Delores Williams, "Black Women, Surrogacy Experience, and Christian Notions of Redemption," in Paula M. Cooey and William Eakin, eds., *After Patriarchy* (Maryknoll, N.Y.: Orbis Books, forthcoming); Savina Teubal, *Sarah the Priestess: The First Matriarch of Genesis* (Athens, Ohio: Swallow, 1984).
13. Teubal, in *Sarah the Priestess,* suggests that the issue of a son is more complicated than most commentators have thought. Sarah may have been a

member of a religious order whose members did not usually have children of their own but had children through handmaids. She suggests that the issue of whether the children in this family belonged to the priestess or to the patriarch is part of the story's drama.

14. Renita Weems, *Just a Sister Away: A Womanist Vision of Women's Relationships in the Bible* (San Diego, Calif.: LuraMedia, 1988). *See also* Trible, *Texts of Terror;* Williams, "Black Women."
15. The historical background of this text is complicated and ambiguous at many points, and scholars disagree about its meaning. The binding of Isaac has other interpretations than the ones I have mentioned here. *See* Brueggemann, *Genesis.*
16. Alice Miller, *The Untouched Key: Tracing Childhood Trauma in Creativity and Destructiveness* (New York: Doubleday & Co., 1990), pp. 137-39: "In [two Rembrandt paintings of the sacrifice of Isaac], the father's hand completely covers the son's face, obstructing his sight, his speech, even his breathing. . . . Abraham is grasping his son's head with his left hand and raising a knife with his right; his eyes, however, are not resting on his son but are turned upward, as though he is asking God if he is carrying out His will correctly. At first I thought that this was Rembrandt's own interpretation and that there must be others, but I was unable to find any. In all the portrayals of this scene that I found, Abraham's face or entire torso is turned away from his son and directed upward. Only his hands are occupied with the sacrifice. As I looked at the pictures, I thought to myself, 'The son, an adult at the peak of his manhood, is simply lying there, quietly waiting to be murdered by his father. In some of the versions he is calm and obedient; in only one is he in tears, but not in a single one is he rebellious.' . . . How can a person lying on a sacrificial altar with his hands bound . . . ask questions when his father's hand keeps him from seeing or speaking and hinders his breathing? . . . He has been dehumanized by being made a sacrifice; he no longer has a right to ask questions and will scarcely even be able to articulate them to himself, for there is no room in him for anything besides fear."
17. *See* Teubal, *Sarah the Priestess,* for a discussion of a possible struggle between patriarchy and goddess religion, which may underly some of the dynamics of this story.
18. For a summary of the basic elements of social systems theory, *see* Lynn Hoffman, *Foundations of Family Therapy* (New York: Basic Books, 1981).
19. The relationship between Sarah and Hagar is probably more complicated than is usually thought. *See* Teubal, *Sarah the Priestess.*
20. For summaries of attachment theory, *see* John Bowlby, *Attachment* (New York: Basic Books, 1969).
21. For commentary on the surrogate role of black women, *see* Williams, "Black Women," and Margaret Atwood's novel, *The Handmaid's Tale* (New York: Fawcett Crest, 1985).

22. For summaries of narcissistic overinvestment, *see* Alice Miller, *Thou Shalt Not Be Aware* (New York: Farrar, Straus & Giroux, 1984).
23. *See* Walter Brueggemann, *Genesis* (Atlanta: John Knox Press, 1982); E. A. Speiser, *Genesis* (Anchor Bible) (New York: Doubleday & Co., 1982); Gerard van Rad, *Genesis* (Philadelphia: Westminster Press, 1961).
24. Hans Walter Wolfe, *Hosea* (Philadelphia: Fortress Press, 1973); Friedman and Anderson, *Hosea* (Anchor Bible) (New York: Doubleday & Co., 1982).
25. *See* Raymund Schwager, *Must There Be Scapegoats? Violence and Redemption in the Bible* (New York: Harper and Row, 1987).
26. *See* Walter Wink, "Prayer and the Powers," *Sojourners* (October 10, 1990), p. 10, in which the issue of God's repentance for violence is highlighted.
27. *See* Daniel Day Williams, *The Spirit and the Forms of Love* (New York: Harper and Row, 1968).
28. Gerhard Kittel, *Theological Word Book of the New Testament* vol. 3 (Grand Rapids, Mich.: Wm. B. Eerdman's Publishing Co., 1965), p. 167.
29. Fortune, *Sexual Violence,* pp. 56-57.
30. *See* Elisabeth Schüssler Fiorenza, *In Memory of Her* (New York: Crossroad Publishing Co., 1984), for discussion of the household codes in Corinthians and Ephesians. Some new research challenges the consensus that women did not assume significant leadership positions in ancient Jewish communities of faith. *See* Bernadette Brooten, *Women Leaders in the Ancient Synagogue* (Chico, Calif.: Scholars Press, 1982).
31. Joanne Brown and Carole Bohn, eds., *Christianity, Patriarchy, and Abuse: A Feminist Critique* (New York: Pilgrim Press, 1989). *See* esp. chap. l, on problems with the metaphor of the suffering God for victims of abuse.
32. For summaries of theories of atonement, *see* Williams, *Spirit and Forms of Love,* pp. 173ff.; Rita Brock, *Journeys by Heart* (New York: Crossroad Publishing Co., 1988), pp. 53ff.; Brown and Bohn, *Christianity, Patriarchy, and Abuse,* pp. 4ff.; Catherine Keller, *From a Broken Web* (Boston: Beacon Press, 1986), pp. 164-65.
33. Brown and Bohn, *Christianity, Patriarchy, and Abuse,* pp. 7ff.
34. Williams, *Spirit and Forms of Love,* p. 175.
35. Brock, *Journeys by Heart,* p. 55.
36. Hal Lindsey, *The Late Great Planet Earth* (Grand Rapids, Mich.: Zondervan, 1970).
37. Williams, *Spirit and Forms of Love,* p. 174.
38. Ibid., pp. 185-86.
39. Brown and Bohn, *Christianity, Patriarchy, and Abuse,* pp. 1ff.
40. Loomer, "Size of God," p. 41.
41. Ibid., p. 43.
42. Jacquelyn Grant, *White Women's Christ and Black Women's Jesus* (Chico, Calif.: Scholars Press, 1989), p. 212.

43. Joanne Carlson Brown and Rebecca Parker, "For God so Loved the World?" in Brown and Bohn, *Christianity, Patriarchy, and Abuse,* pp. 1ff.
44. Bernard Loomer, "Two Dimensions of Power," *Criterion* (1976), p. 28.
45. Walter Wink, *Unmasking the Powers* (Philadelphia: Fortress Press, 1986), p. 40.
46. Grant, *White Women's Christ and Black Women's Jesus,* p. 214.

CHAPTER 9: MINISTRY PRACTICE AND PRACTICAL THEOLOGY

1. The following books deal with intervention and treatment issues for victims of sexual violence: Marie Fortune, *Sexual Violence: The Unmentionable Sin: An Ethical and Pastoral Perspective* (New York: Pilgrim Press, 1983); Mary Pellauer, et al., eds., *Sexual Assault and Abuse: A Handbook for Clergy and Religious Professionals* (New York: Harper and Row, 1987); Suzanne N. Sgroi, ed., *Handbook of Clinical Intervention in Child Sexual Abuse* (Lexington, Mass.: Lexington Books, 1982); Ellen Bass and Laura Davis, *The Courage to Heal: A Guide for Women Survivors of Child Sexual Abuse* (New York: Harper and Row, 1988); Gil Eliana, *Outgrowing the Pain: A Book for and About Adults Abused as Children* (New York: Launch Press, 1983); Linda Ledray, *Recovering from Rape* (New York: Henry Holt, 1986); Wendy Waltz and Beverly Holman, *Incest and Sexuality: A Guide to Understanding and Healing* (Lexington, Mass.: Lexington Books, 1987).
2. The following give guidelines from various perspectives for confronting and working with sexually abusive men: Suzanne Sgroi, ed., *Handbook for Clinical Intervention in Child Sexual Abuse* (complete biblio.); George W. Barnard, et al., eds., *The Child Molester: An Integrated Approach to Evaluation and Treatment* (New York: Brunner/Mazel, 1989); David Finkelhor, *Child Sexual Abuse* (New York: Free Press, 1984); Nicholas Groth, *Men Who Rape* (New York: Plenum Press, 1979); Richard Gelles and Murray Straus, *Intimate Violence* (New York: Simon and Schuster, 1988).
3. For suggestions on changing institutional policies and procedures, *see* Marie Fortune, *Is Nothing Sacred? When Sex Invades the Pastoral Relationship* (New York: Harper and Row, 1989); Peter Rutter, *Sex in the Forbidden Zone: When Men in Power—Therapists, Doctors, Clergy, Teachers, and Others—Betray Women's Trust* (Los Angeles: Jeremy Tarcher, 1989).
4. *See* notes for chap. 5 for references on these issues.
5. For cogent analyses of how theological metaphors help foster an environment that encourages sexual violence, *see* Joanne Carlson Brown and Carole R. Bohn, *Christianity, Patriarchy, and Abuse: A Feminist Critique* (New York: Pilgrim Press, 1989); Rita Brock, *Journeys by Heart* (New York:

Crossroad Publishing Co., 1988); Raymund Schwager, *Must There Be Scapegoats? Violence and Redemption in the Bible* (New York: Harper and Row, 1987); *see also* the references and notes for chap. 8.

6. James N. Poling and Donald E. Miller, *Foundations for a Practical Theology of Ministry* (Nashville: Abingdon Press, 1985), p. 62.
7. Ibid., p. 69.
8. "The elucidation of immediate experience is the sole justification for any thought; and the starting point for thought is the analytic observation of components of this experience. But we are not conscious of any clear-cut complete analysis of immediate experience, in terms of the various details which comprise its definiteness. We habitually observe by the method of difference. Sometimes we see an elephant, and sometimes we do not. The result is that an elephant, when present, is noticed. Facility of observation depends on the fact that the object observed is important when present, and sometimes is absent." Alfred North Whitehead, *Process and Reality: An Essay in Cosmology* (New York: Free Press, 1978), p. 4. *See also* Ellen K. Wondra, "Theology in a Postmodern Key," *Plumbline: A Journal of Ministry in Higher Education* (December 1989), 4-16.
9. The critical theories that have most informed my work are psychoanalytic theory as reinterpreted by postmodern criticism, feminist theology, and black theology.
10. This section is heavily dependent on the constructive theology of Bernard Meland, *Essays in Constructive Theology: A Process Perspective* (Chicago: Exploration Press, 1988). P. 5: "Within the Creative Passage there occurs the passage of history, not as a single stream, but as diverse cultural currents, each of which has its own dynamic structure, integrating through memory, precedent, custom and much more, the sequences of events and actualities that have constituted its living stream. The dynamic passage of events within each culture has given form to a *Structure of Experience,* which can be said to be the enduring structural residue of the cultural history within its particular orbit of meaning, as seen from within the perspective of every present moment of that history. The Structure of Experience is thus the present immediacy within the total and inclusive Creative Passage. . . . Within each Structure of Experience there is to be found a persisting, elemental myth, giving shape to its cultural *mythos,* expressive of the hard-earned, endurable modes of response, subliminal for the most part, which have formed within that orbit of meaning."
11. James N. Poling, "Empirical Theology," in *Dictionary of Pastoral Care and Counseling,* ed. Rodney Hunter (Nashville: Abingdon Press, 1990), pp. 356-58.
12. Bernard Meland, *The Future of Empirical Theology* (Chicago: University of Chicago Press, 1969), pp. 13, 297.
13. *See* chap. 6 for a more detailed discussion of the rhythm of sensitivity and creativity.

BIBLIOGRAPHY

Allen, Charlotte Vale. *Daddy's Girl.* Wyndham Books, 1980.

Andolsen, Barbara, et al., eds. *Women's Consciousness, Women's Conscience.* Harper and Row, 1985.

Angelou, Maya. *I Know Why the Caged Bird Sings.* Random House, 1970.

Aries, Philippe. *Centuries of Childhood: A Social History of Family Life.* Vintage, 1962.

Atwood, Margaret. *The Handmaid's Tale.* Fawcett Crest, 1985.

Bal, Mieke. *Lethal Love: Feminist Literary Readings of Biblical Love Stories.* Indiana University Press, 1987.

Barnard, George, et al. *The Child Molester.* Brunner/Mazel, 1989.

Baron, Larry, and Murray Strauss. *Four Theories of Rape in American Society.* Yale University Press, 1989.

Bass, Ellen, and Laura Davis. *The Courage to Heal: A Guide for Women Survivors of Child Sexual Abuse.* Harper and Row, 1988.

Bass, Ellen, and Louise Thornton, eds. *I Never Told Anyone: Writings by Women Survivors of Child Sexual Abuse.* Harper and Row, 1983.

Becker, Ernest. *Escape from Evil.* Free Press, 1975.

Bernheimer, Charles, and Clair Kahane, eds. *Dora: Freud, Women, and Hysteria.* Columbia University Press, 1985.

Blanck, Gertrude, and Rubin Blanck. *Beyond Ego Psychology.* Columbia University Press, 1986.

______. *Ego Psychology: Theory and Practice.* Columbia University Press, 1974.

______. *Ego Psychology II: Psychoanalytic Developmental Psychology.* Columbia University Press, 1979.

Blumenthal, David R. *God at the Center: Meditations on Jewish Spirituality.* Harper and Row, 1988.

Boswell, John. *The Kindness of Strangers: The Abandonment of Children in Western Europe from Late Antiquity to the Renaissance.* Pantheon Books, 1988.
Bowlby, John. *Attachment.* Basic Books, 1969.
Breger, Louis. "Daniel Paul Schreber: From Male into Female," *Journal of the American Academy of Psychoanalysis* 6-2 (1978): 123-56.
Bregman, Lucy. "Religion and Madness: Schreber's Memoirs as Personal Myth," *Journal of Religion and Health* 16-2 (1977): 119-34.
Brock, Rita. *Journeys by Heart.* Crossroad, 1988.
Brown, Delwin, et al., eds. *Process Philosophy and Christian Thought.* Bobbs-Merrill, 1971.
Brown, Joanne Carlson, and Carole R. Bohn, eds. *Christianity, Patriarchy, and Abuse: A Feminist Critique.* Pilgrim Press, 1989.
Browning, Don S., ed. *Practical Theology: The Emerging Field in Theology, Church, and World.* Harper and Row, 1983.
Brownmiller, Susan. *Against Our Will: Men, Women, and Rape.* Simon and Schuster, 1975.
Brueggemann, Walter. *Genesis.* John Knox Press, 1982.

Cannon, Katie G. *Black Womanist Ethics.* Scholars Press, 1988.
Chesler, Phyllis. *Women and Madness.* Doubleday, 1972.
Childs, Brevard S. *Biblical Theology in Crisis.* Westminster Press, 1970.
______. *Old Testament Theology in a Canonical Context.* Fortress Press, 1985.
Chodorow, Nancy. *The Reproduction of Mothering: Psychoanalysis and the Sociology of Gender.* University of California Press, 1978.
Cicchetti, Dante, and Vicki Carlson, eds. *Child Maltreatment: Theory and Research on the Causes and Consequences of Child Abuse and Neglect.* Cambridge University Press, 1989.
Cobb, John. *Christ in a Pluralistic Age.* Westminster Press, 1975.
______. *A Christian Natural Theology.* Westminster Press, 1965.
Cobb, John, and David Griffin. *Process Theology: An Introductory Exposition.* Westminster Press, 1976.
Condren, Mary. *The Serpent and the Goddess: Women, Religion, and Power in Celtic Ireland.* Harper and Row, 1989.
Cooey, Paula M., William R. Eakin, and Jay B. McDaniel, eds. *After Patriarchy.* Orbis Books (forthcoming).
Cornwall Collective, *Your Daughters Shall Prophesy: Feminist Alternatives in Theological Education.* Pilgrim Press, 1979.

Daly, Mary. *Beyond God the Father.* Beacon Press, 1973.
Davis, Angela. *Women, Culture, Politics.* Vintage, 1990.
______. *Women, Race, and Class.* Vintage, 1983.
Davis, Stephen, ed. *Encountering Evil: Live Options in Theodicy.* John Knox Press, 1981.

Dean, William, and Larry Axel. *The Size of God: The Theology of Bernard Loomer in Context.* Mercer University Press, 1987.
D'Emila, John, and Estelle B. Freedman. *Intimate Matters: A History of Sexuality in America.* Harper and Row, 1988.
Diagnostic and Statistical Manual of Mental Disorders (3rd, rev. ed.). American Psychiatric Association, 1987.
Dinnerstein, Dorothy. *The Mermaid and the Minotaur: Sexual Arrangements and Human Malaise.* Harper and Row, 1977.
DuBois, Ellen Carol, ed. *Elizabeth Cady Stanton, Susan B. Anthony: Correspondence, Writings, Speeches.* Schocken Books, 1981.
Dworkin, Andrea. *Pornography: Men Possessing Women.* Perigee/Putnam, 1981.

Eisenstein, Hester. *Contemporary Feminist Thought.* Hall and Co., 1983.
Eisler, Riane. *The Chalice and the Blade: Our History, Our Future.* Harper and Row, 1987.
Eliana, Gil. *Outgrowing the Pain: A Book for and About Adults Abused as Children.* Launch Press, 1983.
Erikson, Erik. *Childhood and Society.* W. W. Norton & Co., 1963.
Eugene, Toinette. "Moral Values and Black Womanists," *Journal of Religious Thought* (Spring 1988).

Finkelhor, David. *Child Sexual Abuse.* Free Press, 1984.
Fortune, Marie. *Is Nothing Sacred? When Sex Invades the Pastoral Relationship.* Harper and Row, 1989.
______. *Sexual Violence: The Unmentionable Sin: An Ethical and Pastoral Perspective.* Pilgrim Press, 1983.
Freud, Sigmund. "Beyond the Pleasure Principle," *The Standard Edition of the Complete Psychological Works of Sigmund Freud.* 18:3-64. Hogarth Press, 1955.
______. *Dora: An Analysis of a Case of Hysteria.* Collier Books, 1963.
______. *A General Selection from the Works of Freud.* Doubleday & Co., 1957.
______. *The Interpretation of Dreams.* Avon Books, 1965.
______. *Sexuality and the Psychology of Love.* Collier Books, 1963.
______. *Three Case Histories.* Collier Books, 1963.
Friedman, David, and Frances Andersen. *Hosea* (Anchor Bible). Doubleday & Co., 1980.

Gallop, Jane. *The Daughter's Seduction: Feminism and Psychoanalysis.* Cornell University Press, 1982.
Garner, Shirley Nelson, et al., eds. *The (M)other Tongue: Essays in Psychoanalytic Interpretation.* Cornell University Press, 1985.
Gelles, Richard, and Murray Straus. *Intimate Violence.* Simon and Schuster, 1988.
Genovese, Eugene, ed. *The Slave Economy of the Old South: Selected Essays in Economic and Social History.* Louisiana State University Press, 1968.

Gilligan, Carol. *In a Different Voice.* Harvard University Press, 1982.

Grant, Jacquelyn. *White Women's Christ and Black Women's Jesus.* Scholars Press, 1989.

Griffin, David. *God, Power, and Evil: A Process Theodicy.* Westminster Press, 1976.

Griffin, Susan. *Pornography and Silence: Culture's Revenge Against Nature.* Harper and Row, 1981.

______. *Rape: The Politics of Consciousness.* Harper and Row, 1986.

______. *Women and Nature: The Roaring Inside Her.* Harper and Row, 1978.

Groth, Nicholas. *Men Who Rape.* Plenum Press, 1979.

Gurko, Miriam. *The Ladies of Seneca Falls: The Birth of the Women's Rights Movement.* Schocken Books, 1976.

Gutman, Herbert. *The Black Family in Slavery and Freedom: 1750-1925.* Vintage, 1976.

Hewitt, Nancy. *Women's Activism and Social Change: Rochester, NY, 1822-1872.* Cornell University Press, 1984.

Hoffman, Lynn. *Foundations of Family Therapy.* Basic Books, 1981.

The Holy Bible (New Revised Standard Version). N.C.C.C., 1989.

Horner, Althea. *Object Relations and the Developing Ego in Therapy.* Jason Aronson, 1984.

Hunter, Mic. *Abused Boys: The Neglected Victims of Sexual Abuse.* Lexington, 1990.

Kegan, Robert. *The Evolving Self.* Harvard University Press, 1982.

Keller, Catherine. *From a Broken Web: Separation, Sexism, and Self.* Beacon Press, 1986.

Kernberg, Otto. *Borderline Conditions and Pathological Narcissism.* Jason Aronson, 1975.

______. *Internal World and External Reality.* Jason Aronson, 1980.

______. *Severe Personality Disorders: Psycho-therapeutic Strategies.* Yale University Press, 1984.

Kittel, Gerhard. *Theological Dictionary of the New Testament* (vol. 3). Wm. B. Eerdmans Publishing Co., 1965.

Kohut, Heinz. *The Analysis of the Self.* International Universities Press, 1971.

______. *How Does Analysis Cure?* University of Chicago Press, 1984.

______. *The Restoration of the Self.* International Universities Press, 1977.

______. *Self Psychology and the Humanities.* W. W. Norton & Co., 1985.

Koontz, Gayle, and Willard Swartley, eds. *Perspectives on Feminist Hermeneutics.* Institute of Mennonite Studies, 1987.

Lamb, Matthew L. *Solidarity with Victims: Toward a Theology of Social Transformation.* Crossroad, 1982.

Lax, Ruth, et al., eds. *Rapprochement: The Critical Phase of Separation Individuation.* Jason Aronson, 1980.

Lederer, Laura, ed. *Take Back the Night: Women on Pornography.* Wm. Morrow, 1980.

Ledray, Linda. *Recovering from Rape.* Henry Holt, 1986.

Lerner, Gerda. *The Creation of Patriarchy.* Oxford University Press, 1986.

Levi-Strauss, Claude. *The Elementary Structures of Kinship.* Beacon Press, 1969.

Lew, Mike. *Victims No Longer: Men Recovering from Incest and Other Sexual Child Abuse.* Nevramont, 1988.

Lindsey, Hal. *The Late Great Planet Earth.* Zondervan, 1970.

Loomer, Bernard. "The Free and Relational Self," in *Belief and Ethics,* ed. W. W. Schroeder and Gibson Winter. Center for the Scientific Study of Religion, 1978.

______. "On Committing Yourself to a Relationship," *Process Studies* 16-4 (Winter 1987).

______. "Two Conceptions of Power," *Criterion* 15 (1976), pp. 12-29.

Lystad, Mary, ed. *Violence in the Home: Interdisciplinary Perspectives.* Brunner/Mazel, 1986.

McFague, Sallie. *Models of God.* Fortress Press, 1987.

McGoldrick, Monica, et al., eds. *Women in Families: A Framework for Family Therapy.* W. W. Norton & Co., 1989.

Mahler, Margaret, et al. *The Psychological Birth of the Human Infant.* Basic Books, 1975.

Mause, Lloyd de. *The History of Childhood.* Psychohistory Press, 1974.

Mead, George Herbert. *Mind, Self, and Society,* ed. Charles W. Morris. University of Chicago Press, 1934, 1962.

Meissner, W. W. *The Borderline Spectrum: Differential Diagnosis and Development Issues.* Jason Aronson, 1984.

______. *Internalization in Psychoanalysis.* International Universities Press, 1981.

______. *Treatment of Patients in the Borderline Spectrum.* Jason Aronson, 1988.

Meland, Bernard. *Essays in Constructive Theology: A Process Perspective.* Exploration Press, 1988.

______. *Faith and Culture.* Southern Illinois University, 1953.

______. *Fallible Forms and Symbols.* Fortress Press, 1976.

______. *The Realities of Faith.* Oxford University Press, 1962.

______. *The Secularization of Modern Cultures.* Oxford University Press, 1966.

Meland, Bernard, ed. *The Future of Empirical Theology.* University of Chicago Press, 1989.

Miller, Alice. *Banished Knowledge: Facing Childhood Injuries.* Doubleday & Co., 1990.

______. *The Drama of the Gifted Child.* Basic Books, 1981.

______. *For Your Own Good: Hidden Cruelty in Child-rearing and the Roots of Violence.* Farrar, Straus & Giroux, 1984.

______. *Thou Shalt Not Be Aware: Society's Betrayal of the Child.* Farrar, Straus & Giroux, 1984.

______. *The Untouched Key: Tracing Childhood Trauma in Creativity and Destructiveness.* Doubleday & Co., 1990.

Miller, Jean Baker, ed. *Psychoanalysis and Women.* Penguin Books, 1973.

Mitchell, Juliet. *The Longest Revolution.* Pantheon Books, 1984.

Morrison, Toni. *Beloved.* New American Library, 1987.

______. *Song of Solomon.* New American Library, 1977.

Morton, Nelle. *The Journey Is Home.* Beacon Press, 1985.

Moynihan, Daniel P. *The Negro Family: The Case for National Action.* United States Dept. of Labor, 1965.

Mud Flower Collective. *God's Fierce Whimsy: Christian Feminism and Theological Education.* Pilgrim Press, 1985.

Neiderland, William. *The Schreber Case: Psychoanalytic Profile of a Paranoid Personality.* Analytic Press, 1984.

Nelson, James. *Embodiment: An Approach to Sexuality and Christian Theology.* Pilgrim Press, 1976.

______. *The Intimate Connection: Male Sexuality, Masculine Spirituality.* Westminster Press, 1988.

Pellauer, Mary, et al., eds. *Sexual Assault and Abuse: A Handbook for Clergy and Religious Professionals.* Harper and Row, 1987.

Piaget, Jean. *The Construction of Reality in the Child.* Basic Books, 1937, 1954.

Poling, James N. "Child Sexual Abuse: A Rich Context for Thinking About God, Community, and Ministry," *Journal of Pastoral Care* 42-1 (Spring 1988): 58-61.

______. "Issues in the Psychotherapy of Child Molesters," *Journal of Pastoral Care* 8-1 (Spring 1989): 25-32.

______. "Social and Ethical Issues of Child Sexual Abuse," *American Baptist Quarterly* 8-4 (1990): 257-66.

______. "A Theological Integration of the Social and Personal in Pastoral Care and Counseling: A Process View." Unpublished dissertation, School of Theology, Claremont, Calif., 1979.

Poling, James N., and Donald E. Miller. *Foundations for a Practical Theology of Ministry.* Abingdon Press, 1985.

Poling, James N., and Lewis S. Mudge, eds. *Formation and Reflection: The Promise of Practical Theology.* Fortress Press, 1987.

Pollock, Linda. *Forgotten Children: Parent-Child Relations from 1500-1900.* Cambridge University Press, 1983.

Russell, Diana. *Rape in Marriage.* Macmillan, 1982.

______. *The Secret Trauma: Incest in the Lives of Girls and Women.* Basic Books, 1986.

_______. *Sexual Exploitation: Rape, Child Sexual Abuse, and Workplace Harassment.* Beverly HIlls, 1984.

Rutter, Peter. *Sex in the Forbidden Zone: When Men in Power—Therapists, Doctors, Clergy, Teachers, and Others—Betray Women's Trust.* Jeremy Tarcher, 1989.

Sanders, James. *Canon and Community: A Guide to Canonical Criticism.* Fortress Press, 1984.

Schatzman, Morton. *Soul Murder: Persecution in the Family.* New American Library, 1973.

Schreber, Daniel Paul. *Memoirs of My Mental Illness,* trans. Ida Macalpine and Richard Hunter. Wm. Dawson and Sons, 1955.

Schüssler Fiorenza, Elisabeth. *In Memory of Her.* Crossroad, 1983.

Schwager, Raymund. *Must There Be Scapegoats? Violence and Redemption in the Bible.* Harper and Row, 1987.

Sgroi, Suzanne N., ed. *Handbook of Clinical Intervention in Child Sexual Abuse.* Lexington, 1982.

Smith, Wallace. *The Church in the Life of the Black Family.* Judson Press, 1985.

Speiser, E. A. *Genesis:* Doubleday & Co., 1982.

Stanton, Elizabeth Cady. *Eighty Years and More: Reminiscences, 1815–1897.* Schocken Books, 1971.

Stern, Daniel. *The Interpersonal World of the Infant.* Basic Books, 1985.

Stone, Howard, and William Clements, eds. *Handbook for Basic Types of Pastoral Care and Counseling.* Abingdon Press, 1991.

Straus, Murray. *Behind Closed Doors: Violence in the American Family.* Anchor, 1980.

Suchocki, Marjorie Hewitt. *The End of Evil.* State University of New York, 1988.

Teubal, Savina J. *Hagar the Handmaid.* Harper and Row, 1989.

_______. *Sarah the Priestess: The First Matriarch of Genesis.* Swallow Press, 1984.

Thistlethwaite, Susan Brooks. *Sex, Race, and God: Christian Feminism in Black and White.* Crossroad, 1989.

Tracy, David, *Plurality and Ambiguity: Hermeneutics, Religion, and Hope.* Harper and Row, 1987.

Trible, Phyllis. *Texts of Terror.* Fortress Press, 1984.

"The Unique Death of Eli Creekmore." Videotape produced by KCTS, Seattle, Wash., 1987.

van Kessel, Rob. *Zes Kruiken Water: Enkele Theologische Bijdragn Voor Kerkopbouw.* Gool and Sticht, Netherlands, 1989.

von Rad, Gerhard. *Genesis.* Westminster Press, 1961.

Walters, Marianne, et al. *The Invisible Web: Gender Patterns in Family Relationships.* Guilford, 1988.

Waltz, Wendy, and Beverly Holman. *Incest and Sexuality: A Guide to Understanding and Healing.* Lexington, 1987.

Washington, Mary Helen. *Invented Lives: Narratives of Black Women, 1860-1960.* Vintage, 1987.

Weems, Renita. *Just a Sister Away: A Womanist Vision of Women's Relationships in the Bible.* LuraMedia, 1988.

Whitehead, Alfred North. *Process and Reality.* ed. D. R. Griffin and D. W. Sherburne. Free Press, 1929, 1978.

Wilden, Anthony. *System and Structure: Essays in Communication and Exchange.* Tavistock, 1972.

Williams, Daniel Day. *The Minister and the Care of Souls.* Harper and Row, 1961.

______. *The Spirit and Forms of Love.* Harper and Row, 1968.

Wilmore, Gayraud, and James Cone, eds. *Black Theology: A Documentary History, 1966-1979.* Orbis Books, 1979.

Wink, Walter. *Naming the Powers: The Language of Power in the New Testament.* Fortress Press, 1984.

______. *Unmasking the Powers: The Invisible Forces That Determine Human Existence.* Fortress Press, 1986.

______. "Prayer and the Powers," *Sojourners* (October 10, 1990).

Winnicott, D. W. *Deprivation and Delinquency.* Tavistock, 1984.

Winquist, Charles. *Practical Hermeneutics: A Revised Agenda for Ministry.* Scholars Press, 1980.

Wolff, Hans Walter. *Hosea.* Fortress Press, 1974.

Wondra, Ellen. "The Dialogue Which We Are." Unpublished essay, Rochester, N.Y., 1990.

______. "Theology in a Postmodern Key," *Plumbline: A Journal of Ministry in Higher Education* (December 1989), 4-15.

INDEX